The Ghosts of Virginia

Volume I

by L. B. Taylor, Jr.

Photographs by the Author
Illustrations by
Brenda Goens,
Lisa Sullivan &
Isobel Donovan

Sixth Printing
2009

www.vaghosts.com

Copyright © 1993 by L. B. Taylor, Jr.
Printed in the U.S.A. by Progress Printing Co., Inc.

ISBN 0-9628271-5-0

Contents

CHARLOTTESVILLE AREA

CENTRAL AND SOUTHWESTERN VIRGINIA

RICHMOND AREA

Author's Note

I began writing about Virginia ghosts a dozen years or so ago, more or less by accident. I had been writing non-fiction books for New York publishers for some time, on every conceivable subject — from America's space program, to treasure hunting in Florida, to the nuclear arms race. One day an editor called me and asked if I would be interested in doing a book on haunted houses. I was.

It was to be a book national in scope; that is, it was to include spectral phenomena all across the country, from New England to California. I quickly became fascinated with this field, and in doing the research, I came across scores of ghostly accounts and experiences here in my home state. I could only include a couple of these in the book, but I felt there had to be an outlet for so much rich Virginia history and anecdotal material.

And this is how I came to write and publish a book on the "Ghosts of Williamsburg." From a purely business standpoint, it was not a good idea. In fact, my editors in New York thought I was crazy. They said that since it was regional in nature, it would have only limited success. I figured that since three or four million people, possibly more, visit the historic Williamsburg area each year, and that since the subject of ghosts is not exactly topical, and would last, that it might be a good gamble. Luckily, I was right. The Williamsburg book was first published in 1982, and has been through nine printings to date.

Three years later I wrote "The Ghosts of Richmond," and then followed, "The Ghosts of Tidewater" (1990), "The Ghosts of Fredericksburg" (1991), and "The Ghosts of Charlottesville and Lynchburg" (1992).

Sometime in the fall and early winter of 1992, the idea came to me to do a "big" book on all the ghosts of Virginia. It just seemed to make sense. I already had done most of the research and I had covered most of the state. So I decided to select the best three to six or so chapters from my five regional books, and then add the other parts of Virginia not previously included — Northern Virginia, the Shenandoah Valley, Southern Virginia, and from Roanoke down to the Southwestern tip of the Commonwealth.

It has been a profound and extremely gratifying experience. I have travelled the breadth and depth of the land. I have met and talked to hundreds of interesting people gracious enough to share their brushes with the supernatural with me. I have stalked the great and small libraries of the state, poring through obscure and all-but-forgotten volumes on county histories and town profiles. Sometimes I found lost legends which to me, as a writer, were like unearthing a hidden vein of gold ore.

In the Alderman Library of the University of Virginia, for example, I came across an 1868 newspaper account of the once-famous Scottsville ghost, which somehow had gotten lost in the technological rush of the 20th century. In the William and Mary libraries, I uncovered the extraordinary account of the murders of the two brothers in Buckingham County, and how an otherworldly experience helped bring their killers to trial. In a dusty volume, I discovered the phantasmal tale of the notorious "Red Fox of the Cumberland Mountains." And in the yellowed pages of a 1940 historical society publication I became entranced with family recollections of possibly the most famous of all Virginia Ghosts — the frightening poltergeist of Augusta County.

And I learned so much about the splendid history of our great state and its storied leaders. I have visited a large number of the magnificent plantations...Shirley, Berkeley, Sherwood Forest, Westover and Brandon on the James River...Woodlawn and Gunston Hall in Northern Virginia, and others throughout the state...Carter Hall...Belle Grove...Stratford Hall...Tuckahoe...

I have learned of haunting encounters involving such giants as William Byrd II and John Tyler...Thomas Jefferson and Robert E. Lee. I have driven over the byroads and backroads from the shore to the mountains and through the valleys in between. And I have been able to go home in the process — to Amherst County and to Lynchburg where my parents and grandparents are from.

It has been an absorbing and enriching endeavor.

There is another, more commercial reason for my writing this book. I believe it will sell. More than 60 years ago, a remarkable woman named Marguerite DuPont Lee penned a book called "Virginia Ghosts." It must have taken her a long time to complete it, because she got most of her material by correspondence, much of it from the grand manor homes and families across the state. Her book is a classic. Whenever I give talks about my books, or do a craft show, people invariably ask me where they can get a copy of Ms. Lee's volume. Unfortunately, it has been out of print for some time now. I don't know why. Once in a while you can find a copy in a used book store.

Marguerite Lee provided a number of key leads for my research. I wish I could have known her. She had a style and grace which has become a great rarity in our day and age. Which brings me to another reason why I wanted to write this. We are fast losing a wonderful part of our heritage; the legend and lore of our ancestors. We are losing it because of our fast-paced, high-tech, television-era society. We don't seem to have time anymore for such time-honored traditions as story telling and the passing along of life's experiences. We are in too big a hurry, and I, for one, think that's a shame. I have a young granddaughter, Emily Megan Taylor — three years old at the time of this writing — and I want her to someday read and enjoy these colorful vignettes of our past.

As I said, I believe there is a market for such. I am continually surprised at the intense interest people have in true psychic encounters whenever I meet with the public. There seems to be a sort of ethereal fascination. It is evident in the growing popularity of ghost tours all across Virginia.

I get letters and telephone calls from all over the nation — from Washington State to Miami, Florida. Most are from people who just want to talk about some strange event which happened to them and they seem appreciative to have someone listen. I enjoy them. I'm pleased that people are becoming no longer afraid to talk about their ghosts; that through my books and others they realize many others have had similar things happen to them.

A few ask for advice. Some are afraid of what they can't explain. I tell them that the overwhelming percentage of ghosts are benign, if not downright friendly. What do you do if you have a spirit in the house that is bothersome? You could have the house exorcised, or call in a psychic expert to diagnose the characteristics of your "extra tenant." But people have told me the most effective measure they have tried is just simply sitting down and talking to ghosts. That seems to get the best results.

Why do I write these books?

Just one letter and one phone call have made all my efforts all the endless hours of research, all the endless hours of staring at blank pages of paper trying to find the right words — more than worthwhile. The letter came from Carolyn Kim, then executive secretary to Charles Thomas Cayce, who was at the time President of the Association for Research and Enlightenment in Virginia Beach. "I feel," she wrote, "besides being entertaining, that you are rendering a great service. It could only be to the advantage of all of us to be aware of the phenomena. Who knows how many ways we could help these poor souls if we were only more open to their existence, and could feel free to share our knowledge and experiences."

And so I then realized the prophetic words of Margaret DuPont Lee which she included in the introduction of her second book on ghosts more than 60 years ago. She wrote: "The very generous words of approval accorded my little edition of 'Virginia Ghosts' by friends, and particularly the many gracious testimonials from strangers, renders the adventuring after yet further evidence of spirit return a happy quest."

And lastly, I got a phone call one night from a nurse at the Medical College of Virginia in Richmond. She told me of a young boy who was critically ill in New Mexico, and who came to MCV twice a year for treatment of a rare disease. She said they had asked him what he wanted on his next trip to the hospital. He said he wanted two things. One, he wanted to ride on some long rides at an amusement park, so the nurse said they would take him to King's Dominion and to Busch Gardens. He said the other thing he would like most was a copy of "The Ghosts of Richmond."

There was my answer.

Among the more intriguing letters I have gotten over the past year or so was one from a young lady named Ann Smathers from Albuquerque, New Mexico, of all places. Her parents apparently had visited Williamsburg, Virginia, sometime during the summer and fall of 1992 and had taken Ann a copy of "The Ghosts of Tidewater."

So she wrote: "In your book you have a curious photograph on page 57 of the old mansion of Evelynton. Near the main door to the mansion there looks like a lady dressed in white and she appears to be sitting on the front porch. When, on page 61, you wrote, '...Nor does it explain why she (Evelyn Byrd) has reappeared, as recently as when this book was going to press, at Evelynton...' were you referring to that picture?

"I don't know for sure if I believe in ghosts or not, but I have never ruled out the possibility and I'm not offended if anyone ever suggests it to me. If you weren't talking about the picture, there could be many other explanations for what I see in it.

"It could be dust on the negative.

"There could be weird lighting.

"You, or whoever did the photograph, could have had someone there.

"It could be other things.

"It could be Evelyn Byrd."

Her letter fascinated me. Evelyn Byrd was a lady who allegedly died of a broken heart in the 18th century because her father
would not let her marry the man she loved. She was only 29 when
she departed this earth, and many claim she frequently returns not
only to her home at Westover Plantation on Route 5 between
Richmond and Williamsburg, but also to the mansion which has
been named for her — Evelynton.

I had photographed the house in 1989 when I was doing
research for "The Ghosts of Tidewater." I dug through dusty files
in my storage room to find the original photograph, and sure
enough, there was "something" on the porch of the house that I
had not noticed before. I got a little excited.

Under a large magnifying glass, it appears that what is there
may be a child or young girl, with blonde hair, with her back to the
camera, dressed all in white. I didn't recall seeing anyone on the
porch the day I took the picture, but it is possible there was a
tourist or someone seated on a bench there.

But then again, if it isn't a person, who or what is it? Was Miss
Evelyn Byrd playing tricks with me? Anyway, judge for yourself.
Below is the photo.

Evelynton Plantation

Introduction

Virginia abounds in ghosts!

Why?

No one can say for certain. Possibly it is because it was the oldest colony in the New World and therefore has a longer and richer history. Certainly, it has a great number of old houses, manor homes, mansions and plantations, many dating back two and three centuries. Such edifices often are fertile haunting grounds for ghosts. Virginia, too, has seen its share of tragedy and traumatic events. In the early settler days there was horrible famine, disease and bloody Indian massacres. The Revolutionary War caused great suffering, and countless thousands of native sons and others either died or were grievously wounded during the Civil War.

Another possible cause for the preponderance of ethereal spirits in the Old Dominion is because Virginians seem to have a keen sense of history and tradition. Many legends have been carefully preserved and passed down from generation to generation. Whatever the reason, we are fortunate that so many of these ghostly treasures have survived so that yet others may enjoy the thrill of the unexplained, the strange, and the mystic.

Historically, we know that ghosts have been talked and written about for thousands of years. Plato discussed them in the 4th century BC. The chain-rattling fictional ghost in Charles Dickens' "A Christmas Carol," reportedly was derived from a true experience related by the Roman scholar, Pliny the Younger.

What exactly is a ghost? I am asked this question all the time. After more than 12 years of talking to hundreds of people who have experienced the presence of spectral phenomena, and reading extensively on the subject, I am convinced that no one really knows! The people who have seen, heard, felt or otherwise sensed ghosts don't know who or what for sure they are; parapsychology scientists can't seem to agree on a single definition; and even psychics are uncertain.

All that considered, following are some of the more commonly offered explanations.

** A ghost appears to be a surviving emotional memory of someone who has died traumatically, and usually tragically, but is unaware of his or her death.

** Ghosts are apparitions of dead persons. Apparitions, in turn, are visual paranormal appearances, generally spontaneous, that suggest the real presence of someone distant or dead.

** A ghost is the spirit of a deceased person who still actually lives in some other sphere of existence, and is occasionally able to manifest itself to certain individuals on earth.

** Ghosts are the souls of the dead.

** Ghosts are manifestations of assorted unconscious wishes, unresolved guilts or patchwork imaginings.

** A ghost is a disembodied spirit or energy that manifests itself over a period of time in one place, called a haunt.

** A ghost is consistent with the known characteristics of someone who has died in a certain place, and it is as if an aggregate of the deceased's personality is still functioning.

** A ghost can be visual, auditory, olfactory, or tactile.You see a ghost as an apparition, or hear its noise, or smell its fragrance, or observe its manipulation of objects, or feel its cold breath. Or it is felt as an unseen presence by a sixth sense.

** A ghost is manifestation of persistent personal energy — an indication that some kind of force is being exercised after death which is in some way connected with a person previously known on earth.

** Ghosts are illusions created by a powerful class of beings — angelic or demonic or both — who appear to us in the masquerade of dead humans for the purpose of contacting, helping or hurting us.

** Ghosts are images, somehow recorded on a sensitive medium, like a camera records pictures on film, that are visible under certain conditions to people with a certain state of mind. In other words, you are watching an instant replay of a past person or event.

** The great Greek philosopher Plato said a ghost is the soul which survives the body. Sometimes it is wrapped in an "earth covering" which make s it heavy and visible, and drags it down to the visible region.

** A ghost is the soul which leaves the body at death, but under certain circumstances "it" may tarry on earth instead of proceeding to the "other side."

** Ghosts are not the souls of the dead, but are rather telepathic messages from their lingering bodiless minds.

** The question is (regarding ghosts), is there a real human being who died in an unfortunate circumstance, and somehow missed the bus, and stopped where he or she shouldn't be? They're stuck...

So, take your pick. Of all the attempts at explaining ghosts, I tend to like what Professor Henry Habbeley Price of Oxford University once said. Ghosts exist "in a dimension or dimensions unknown to us."

Are ghosts real? Who can say? Certainly most suspected ghostly phenomena can be explained by rational means. Old houses do creak and groan. Passing trucks and trains can stir up all sorts of creepy noises. The sounds of rats and cats and birds and other creatures can easily be misinterpreted in the dark hours.The glare of sunlight, or moonlight on a distant window at just the right angle can play tricks on human eyes at times. Fertile imaginations can create all sorts of perceived demons. So can grief. Marsh gas and other physical phenomena can cause apparent apparitions. Alcohol and other stimulants can conjure up wild visions.

Thus common sense and the application of simple logic can explain most mysteries. But not all. There is still a small percentage of extraordinary happenings which defy explanation. And who are we to dismiss them. Are not our rational arguments locked within the present and limited boundaries of human understanding?How can anyone say for sure that there is not a psychic realm which still lurks in the dark recesses of the unknown — the key to which may lie somewhere in the future? One thing we do know: some people are more sensitive, more receptive to emissions from this other world than most of us.

We don't yet know why this is. Perhaps someday we will. I know that I am not among those so "gifted." I have not personally experienced a ghost.

Nor, as I have often said, do I try to make believers out of anyone. A Gallop poll taken a few years ago found that one of every four Americans queried said they believed in ghosts, and one in six said they have been in touch with someone who had already died. I suspect these numbers are conservative, because some people are reluctant to admit such experiences.

I like what the noted psychic expert Hans Holzer has said: "Throughout the centuries, the skeptical, the scientific and the credulous have attempted to solve the mystery of ghosts and hauntings. There are theories, but no proofs, as to why things happen. But that the incidence of such happenings exceeds the laws of probability, and that their number establishes that there is something to investigate, is beyond dispute."

Perhaps the great television magician of a generation ago, Dunninger, summed it up best. He said, "to those who believe, no explanation is necessary. To those who don't believe, no explanation is possible." I can only add this. I have, over the years, interviewed hundreds of people, from all walks of life, who claim they saw, felt or heard ghosts, and I deeply believe they were sincere. I feel this, too. Some of the strange events, happenings and occurrences recorded in this book would have been all but impossible to make up. Even Edgar Allen Poe would have had difficulty topping what I believe to be the simple truth told by people just like you and me.

One of the most eloquent quotes I have ever read on this subject was by the noted author H. P. Lovecroft. He wrote: "There is something marvelous beyond the horizon of death and the limit of our sight. It becomes personal knowledge when our minds are coaxed out of the shadows of the purely material world and into the brilliance and brightness of the world of spirit...that lies just beyond the limit of our sight."

But as I have repeatedly said, my task is not to make converts to the believability of ghosts. It is merely to entertain; to pass along the fascinating accounts I have heard. So whatever your persuasion is or isn't, I hope you will find the following accounts as interesting and entertaining as I did.

Enjoy!

While there still may be much argument about *what* a ghost is or isn't, there seems to be more agreement, at least among the so-called experts, as to *why* ghosts appear. Here are a few of the more often-quoted reasons:

** They were associated with a particular house all or most of their lives and feel it still belongs to them and current tenants may be thought of as intruders. Ghosts seem to be especially concerned about renovations or alterations of "their" house, and often may display their displeasure if they don't agree with what is being done.

** They return to search for a lost lover in life. Example: "Miss Lizzie" dead now for more than 100 years, has been seen holding a candle in the upstairs window of Edgewood, a Victorian house in Charles City County. She is looking for her fiancé who rode off to the Civil War and never came back.

** They come back to complete some business they left unfinished in life. Example: to complete or rewrite a will that is outdated or misdirected.

** Ghosts are sometimes found reenacting activities or events of the past, perhaps bound to their haunting ground by a powerful emotion or event that prevents them from passing completely to the "other side."

** They appear to right a grievous wrong done to them. Murder victims have been known to return in spirit form either to haunt their killers or to expose them.

** They touch back to atone for some mistake, perceived or real, they feel they committed while living. The "Gray Lady" of Sherwood Forest Plantation near Williamsburg can be heard rocking a baby that died in her care more than a century ago.

One of the problems with doing a book of this sort is just where do you draw the line. Inevitably, some good, absorbing ghost stories will be missed. It was difficult enough selecting only a handful of chapters out of the 30 or so in each of my five regional books. And in travelling through the state, many other potential gems slipped away. Some I just couldn't track down. I would, for example, have liked to have found out more about: an alleged talking cat who spooked a house in Danville in the 1940s era; the human lightning rod of Waynesboro, a man said to have been struck seven times by lightning during his lifetime; and the bleeding house in the Fairfax area where blood supposedly ran out of light sockets, faucets and the shower. They sound intriguing, don't they? But it is frustrating when you can't track them down. So, if I missed your favorite legend, forgive me. But do call or write me about it. If this book proves successful, who knows? Maybe there will be a Volume II!

And, finally, a brief word about "logistics." How do you organize more than 60 chapters and over 90 individual ghostly experiences. Where do you start and where do you end? Perhaps just a random, out-of-the-hat scramble would have been as good as any plan. However, in the final analysis, the decision was to try to bring some cohesion to this mass of spectral material.

Where to begin? Would it not be fitting to start where the first settlers did nearly 400 years ago — on Jamestown Island? After all, there is an authentic and charming encounter there called "Caught in a Colonial Time Warp." And so the journey commences there and spreads to the splendid "Plantation Row," on the north side of the James River in Charles City County, through West Point, and over to historic Williamsburg. From there we move east to the sprawling Tidewater Virginia area, ranging from Portsmouth, Norfolk and Virginia Beach, up through Forts Eustis and Monroe to Poquoson, then Gloucester, Mathews, Deltaville and the Eastern Shore.

Interspersed throughout the book are "summary chapters" on specific specialized subjects, each containing multiple stories. The route next heads north via Colonial Beach, Fredericksburg and Aquia, and meanders into Northern Virginia, covering everything from rural country mansions to Old Town Alexandria. The trek then winds through the Shenandoah Valley, starting near Winchester and running down through Harrisonburg to the charismatic Charlottesville area. Central state coverage runs from Lynchburg to Roanoke with side trips to Augusta, Botetourt and other counties. The road stretches all the way south to Abingdon and the Cumberland Gap "toe" of the Commonwealth, and then comes back north to the psychically rich Richmond region.

This otherworldly odyssey closes the loop near where it began, this time on the South side of the James. And so, now, it is time to begin your travels. Happy hauntings!

Caught in a Colonial Time Warp

(Jamestown Island)

I t was on historic Jamestown Island, a spit of heavily-wooded land jutting into the mighty James River, that America's first band of settlers chose to begin a new life. It was here that they anchored and came ashore for good in May 1607. And, it was here, 364 years later, that a small group of the early adventurers apparently "returned" for a brief period in an extraordinary occurrence witnessed by Gerry McDowell of Virginia Beach and her late husband, Gus.

Both Gerry and Gus liked to travel, and often visited regional sites in the off season. It was on such an excursion to Jamestown Island in 1971 that the "event" happened. They were there very early on a chilly autumn morning, because, as Gerry says, "we liked to be out when no one was around so we could enjoy the solitude, and Gus liked to feed the animals."

The story is best told in Gerry's own words, as follows: "I can remember it as clearly as if it happened yesterday, although it now has been more than 20 years. It was real early on a Sunday morning, about 6 a.m. It was damp and misty. You could see the fog coming off the river. I was listening to one of those audio recordings which told all about the first settlement, when I had the strangest sensation. There was a deathly stillness in the air.

"I turned around and there, coming down a path toward us was a group of about 20 people, men, women and children. They were all dressed in colonial costume. The men wore knickers with either black or white stockings and shoes with buckles. They had on jacket blouses with wide white collars and very broad brimmed hats. The ladies were wearing long gray or black dresses, with shawls over their shoulders, and bonnets.

"They were very animated. The men and women were talking and laughing, and waving their arms as they walked. The children were running in and out of the group. I thought at first that it might be a troop of actors who were coming to participate in a play or something. I looked at Gus, and he saw them, too. We stood together and watched as they approached us.

"It was then that we realized there was something different. While they seemed to be talking, there was no sound whatsoever. Instead there was only an icy silence. They didn't appear to be ghosts, because I think most ghosts are wispy or transparent, and they weren't. You couldn't see through them. And then we noticed. They were ghosts, because they were not walking on the ground! They were elevated above it by a few inches.

"Gus and I froze. We stood still and didn't say a thing. We felt together that any movement or sound on our part would dissolve them. On they came. They marched right by us without noticing

Jamestown Church

2

us. It was as if we weren't there. We could have reached out and touched them, but we didn't. They moved past us and walked straight up the path to the church. When we turned to follow them, we could barely believe our eyes. The church had transformed from its present state to how it must have looked in the early 1600s, complete with steeple and all! Gus and I both gasped.

"They opened the door and, one by one, went inside. When the last gentleman entered, he turned and appeared to stare at us. Gus said he had a smile on his face. I didn't see that, but he slammed the door forcefully. Again, there was no sound. We stood there for a few seconds in silence, transfixed. And then the church appeared in its present state again.

"Neither one of us was afraid of ghosts, so we were not really scared. Still, it was minutes before either of us could speak. Then Gus finally said, 'nobody is going to believe this!' I don't know much about such things, but I think now that we had somehow gotten into a time warp for that brief instant. I have heard about such things, although I don't really understand them. But how else can you explain what happened! All I know is that it was a once in a lifetime experience that I will never forget."

The Curse Tree of Jamestown Island

(Jamestown)

I t would be highly unlikely that you would find the story in any of the countless history books which chronicle the life and times of the settlers at Jamestown and the colonists at Williamsburg. Nor would you be apt to hear tour guides relate this strange tale if you visit the major attractions at Jamestown Festival Park or Colonial Williamsburg.

Rather, you must travel somewhat off the beaten track, to Jamestown Island itself, about a mile or so away from the Park. The area today is maintained jointly by the Association for the Preservation of Virginia Antiquities and the National Park Service.

Just beyond Jamestown Memorial Church, which was built in 1907 upon the foundation of an original church erected in 1617, lies a small, quiet, tree-shaded cemetery containing only a handful of graves. It is here that James and Sarah Harrison Blair are buried.

Chances are, unless you are more than a casual buff of colonial history, the name of James Blair is unfamiliar. This is an unfortunate injustice to the man, for he was an important figure in Virginia's history during the latter days of the 17th century and well into the 18th century. Born in Scotland and educated at the University of Edinburgh, he filled, according to the markings on his tombstone, "the offices of preacher of the gospel for 54 years."

He also served as a faithful "councillor" to the British Governor and subsequently as a Governor of the Colony. Further, he has been described by biographers as a "very powerful man,"

4

and as the "chief force" behind the founding of the College of William and Mary, the second oldest institution of higher learning in the country.

On a more personal note, his tombstone points out that "the comliness (sic) of a handsome face adorned him...he entertained elegantly in a cheerful, hospitable manner without luxury...in affability, he excelled." And it is in the combination of these attractive features that this tale has it origins.

It was in the year 1687. Sarah Harrison, by popular accounts, was then a strikingly beautiful young lady of 17, who, because of the relatively comfortable financial position of her parents, was an active participant in the plantation-circle social life along the lower James River. The oldest daughter of the "mighty" Colonel Benjamin Harrison of Wakefield Plantation, a wealthy land owner, she has been variously described as vivacious, full of life, and head strong. Some intimate that she was a forerunner to the late 20th century women's liberation movement because it is alleged she spoke her piece whenever she felt slighted by the young men of the day.

Despite this strongly independent nature — or perhaps because of it — in conjunction with her natural beauty, Sarah Harrison was actively wooed by a number of handsome and eligible suitors. It was in 1687, according to Sam Robinson, a long time caretaker at Jamestown Island, that "she firs' sign a (marriage) contract with a young gennelman by name of William Roscoe. He was 22 and she was in her 17." The contract, Robinson said, stated that "she would never marry to any man on earth (other than Roscoe) as long as he was alive, so hep her God, signed Sarah Harrison."

However, three weeks later she met the handsome, charismatic Blair. She was swept off her feet. Her parents were not so enchanted. There were two immediate problems. She already was engaged to a perfectly acceptable (to them) young man. Secondly, James Blair at the time was 31 years old, nearly twice Sarah's age. As Robinson colorfully phrased it, "in olden day iffon young girl was to marry elder gennelman (it) was called a disgrace to her parents. 'Course now day an' time it (doesn't) make any diffen (difference) how old dey is jes as dey has de money."

What immediately ensued was the expected; a bitter rift between daughter and parents. This intensified when Sarah broke her initial engagement and told them she planned to marry the Reverend Blair. Through reasoning, arguments and threats, her parents tried everything to discourage the union, but Sarah's mind

5

Curse Tree at Jamestown Island

was made up.

As Robinson recounted the story: "She break the contract then her lover William Roscoe, causin' his death made her hearbreakin' and marry to Dr. Blair." It is not known if her parents even attended the affair. One version, though, has it that Sarah refused to utter the words "to obey" at the ceremony. As it was said, she had a mind of her own, this girl.

Her parents would not give up even after the wedding. They sought to have the marriage annulled. But here, fate took a curious hand. In Robinson's words: "...Colonel Benjamin, Mrs. Hannah his wife, and his baby daughter, — all three of them was kill up on Route 5 up at Berkeley by lightning...so they didn't get a chance in life to separate Miss Sarah from Dr. Blair."

Sarah and James Blair, it is said, lived a happy life together as man and wife. She died in 1713 at the age of 42 still unforgiven by her family. Says Robinson: "By disobeying her parents in life and marry to Dr. Blair again' her family consent, the Harrison family...buried her away from her family." On her tombstone are the Latin words which, translated, say, "In sacred memory, here lies in the hope of blessed resurrection the body of Mrs. Sarah Blair...exceedingly beloved and lamented."

Her husband lived on for 30 years, contributing significantly to the continued growth and prosperity of the young colony. When he died in 1743, he was laid to rest at a site "six inches beyond" on "The left hand side" of his wife's grave.

In the year 1750, seven years after Blair's death, fate intervened again. Robinson told what happened this way: "Was a stoned in fence around the two graves six inches apart side by side." A sycamore tree "came up between 'em as a little wild sapling. Wasn't anythin' deed (did) to prevent de tree or protect de grave so as it growed it caught in the center tomb there by Dr. Blair, break the stones then in two both ends, right where her stone were joined to Dr. Blair stone, push her tomb up out de grown' above Dr. Blair and push de back on the head end seven feet from her husband back over to de right within six inches of her (third) elder sister, Mother, Father and younger sister...and leave Dr. Blair on de left hand side in a stone by himself."

And so, as the legend went, Sarah's parents, who could not dissolve her marriage with Blair while they were alive, were finally able to separate the lovers after death. The late Robert L. Ripley wrote about this odd incident in his "Believe it or not" column, calling the sycamore the "mother-in-law tree." Others have referred to it as the "curse tree." Robinson, who told the story many times, once to Queen Elizabeth of England during her visit to Jamestown Island in 1957 upon the 350th anniversary of the first settlers' landing, said: "the mother-in-law didn't get a chance in life to separate her daughter Sarah from Dr. Blair, but...she did come back and plant the old sycamore to separate her."

There is a bizarre footnote to the story. Several years ago the old sycamore tree, which had grown to considerable size, died and was cut out of the site, although the broken bricks and cracked tombs were left as they were, pushed apart.

Soon after, a new sycamore sapling sprang up in the exact same spot where the original tree had stood, and flourishes today. It is, some say, the strong will of Sarah's parents reasserting itself from beyond the graves. The legend lives on.

*"Wretches! ye loved her for her
wealth and hated her for her
pride, And when she fell in
feeble health, ye blessed her —
that she died!*

(Lenore)

The Ethereal Reappearance of Miss Evelyn Byrd

(Charles City County)

wo large metallic eagles adorn the gateposts leading into Westover Plantation, in Charles City County, Virginia, set majestically along a beautiful stretch of the James River. Not as well known as the neighboring Berkeley Plantation, Westover, nevertheless is considered an outstanding example of Georgian architecture in America. Built in the early 18th century, it was, for generations, the ancestral home of the William Byrd family, one of the most powerful and influential clans in the colonies.

The mansion features a steeply sloping roof flanked by tall chimneys in pairs at both ends. A surrounding wrought iron fence has supporting columns topped by unusual stone finials cut to represent: an acorn for perseverance (from little acorns great oaks grow); a pineapple for hospitality; a green key to the world for knowledge; a cornucopia or horn of plenty; a beehive for industry; grapes for mirth; and an urn of flowers for beauty.

Westover was the scene of lavish social entertainment among the more affluent colonists during the 18th century. Great parties were held there with the rich and famous as frequent guests. But the house also is filled with a history of sadness and tragedy.

If there is such a thing as a "benevolent" spirit, or at least one who is dedicated not to frighten those who see it, then there is perhaps no better example than the gentle, almost fragile spirit of Evelyn Byrd of Westover. Though she has been dead for nearly 250 years, her apparition still occasionally reappears there; a wraith-like figure most often dressed in white; sad and haunting as if still seeking the happiness which eluded her in life so long ago.

Born in 1707, she was a bright child, a bit spoiled, precocious and high spirited. She was the daughter of William Byrd II, master of Westover and one of the most prominent statesmen of his time;

Westover

secretary of the Virginia colony for years; advisor to the governor; founder of the city of Richmond; wealthy land owner; and country squire.

When she was just 10, her father took her to England so she could be properly schooled. There, she flowered into a beautiful young woman with porcelain-white skin, shining chestnut hair, slanting, almost-Oriental blue-green eyes, and an enigmatic, Mona Lisa-like smile. It is told that when she was presented at court at age 16 the King of England remarked: "I am not surprised why our young men are going to Virginia if there are so many pretty Byrds there."

It was in London that Evelyn fell deeply in love with a handsome Englishman. Most historians believe he was Charles Morduant, the grandson of Lord Peterborough. Her father violently objected to the romance, telling her that if she proceeded with it, "as to any expectation you may fondly entertain of a fortune from me, you are not to look for one brass farthing...Nay besides all that I will avoid the sight of you as of a creature detested."

And so, against the desires of her heart, Evelyn Byrd returned to Westover in 1726 a different young woman. The spark of her personality was diminished and she spent long hours by herself, withdrawn, almost reclusive. A number of potential suitors from nearby plantations paid her visits over the next few years, but she spurned them all, much to the chagrin of her father. He referred to her as the "antique virgin."

She confided only in her close friend, Anne Carter Harrison of nearby Berkeley Plantation. They would walk in the formal gardens and talk among the giant boxwoods, passing the afternoons away. It was amid a poplar grove one day that the two young ladies made a pact. Whichever one died first would try to return to visit "in such a fashion not to frighten anyone." Did Evelyn have a premonition? For soon after, she passed away, some say, of a broken heart.

On her tombstone was inscribed the following: "Here in the sleep of peace reposes the body of Evelyn Byrd, daughter of the Honorable William Byrd. The various and excellent endowments of nature: improved and perfected by an accomplished education formed her, for the happiness of her friends; for the ornament of her country. Alas Reader! We can detain nothing, however valued, from unrelenting death. Beauty, fortune, or valued honour! So here a proof! And be reminded by this awful tomb that every worldly comfort fleets away. Excepting only, what arises from imitating the virtues of our friends and the contemplation of their happiness. To which, God was pleased to call this Lady on the 13th day of November, 1737, in the 29th year of her age."

For months the saddened Anne Harrison did not venture among the trails and trees they had so often walked together. But one day she finally did go to the poplar grove and felt "a presence." She turned and saw a figure approaching. It was Evelyn. She was "dressed in white, dazzling in the ethereal loveliness. She drifted forward a few steps, kissed her hand to the beholder, smiling happily, and vanished."

In the intervening generations, many others have caught fleeting glimpses of Evelyn, among them former Westover owners and guests. In 1856, for example, one woman told the John Seldens, who then lived at Westover, that she had awakened in the night and found a young lady standing in the room who quickly went out the door. The woman described the lady and her dress. "Oh, yes," Mr. Selden remarked, "that was Evelyn Byrd." In the 1920s a young girl sleeping in the same third floor bedroom proclaimed the identical experience.

In the early 1900s a workman was dispatched to do some repair work in that bedroom. Minutes later he came running down the stairs saying to the owner, "you didn't tell me there was a young lady up there." He had seen her combing her hair before a mirror. But when they went back upstairs there was no one there.

In December 1929, a guest of the Richard Cranes, who then owned the plantation, reported seeing the "filmy, nebulous and cloudy figure of a woman, so transparent no features could be distinguished, only the gauzy texture of a woman's form." It seemed, the guest said, "to be floating a little above the lawn."

In fact, when the Cranes bought Westover around 1920, Mrs. Crane said, "Oh dear, we'll never get any help because of the ghost." But they had no trouble, because even though the legend of Evelyn's reappearances was known throughout Charles City County, servants also believed her to be a friendly spirit.

And indeed, servants, too, have experienced the phenomenon. One old butler was coming through a narrow passageway in the hall when he saw a lady. Presuming it to be Mrs. Crane, he stepped aside to let her pass. She disappeared before his eyes. Another time a cook saw the apparition of a woman without a head, her view partially blocked by pantry shelves.

More recently, Mr. Bagby, who lives in a small house between the mansion and the cemetery where Evelyn is buried, was in his

Miss Evelyn Byrd

kitchen one evening when he saw a woman at eye level outside on the lawn. Thinking it was Mrs. Bruce Crane Fisher, then mistress of Westover, he went outside to say hello. There was no one there. Then, he thought that if he had seen a woman at eye level, since his kitchen is raised, she would have had to be at least 10 feet tall!

But of all who have claimed sightings of Evelyn, no one yet has offered a reasonable explanation as to why her restless spirit would want to periodically return to a place which apparently caused her so much unhappiness in life. Some people speculate that ghosts return to the world of the living to carry out some "unfinished business." Could it possibly be that Evelyn comes back to "announce" that she has been reunited with her English lover; that she has found in death the bliss she had been denied in life?

The Strange Saga of Aunt Pratt

(Charles City County)

I t is, unquestionably, one of the most magnificent original colonial mansions in the United States. Architectural historians believe that parts of its impressive design were inspired by the second governor's palace at Williamsburg.

The site upon which the great house sits is steeped in early Virginia history and tradition. It was, in fact, founded in 1613 — just six years after the first settlers landed at nearby Jamestown, and a full seven years *before* the Pilgrims arrived at Plymouth Rock.

This is Shirley Plantation, located at a point overlooking a scenic bend in the James River about halfway between Williamsburg and Richmond.

It was originally owned by Sir Thomas West, the first Royal Governor of the Colony of Virginia. He named it in honor of his wife's father, Sir Thomas Shirley of Whiston, England. Later, the plantation gained eminence as the home of Colonel Edward Hill, who held many high offices in the colony through the mid-17th century, including speaker of the Assembly of Burgesses and treasurer of Virginia. The estate has been in the Hill and Carter families for more than 300 years.

The present house was begun in 1723 by the third Edward Hill, also a man of status in the colony. He built it for his daughter, Elizabeth, who married John Carter, son of the legendary King Carter. It took nearly 50 years to complete the construction and

Shirley Plantation

was done as one author described it, "with a lavish disregard for cost seldom displayed in the building of even great mansions."

The handsome brick house stands three stories tall with rows of dormer windows projecting from the roof on all sides. It has huge twin chimneys which flank a large carved pineapple, the colonial symbol for hospitality. Two splendid, two-story porticos, each with four white pillars, set off the front of the building with stylish grace.

Inside, 18th century artisans fashioned superb panelling and delicate carvings. A major design feature is an elegant carved walnut staircase which rises for three stories without visible support — the only one of its kind in America. The entire house is filled with exquisite furnishings, crested silver, and interesting memorabilia assembled from the nine generations of the families which have lived there.

Shirley was a well-known center of hospitality 100 years before and during the American Revolution. George Washington and Thomas Jefferson were guests there as were numerous other prominent Virginians. There are also many interesting anecdotes and stories about events which have transpired at Shirley.

One of the more charming concerns the time a young and beautiful Anne Hill Carter was carrying a punch bowl across the dining room when it began slipping from her fingers. She was rescued by a dashing young military officer — "Light Horse" Harry Lee. Not long afterwards they were married at Shirley. Their son became one of the most famous of all Virginians — and Americans. He was Robert E. Lee.

Perhaps the most compelling legend of Shirley revolves around the ghost of a former resident and family member. For Shirley, like a number of its neighboring plantations along the James, is haunted.

This is the fascinating, and, to this day, the inexplicable story of "Aunt Pratt," or more specifically, of her famous portrait. She was reportedly a sister of Edward Hill, and was born late in the 17th century. Little is known of her, but it is said there always was a certain air of mystery about the woman.

Whatever, one of the things for which Shirley is noted for is its fine collection of family portraits. Apparently, Aunt Pratt's portrait occupied a suitable place in a downstairs room for a number of years after her death. Then, as a new generation of the family took over occupancy and decided to redecorate, the portrait was taken down and banished to the obscurity of the attic

Aunt Pratt, or, if you will, her spirit, did not take kindly to this. In fact, she made what family members described as a "mighty disturbance." This usually took the form of the sound of a woman rocking in the attic late at night. A number of guests, as well as Hills and Carters, told of hearing the incessant rocking on certain nights. Yet when they summoned courage to check the attic, all was still and quiet. Nothing was amiss, although they admitted getting chills up their spines when they looked into the eyes of

Aunt Pratt's portrait amidst the dust, cobwebs and clutter of the attic.

Eventually, the restlessness of her spirit proved too much for the occupants of the house. Prudently, they chose to bring the portrait back down and hang it in its rightful place. Once this was done, the strange rocking sounds were never heard again.

Intriguingly, however, this did not end the troubled travels of Aunt Pratt. A few years ago the Virginia Travel Council scoured about the Commonwealth in search of relics, antiques, and other items associated with psychic phenomena for a tourist promotion they were assembling in New York City. Council officials, having heard the story of Aunt Pratt's ghostly rocking, asked if they might

"Aunt Pratt"

borrow her portrait for the exhibit. And so, "she" was crated and shipped north. But no sooner had she been hung on a wall when she once again "came to life," openly venting her displeasures at being so far away from home.

According to credible accounts, the portrait was once observed "swinging" in its display case. Then one morning workmen found the portrait lying on the floor several feet away from the case, and, in their words, "heading toward the exit."

As a security measure, officials had Aunt Pratt locked up in a closet when not on exhibit. One night a maintenance crew became unnerved when they heard "knocking and crying" coming from the locked closet. No one was inside. The next morning the portrait mysteriously had escaped from the closet and was lying on the floor outside.

At this point a psychic expert was called in. She studied the portrait carefully and felt strong sensations. The psychic believed there were two women involved in the portrait, and two theories were offered in possible explanation. One contended that there are actually two portraits, one painted on top of the other. The supposition here is that the original lady involved has, perhaps for centuries, been struggling to regain her identity and respect. The other consideration is that a model perhaps sat in for Aunt Pratt during the original painting, again pointing to the conceivability of a deep-rooted identity crisis.

Whether or not either of these ideas has any validity, the psychic expert was convinced that there was indeed a powerful spiritual phenomenon associated with the portrait; that the person involved was somehow trying to convey her irritancy at being, to her mind, indignantly displayed.

Many experts agree that spirits which manifest themselves in the manner Aunt Pratt did, are actually ghosts of residences who believe, even though they are dead and gone, that the house they lived in still belongs to them. This seems the most plausible explanation in Aunt Pratt's instance.

Subsequent events added credence to this line of thought. On its way back south from the New York showing, the portrait was taken to a shop in Richmond so repairs could be made on the now battered frame. When it was picked up, the shop owner said that ever since Aunt Pratt has been in his care, he heard bells ringing. This, he deemed at best odd, and at worst, eerily haunting, because, he added, there were no bells of any kind in his shop.

The portrait was then restored once more to its proper place on a wall in the downstairs room. Since that time, there have been no further strange occurrences at Shirley.

Aunt Pratt, at last, was home.

Unearthly Lights in the Night

(West Point)

ost forms of psychic phenomena are quite limited in scope. Generally, whatever the manifestation, be it the sighting of a milky apparition, the sound of muffled footsteps in the attic, or a blood stain that cannot be scrubbed clean — the particular characteristic is experienced only by a relatively few people. In some cases, only one person, usually psychically sensitive, is involved. In old ancestral homes, often just the immediate family members encounter the extraordinary. Only in a few instances are the occurrences seen, heard, smelled, felt or tasted by appreciable numbers of people.

That is why the mysterious light at West Point is such a rare example. Over the past 100 years or so literally thousands of Tidewater residents swear they have witnessed the light that seemingly appears and disappears before their eyes. In fact, this sensation is so well known and so reliable in its recurrences, that, for decades area teenagers considered it a "cool" thing to drive to the site late at night and wait for it to show up. As often as not they were not disappointed. It is a story that has been retold generation to generation with many common threads, but with conflicting accounts as to what the actual source is.

Skeptics scoff that what is seen is marsh gas, which is common in the area near West Point at a crossroads called Cohoke. Others say that many of those who come looking for the light are well fortified with "liquid courage" and are likely to see anything. But the majority of those who have been there don't buy these explanations.

"There is definitely a light there," counters Mac Germain, a mechanic in Hopewell. "I've seen it and I wasn't drunk and it wasn't swamp gas. If it was swamp gas then why would people have seen the light at all times of the year?" he asks.

"I've seen it and it's real," adds Mrs. Thomas Whitmore of West Point. "It was so bright. When it got close to us we got off the railroad tracks real fast, but nothing came by."

Ed Jenkins, a native of Gloucester says, "We used to go up there (Cohoke) when we were teenagers. It was the thing to do. I saw it. It would come closer and closer and would almost get to you, then it would vanish. Was I scared? Absolutely! One time I shot at it with a shotgun and it disappeared. But it always came back."

"I've seen it a hundred times," says John Waggoner, who grew up in Newport News and is now a plant manager in Georgia. "It was just a big old light and it came straight down the tracks, but when it got to you there was nothing there. It used to scare the hell out of the girls I took there. That's what I liked about it."

One person who firmly rules out a spectral source is Lon Dill, a local historian who has written extensively of the area, and is the author of "York River Yesterdays." "Oh, there is something there," he says. "There is a light. I've never seen it, but a friend of mine has and I believe him. But it is some form of luminescence, which can be caused in several ways. Your eyes can fool you at times, especially at night. The best way to see the light is to be young and take your girl friend and a six-pack to the site," Dill chuckles.

Another person who has tried, with some success, to play down the supernatural aspects of the light at West Point is King William County sheriff W. W. Healy. He recalls that in the 1960s and '70s, "It was almost like a state fair down there. People would come by the carload to see it. It got to the point where the road was blocked." Healy has done his best to discourage curiosity seekers. He even dissuaded NBC Television's "Unsolved Mysteries" crew from coming to film the phenomenon. "For the past few years we haven't had too many problems because there has been nothing written about it," he says. "Personally, I'd be scared to go down there at night. I've known people to go down there with shotguns and shoot at anything resembling the light!"

Bruce Johnson is a local farmer who grew up in the Cohoke area and still lives there. His father's farm is within a stone's throw

West Point Light

of where the light is most often seen. "A lot of people have gone to see it," Bruce says. "I've seen license plates from all over the country. It seems like it's most often sighted on cloudy or rainy, dismal nights. I only saw it once. It was back when I was in high school, and I was driving home alone one night after a football game. I stopped at the tracks and I definitely saw some type of light. It looked to me like some sort of welder's arc. It had a gaseous type glow. It was kind of scary actually. I didn't stay long." Bruce's wife, Kay, saw it once, too. She described it as a "big bright round ball of light."

Most everyone who has seen the light (or lights) is pretty much in agreement as to its method of appearance. It first shows up far off, maybe several hundred yards down the tracks, then noiselessly, it approaches, glaring ever brighter as it nears, until its frightening closeness scares off viewers. Its relentless journey can only be impeded by the foolhardy actions of those who either try to run it down or shoot at it. This causes its instant disappearance. Also, although many have tried, including a national magazine film crew, no one has successfully photographed the light.

The source of the light, however, remains a mystery, and, to this day, stirs heated arguments. Many who have seen it contend it is a large lantern, carried by a conductor or brakeman, who allegedly lost his head, (literally), in an unspeakable accident and returns to search for it. One might reasonably ask, why does he look only at night? Others who believe the decapitation story say the light is too large and too bright to be a lantern; that it definitely is a train headlight.

But just as many people believe in the "lost train" theory. They have heard that after the battle of Richmond during the Civil War, in 1864, a train was loaded with wounded Confederate soldiers and dispatched to West Point, where they could recuperate or be sent by ship farther south for recovery and regrouping. The train left Richmond amid a soft chorus of moans but never reached its destination.

One person who has tried to trace the origins of the legend is Bill Travers of Hopewell. He has concluded that there might be two lights involved. "Many people I've talked to say they have seen a bust, that is the head and shoulders of a Confederate soldier, but without distinct features," Travers says. "He is carrying a lantern about 10 feet off the ground. And, beyond the soldier, maybe 300 yards or so, is the large headlight of a train."

The train theory was given some support by the experience of Tom Gulbranson of Oceanview and members of his family one night in 1967. Tom is an amateur psychic sleuth who, over the past 20 years or so, has investigated dozens of haunted houses and sites. He had visited the Cohoke location several times and had seen the light on a few of them. This time he was with his mother, father, brother and a friend.

As they drove up and parked at a strategic point, they noticed another car a few hundred feet away, only about three feet off the tracks, parallel to them. Tom got out his camera equipment and set it up and they waited. It was a bitterly cold night and, after a couple of hours of nothing but silence and darkness, they decided to leave. Just as they were packing up, the light appeared.

"This time it was brighter than I had ever seen it," Tom recalls. "It was an intense light and it came closer and closer. As it neared the other parked car, its startled occupants flicked on their head-lights, and when that happened, we all clearly saw the outline of a train."

Apparently, whatever mission the ghost train is on, it hasn't yet been fulfilled, because accounts of the eerie light persist to this day.

The Legend of Lady Skipwith

(Williamsburg)

he George Wythe (rhymes with Smith) House on the west side of Palace Green is a solid brick mansion that is one of the restored showpieces of Colonial Williamsburg. Built during the middle of the 18th century, the house, along with its outbuildings and gardens form what has been described as a "plantation layout in miniature."

The man for whom the house was named was one of the most famous colonists of his day, although he never received the widespread historic recognition of many of his contemporaries. His public career spanned a half-century and he was a leading force in the American struggle for independence. Wythe, it is said, influenced Thomas Jefferson more than any other man. Jefferson, in fact, referred to him as "my faithful and beloved Mentor in youth, and my most affectionate friend through life."

Wythe died tragically in 1806 as a result of being poisoned, allegedly by a grand nephew who thought he would become heir to a fortune. Wythe, however, lived long enough to write the young man out of his will. This incident occurred not at Wythe House, but in Richmond, so there are no reported hauntings of Wythe's spirit in Williamsburg.

There is, nevertheless, a rather well known ghost in the residence; one who has been glimpsed and heard at various times over the two centuries. This would be Lady Ann Skipwith, the daughter of a Scottish merchant. Born near Petersburg about 1741, she was described by those who knew her as an "attractive yet temperamental young woman of a disposition something uncommon." More candidly interpreted, she had a fiery temper and preceded today's women's rights advocates by more than 200 years by frequently speaking her mind. As one early suitor wrote chauvinistically in his diary: "She had a haughtiness, I may even say a fierceness in her countenance which on any little emotion destroyed in some degree that pretty softness which is so amiable in a young lady."

She married Sir Peyton Skipwith, a wealthy planter, and settled down to a comfortable aristocratic life at Prestwould in Mecklenburg County. Once, in the waning days of Williamsburg's glory in the 1770s, before the Colonial capital was moved to Richmond in 1780, Sir Peyton and Lady Ann attended a gala ball at the Governor's Palace. She was resplendent in a cream satin dress and tiny, high heeled red slippers, "upon which shone buckles of brilliants."

Wythe House

But something happened at the ball — no one is quite sure just what — which triggered Lady Ann's famous temper. Offended by whatever slight it was, she bolted from the Palace unescorted even as the minuets continued, and dashed across the Palace Green toward Wythe House. Why she chose this site for her hasty departure remains unexplained, although she may have been a house guest. Whatever, Lady Ann storytellers agree that while enroute she broke either the strap or heel of one of her slippers and arrived at the house hobbling on one shoe, with the other foot clad only in a silk stocking. Thus, she ascended the wooden stairs sounding somewhat like a person with a peg leg.

It is at this point where the accounts of past writers and actual history part company. According to those who have chronicled the story, Lady Ann then, in a fit of rage, took her own life. The writers contend she was insanely jealous that Sir Peyton cared more for her sister, Jean, than for her, and what happened at the ball was the last straw. They also wrote that Lady Ann lived in Wythe House at the time, and she now is buried in the small graveyard at nearby Bruton Parish Church.

Researchers at Colonial Williamsburg, however, say the facts are otherwise. Sir Peyton and Lady Ann never lived in Wythe

House, although they could have visited there. She did not commit suicide. Rather, she died in childbirth in 1779. And she is not buried at Bruton Parish. Elizabeth Hill Skipwith, wife of Sir Peyton's brother, Henry, lies in rest there.

What the researchers cannot refute, however, is that Wythe House today is haunted with what is most commonly believed to be the spirit of Lady Ann. For nearly 200 years, a number of past residents, visitors, servants and Colonial Williamsburg employees have reported experiencing strikingly similar psychic phenomena in the house.

The most frequent occurrence, almost always at midnight, is the distinct clicking sound of one high heeled slipper on the shallow steps of the broad stairway, alternating with the soft tread of a bare foot. Yet when the stairs and upstairs rooms are searched, no one is ever found. Even today, long time employees speak of such "visitations" in hushed, respectful tones.

Others have witnessed "a beautiful woman, fully gowned in colonial ball costume, come out of a closet in a certain room, look at herself in a mirror and finally pass out of the door" to vanish. No rational explanation for this often repeated sighting has ever been offered.

The gnawing question is if, in fact, this is the spectral reappearance of Lady Ann Skipwith, why does she return to haunt? Was her jealousy over 200 years ago warranted? One telling clue may lie in what occurred after she died. Sir Peyton did, indeed, marry Lady Ann's sister, Jean!

Carter's Grove

C H A P T E R   7

The Puzzling Riddle of the Refusal Room

(James City County)

t has been described by many as the most beautiful house in America. Indeed, the stately Georgian mansion, shaded by a row of enormous old tulip poplar trees overlooking the scenic James River, is a magnificent building even though it is nearly 250 years old. Carter's Grove, in James City County, near Newport News, is rich in history.

Construction of the house itself began in 1750 on a beautiful

1,400 acre tract of land bought by the legendary Virginia colonist Robert "King" Carter, one of the wealthiest and most influential men of his time. At his death he was said to have been owner of more than 300,000 acres of land and over 1,000 slaves. He chose the site for the benefit of his daughter, Elizabeth Carter.

The kitchen was built first, followed by an office at the end of the west wing. "King" Carter died before the building was completed, willing it to Elizabeth's son, Carter Burwell. He also specified that it "in all times to come be called and to go by the name of Carter's Grove." It was Burwell who added the main house, hiring the finest brick masons and carpenters in the area.

The house and grounds today are part of a historic foundation and are open to the public. Tens of thousands of tourists visit the plantation each year, marveling at its beauty. Guides carefully explain the background of the house, describe its elaborate period furnishings, and tell of the many famous guests who visited centuries ago. It was a showpiece residence and many lavish and memorable parties and dinners were held here for rich and famous personages of 18th century Virginia.

Like other plantation homes along the James River, Carter's Grove has its share of colorful legends and anecdotes. There are, for example, deep scars in the handsome hand hewn stair railing leading up from the front hall on the first floor. These were said to have been made during the Revolutionary War by a British cavalryman, Colonel Banastre Tarleton, who rode his horse up the stairway, "hacking the balustrade with his sabre as he ascended."

And if ever there was a site "ripe" for spiritual hauntings of unrestful souls, it would be Carter's Grove. That's because on the grounds is the site at which a great tragedy occurred more than 350 years ago. Here, archaeologists searching for 18th century artifacts, uncovered the remnants of a colony of early settlers dating back to the year 1619. The settlement was known as Martin's Hundred, and all residents of it were massacred by Indians in 1622.

Through the years there have been "occurrences" at the plantation site which lead one to believe psychic phenomena is involved. There is, for instance, the story told by husband and wife caretakers who were alone at the estate one evening. While doing chores in different parts of the west end of the mansion, each distinctly heard "footsteps" emanating from the east end. The man assumed it was his wife, and vice versa.

Later, when they met, they learned to their astonishment that the other had not ventured in the east end of the house. A search revealed nothing.

A supervisor of tour guides tells of an old gardener, now retired, who occasionally heard a woman playing a harp in an upstairs room. No one could ever convince him otherwise, although no known source for the musical interludes was ever found.

But it is in a downstairs drawing room of the house that the "real" ghost of Carter's Grove resides. Long time servants at the mansion are convinced that this room is haunted. It was here that a pretty young woman, Mary Cary, allegedly turned down a proposal for marriage in the mid 18th century from an ardent suitor named George Washington. Some years later, in the same room, Thomas Jefferson offered his hand to "fair" Rebecca Burwell. He, too, was rejected. This parlor subsequently became known as the "refusal room."

In the years since, some peculiar things keep recurring in the room. Most notably, whenever white carnations are placed in it, they are mysteriously ripped to shreds late at night and scattered about. No one knows who does it or why only white carnations are chosen, and only the ones in the refusal room, whereas other flowers in the house remain untouched.

In 1939, the Associated Press carried a nationwide story on the phenomenon, quoting Mrs. Archibald McCrea, then owner of Carter's Grove. She said at the time that it was true that "something" was coming in at night to "blight her blooms." Traps were set for mice but they were never sprung. John Coleman, an elderly butler, said it was "ghosts."

Tour hostesses at the plantation say occasionally even today they find the shredded petals of white carnations littered about the room. No one at the site, present or past, has offered any semblance of an explanation for such strange phenomena. It also is highly doubtful that the torn petals are the work of a prankster, or a succession of pranksters because when the house is open, tour guides are always in or near the room, and when the house is closed at night, security guards keep a close watch, and there are alarm systems throughout which would be triggered by anyone prowling about.

Could it thus be the spirit of one of the two famous spurned lovers, unable to contain his rage of rejection? If you believe in ghosts, it's possible. But some say it more likely may be the return of one of the women who refused. For it is said that when Mary

Refusal Room at Carter's Grove

Cary watched the triumphant Continental Army enter the area after the Yorktown surrender in 1781, commanded by General Washington, she was so overcome by chagrin that she fainted dead away in her husband's arms. So it is speculated that it may be her spirit which sometimes slips into the house late at night to tear the carnations in a fit of anger at what might have been, had she accepted Washington's original bouquet and proposal offer more than two centuries ago.

While I nodded, nearly
napping, suddenly there
came a tapping, As of some
one gently rapping, rapping
at my chamber door.

(*The Raven*)

The Rapping Friend of the Oystermen

(Fort Eustis)

t Fort Eustis, there is a small sheltered cove where the waters of Nell's Creek feed into the James River. Decades ago, before the government purchased the land surrounding this area, Nell's Creek was a haven for Tidewater oystermen. Daily, they would ply their time-honored trade amid the rich oyster beds of the James, nearby, and at night some would stay in the mouth of the creek from Monday night until Friday, when they would take their catch to market and head home.

Local lore has it that this particular creek was named after a young lady named Nell, who lived in the region, probably during the 19th century. No one seems to know her last name. What has been passed down is that she was a spirited, headstrong person who fell in love with a man described as a "straggler," and that her father strongly objected to such a union. In fact, that was putting it mildly. He allegedly told her that if she violated his wishes and married the man, he would kill her and bury her along with all his money.

To make a long story short, despite the warning, she ran off with her love, and her father lived up to his threat. He killed her and buried her, supposedly along with his life savings, at a point on or near the creek beneath two large walnut trees.

Since that time, no one is sure exactly when the sightings began although the consensus of opinion is about the 1880s or 1890s — up to the 1930s — Nell frequently "reappeared," mostly through the psychic manifestation of knockings or rappings, to area oystermen. She was, apparently, a friendly ghost, who provided timely news on where the best oystering was from day to day, and she often played games in which she seemed to enjoy answering questions, mostly concerning numbers and figures. Why she chose to befriend the lonely watermen is a question that remains unanswered.

But from here, the tale is best told by a very real, 79-year-old former oysterman and life-long resident of Poquoson who we shall call "J.P." He doesn't want his real name used because he is afraid the relating of his experience will subject him to crank calls. J.P. is, of course, retired now, but for many years in the 1920s and 1930s, he worked the waters of the James with his father and his brother.

"I definitely believe she was there. There's no doubt in my mind," he says of Nell. "I'm not a superstitious person, or necessarily a believer in ghosts, but in this instance I do believe. I only experienced her presence once, but it was something I will never forget. My father and brother heard her many times, and they believed. And I know they wouldn't tell a lie for anyone. Many say it was a myth, but a lot of people heard her."

As J.P. tells it, the stories about Nell began occurring late in the 19th century. No one ever saw her. They heard her. She "appeared" by knocking on the cabin roofs of the oystermen's boats.

"It was a knock unlike any other I have ever heard," J.P. recalls. "It was different. I can't even describe it. I guess I was about 18 or 20 when I experienced it. We were laid up overnight in the cove and I was standing outside the cabin with my head tucked inside, listening to the conversation. The cabin was full of watermen, talking. There was a very distinct knocking on top of the cabin. When I poked my head outside, it sounded like it came from inside. And when I ducked my head inside the cabin, it sounded like it came from the outside. There was no way it could have been a hoax. I wasn't really scared, but I must have looked concerned, because someone laughed and said, 'that's just ole Nell.' "

J.P. says his father told him many times about the rappings. "He would never volunteer to talk about her, but if someone asked, he would tell you." What J.P.'s father said was that Nell communicated only about things in the past. She would never "discuss" anything in the future.

She talked through her knockings. One rap meant yes, and two was for no. "In those days, people oystered over many sites up and down the James," J.P. continues. "Some would come out of the Warwick River, Deep Creek, Squashers Hole and other places. Every rock in the river had a name and the oystermen knew them all. So they would ask Nell how their peers were doing at other locations. Like, they would ask her, how many bushels of oysters did they get today at Thomas' rock (near the James River Bridge). And Nell would give so many knocks."

If the harvests were better elsewhere, according to J.P., then those asking the questions of Nell would fish those waters the next day. Invariably, their hauls improved. "Only a few of the men took stock in this," J.P. says, "but those who did always benefited from the advice. And she was always right. If she said so many bushels were brought in at such and such a rock, it was so."

Nell apparently amazed the men with all sorts of revelations. "She could answer anything she was asked," J.P. says. "You could ask her how many children someone had, and she would rap out the number in knocks on the cabin. You could ask her someone's age and she knew it exactly. My father said one time a man grabbed a handful of beans out of a sack and asked her how many he had. She told him, to the bean!"

In this manner, Nell carried on conversations with a number of oystermen over the years. She was especially conversant with one man, J.P. says, "and I was told that when he died she even appeared at his funeral by rapping on the coffin."

Robert Forrest, another life-long resident of Poquoson, well remembers his ancestors talking about Nell. "Oh, yes," he says, "I've heard the stories. The one I remember best concerned an old man named John, who was a very religious fellow. He had heard about Nell, too, and he didn't believe the stories until the night he experienced the sensation himself. He went out with some oystermen one time just to prove there was nothing to the tale. He carried his Bible with him.

"Well," Forrest continues, "they laid up in the Deep Creek area that night and tried to rouse her. 'Nell,' they said, 'if you're here, rap twice on the cabin.' Nothing happened. About 30 minutes later they tried again, and, sure enough, this time there were two sharp raps. They asked her several questions and she responded to each of them, but John still wasn't convinced. He thought someone was playing a trick on them, so he went out on deck. There was no one there and no boats nearby. Not only that, but the boat John was on had been untied from its stakes and was drifting freely in the creek. John became a believer right there!"

Occasionally, Nell would become disturbed at something asked or said, and she would quickly make her displeasure known. Randolph Rollins, a retired Poquoson carpenter, said he heard oystermen tell of the time she rocked their boat so violently they thought the tong shafts in the cabin would break. Yet, outside, the waters of the creek were "as smooth as a dish."

J.P. says his brother was reading the Bible to her one night, the chapter of Deuteronomy, when the knockings on the cabin became louder and louder and "got out of control." He stopped reading, and she stopped. "He never read the Bible to her again," J.P. says. Deuteronomy, it may be remembered, includes the ten commandments among which are "Thou shalt not kill," and "Honor thy father (and mother)." No wonder Nell was disturbed.

"All she ever told us was that her father had killed her and buried her nearby with his money," J.P. adds. "So one time, my father and brother went off digging in an area where there were two large walnut trees. Except the whole time they were there, they were pestered by large hornets and wasps, and they had to give it up."

Rollins tells of others who went looking for the lost loot. "One time they were driven off by a swarm of bees. They took that as an omen. Another time, a sudden storm whipped up and the wind nearly took down one of the trees. That scared them off and they never came back."

J.P., however, is not discouraged by all that. He is one who thinks there really is money buried somewhere in the Nell's Creek vicinity. "If I could, I would spend every penny I had to buy some land there now," he says. "But, of course, you can't. The government owns it. I tell you, though, I would like to pitch a tent right under those trees and spend the night. I sure wish I could talk to ole Nell again. I've tried many times, but she's never answered."

In fact, no one has heard from Nell for a number of years. She was a friend of the oystermen for a half century or so, but when the military took over at Ft. Eustis, the knockings ceased. "She must be at peace now," J.P. surmises.

CHAPTER 9

The Revenge of "Dolly Mammy"

(Poquoson)

n all the annals of ghost stories recorded in the United States over the past 400 years, one of the most famous, and one that has most often been talked and written about is the notorious "Bell Witch" of Tennessee. What sets this case apart is not so much the characteristics of the psychic manifestations involved — although they, too, were probably as intense and as varied as any in memory, including rappings, howlings, thrown objects, pinchings, slappings, chokings, blasphemous curses, and even a poisoning, among other things.

What is so different about the Bell Witch, separating it from most other lore and legend, is that this particular haunting was unquestionably the most thoroughly documented instance of violent psychic activity ever recorded at the time — early in the 19th century. Literally hundreds of people, including many experts and even the soon-to-be seventh President of the United States, Andrew Jackson, bore witness to the sheer havoc this she devil wreaked over a sustained period of four years.

It began in 1817 in Robertson County, Tennessee, north of Nashville on the farm of John Bell, who had four sons and a 12-year-old daughter named Betsy. One afternoon, John Bell saw perched on a split-rail fence a black bird of monstrous size. It was much larger than either a vulture or a turkey, and seemed to have an unnerving human gaze. As Bell stood transfixed, the great bird unfolded its wings and flapped across the field, casting a shadow over the skeletal corn stalks that chilled his blood. It was as though he had glimpsed, fleetingly, the shadow of death. This was the harbinger of the witch's arrival.

This was followed soon after by eerie scratchings at the doors and windows of Bell house. The children's hair was pulled, and they were pinched and slapped by unseen hands. At first, the Bells tried to keep their troubles secret, but soon word leaked out and first neighbors, and later others from across the state came to witness the frightening phenomena.

For whatever reason, the specter singled out young Betsy in particular. Her brother, William, wrote about the tormenting in his diary as follows: "This vile, heinous, unknown devil, this torturer of human flesh, that preyed upon the fears of people like a ravenous vulture, spared her (Betsy) not, but rather chose her as a shining mark for an exhibition of its wicked stratagem and devilish tortures."

In time, the witch made herself and her purposes known. She was, she said, Kate Batts, the woman who had sold the farm to the Bells. She claimed to have been cheated in the transaction and had returned from the dead to gain revenge.

When she wasn't harassing Betsy, she turned her wrath on John Bell. He became afflicted with acute pains in his mouth. It was, he said, as if his tongue was growing stiff and then swelling so much that he was neither able to eat nor talk for hours on end. He developed horrible facial contortions and uncontrollable tics. The witch cursed him incessantly, calling him vile names and predicting his imminent death. At the same time she continued to taunt Betsy, dragging her across the room by the hair and slapping her before dozens of terrified witnesses, until her face turned scarlet.

When Andrew Jackson came with an entourage including a psychic consultant, the witch went into such a rage that she drove the expert from the house. John Bell eventually went into a siege of convulsions, and the Bell Witch somehow transformed a doctor's medicine into a murky, toxic potion which caused Bell to lapse into a coma. When he died, and young Betsy's engagement to her childhood sweetheart was broken, four years after the witch had first appeared, the evil spell apparently was broken.

What has all this to do with Virginia ghosts? There is a striking similarity between the Bell Witch of Tennessee, and the ghost of "Dolly Mammy" Messick who surfaced some years later in the town of Poquoson. It was almost as if Kate Batts had come back in a reincarnated spirit.

Poquoson is located on a palette of land between Seaford and Yorktown to the north and west, and just above Hampton to the south and east. It derives its colorful name from the Algonquin Indian word "pocosin," which means a swamp or dismal place. It is nearly surrounded by water and is adjacent to the Plum Tree Island National Wildlife Refuge. Since Colonial times, Poquoson has been the home of rugged and closely-knit clans of watermen and farmers. Many current families can date their ancestors in the area back hundreds of years.

For eons, area residents owning cattle let their animals roam freely in lush, marshy regions known locally as "the Commons." Such was the case with "Dolly Mammy," a no-nonsense, hard working and well-liked woman, whose tragic story and haunting reappearances have been remembered and recounted from generation to generation.

The problem is, some of the details have gotten mixed up in the retelling, principally whether what happened involved one or both of Dolly Mammy's teenagers. One respected area author says

only one was victimized. Many Poquoson old timers, however, including one whose grandparents were directly connected to the bizarre incidents, say both girls were unwilling participants. Since the latter supposition seems to be the more prevalent one, let's follow it.

There also is considerable confusion as to precisely when the incident occurred. One version says the date was March 5, 1856. Yet, according to Bill Forrest, a local resident who says Dolly was his great aunt, there is a mention in the Poquoson Waterman's Book, an unofficial genealogical guide, which says she died in 1904 at age 42.

Whatever, it is agreed that it was a cold, blustery day laden with heavy dark clouds hovering over the low lands. Fearing a snowstorm, Dolly decided to go out into the marshlands to bring in her cows, and asked her daughters, Minnie and Lettie Jane, to go with her. Ensconced comfortably before a fire in the farm house, the girls refused. Some say they were afraid to venture out into howling winds and threatening skies. Others say they sassed their mother.

Angrily flinging on a cloak, Dolly turned to her daughters and told them that if anything happened to her she would return to "haunt" them for the rest of their lives. With that, she disappeared into the gloom. When she had not come back by dark, a search party of friends and neighbors was hastily organized, and they tramped through the marshes with lanterns, calling her name, but they found nothing.

The next morning, a lone fisherman, easing his boat up Bell's Oyster Gut, a narrow estuary near the woman's home, was startled at the sight of a bare leg sticking up out of the marsh grasses. He went for help, and soon after, the body of Dolly Mammy was recovered. She apparently had been sucked into a pocket of quicksand. It appeared that she had struggled desperately for her life, because the rushes and grasses around her body had been pulled up. Her funeral was well attended.

Not long after that, the haunting threat of Dolly Mammy began to be carried out. One day the girls went to visit nearby relations. No sooner had they arrived when ghostly knockings began to echo loudly throughout the house. Suspecting pranksters, a family member grabbed a heavy piece of wood and barred the door.

Incredibly, the bar leaped into the air from its iron fastenings and flew across the room. The knockings, described as "like an iron fist beating on a thin board," continued and grew in intensity, so much so that they were heard a quarter of a mile away by the master of the house. Rushing back home, he found the girls and his family cowering in terror.

While the thunderous knockings, which seemed to follow the girls wherever they went, especially at their house, continued as the main form of spectral manifestation, there were many other incidents as well. "All sorts of things started to happen," says Randolph Rollins, a spry octogenarian and lifelong resident of Poquoson. Rollins' grandfather was a witness to some of the events.

"I can remember him telling me about one night the two girls slept together in a bed and the next morning when they woke up their hair was tightly braided together," he says. "No one could ever explain that." As the months passed, relatives and neighbors spent considerable time at Dolly's house trying to console the distraught daughters. Rollins' grandfather was one of them.

"He told me many a time about being in the house, when a table in the middle of the living room with a lamp on it would start shaking and jumping up and down. Then the lamp would go out and it would be dark, and he could hear the sounds of someone being slapped. When he relit the lamp, the girls would have red marks on their faces with the imprint of a hand. He said that happened a number of times," Rollins says.

Once, witnesses claimed, as the girls lay in deep sleep in their bed, "something" lifted the bed off the floor and shook it. Another time, an unseen hand snatched a Bible from beneath the pillow of one of the girls and flung it against a wall.

As in the case of the Bell Witch of Tennessee, as word of the eerie doings got around, curiosity seekers from all over came to the house. An army officer from nearby Fort Monroe arrived with the intention of debunking the ghost as a myth. He had his men search the house from cellar to attic and then had guards surround it to ward off any tricksters. Yet that evening, as he sat in the parlor, the knockings were so loud they could be heard a half mile away. Then a lamp seemed to lift itself from a table, sail through the room, and land on the mantel. Having seen and heard enough, the bewildered officer wrote in a report, "Whatever causes the disturbance is of supernatural origin."

Rollins reports that once when his grandfather was in the house, two skeptical lawyers showed up. The rappings grew so deafening, normal conversation couldn't be heard and they abruptly fled. And one memorable evening a spirit medium was invited to hold a seance in the home. It was attended by the girls and a large group of people. According to published accounts of the affair, a "shadowy figure" appeared, winding a ball of yarn. As the figure responded to various commands of the medium, the girls fainted. Then the medium said, "If you are the mother of these girls and are connected with these strange rappings, (which were going on simultaneously) speak!" The girls' names were then called out, followed by wild, shrieking laughter. That was enough to clear the room. Everyone except the girls, the medium, and an old Baptist deacon, departed in haste.

This single "appearance" seemed to be the high point of the hauntings. When one of the girls died, the knockings and other phenomena ceased. The mother had made good her threat.

There is a brief epilogue. In the lush marshes and thick grass of the Commons, through which Poquoson cows roamed freely, there is one small patch of land where, curiously, no vegetation has grown since early this century. It is precisely the spot where the body of Dolly Mammy had been found so long ago!

The Celebrity Spirits of Fort Monroe

(Fort Monroe)

here are so many ghosts — famous or otherwise — at historic Fort Monroe in Hampton that it's hard to know where to begin. One can almost take his or her pick of a "celebrity specter" and chances are "it" has been sighted at some point over the past 160 years or so. The star-studded list of apparitions who have allegedly appeared at one time or another include Abraham Lincoln, Jefferson Davis, and his wife, Varina, the Marquis de Lafayette, Ulysses S. Grant, Indian Chief Black Hawk, and a budding young author and poet named Edgar Allan Poe.

In fact, the only major notable who either served or visited the Fort and has not returned in spirit form is Robert E. Lee, who as a young lieutenant helped with the engineering and construction of the facility in the 1830s.

But the list of haunts at Fort Monroe is not limited to the well known. There are numerous nameless ones also, including illicit lovers, and a bevy of perky poltergeists who have been accused of such indignities as smacking officers in the face with flying dish towels, and tossing marble laden tables across rooms. There are even reports — serious ones — of a reptilian monster who has been seen stirring in the ancient moat which surrounds the fort.

Dennis Mroczkowski, Director of the Casemate Museum at the Fort, offers a thought about why so many spirits seem to frequent the site. "With the hundreds of thousands of people who have been assigned to the fort," he says, "there's a large population to draw from for ghosts. There have been numerous sightings of strange apparitions and many tend to repeat themselves and become identified in people's minds with the famous people who have been here." He also believes that the dark and dreary corridors and the thick-walled casemates possibly could have lent some inspiration to the later macabre writings of one-time resident Edgar Allan Poe.

The history of the area dates back to the time of the first English settlement in America. The hardy souls aboard the *Godspeed, Susan Constant*, and *Discovery*, saw Old Point Comfort, where Fort Monroe is located, in April 1607, at least two weeks before they dropped anchor at Jamestown. A small exploration party even rowed ashore and met with local Indians.

In 1608, Captain John Smith checked the area out and deemed it an excellent site for a fort. Consequently, a year later, Captain John Ratcliffe was dispatched from Jamestown to build an earth work fortification that was called Fort Algernourne. By 1611, it was well stockaded and had a battery of seven heavy guns and a garrison of 40 men. A century later, there were 70 cannons at the fort, and in 1728, a new brick facility was constructed at Old Point Comfort and was renamed Fort George. This structure was completely destroyed by a fierce hurricane in 1749.

The strategic military value of the site was recognized by the French under Admiral Comte de Grasse during the Revolutionary War when his men re-erected a battery there. The War of 1812 demonstrated the need for an adequate American coastal defense, and over the next few years plans were drawn up for an elaborate system of forts running from Maine to Louisiana.

Old Point Comfort was selected as a key post in this chain, and the assignment for building a new fort there was given to Brigadier General Simon Bernard, a famous French military engineer and former aide-de-camp to Emperor Napoleon I. Construction extended over 15 years, from 1819 to 1834, and it was named Fort Monroe after James Monroe, a Virginian, and the fifth President of the United States.

Upon its completion, the fort had an armament of nearly 200 guns which controlled the channel into Hampton Roads and dominated the approach to Washington by way of the Chesapeake Bay. In fact, it has often been called "the Gibraltar of Chesapeake Bay." It represented the highest development in the art of seacoast defense at a time when masonry works were still resistant to gunfire, and to this day Fort Monroe remains the largest enclosed fortification in the United States. Standing on the tip of Old Point Comfort, a flat sand spit two and a half miles long, which projects southward from the mainland by Mill Creek, the fort was easily defended and difficult to approach.

So impregnable was this bastion, and so ideally located, it was one of the few Union fortifications in the South that was not captured by the Confederates during the Civil War. It was described as an unassailable base for the Union Army and Navy right in the heart of the Confederacy. Thus President Abraham Lincoln had no qualms about visiting the fort in May 1862 to help plan the attack of Norfolk. It was here, too, in April 1864, that General U. S. Grant outlined the campaign strategy that led to the end of the Civil War.

And it was also at Fort Monroe, a year later, that the imprisonment of Jefferson Davis, the President of the Confederate States of America, led, many believe, to one of the first and most famous ghost stories associated with the site. Davis, who had been planning to reestablish the capital of the Confederacy in Texas with hopes of continuing the war, was captured near Irwinville, Georgia, on May 10, 1865. His devoted wife, Varina, rushed forward when it appeared that a Northern cavalryman was about to

Lee House

shoot down her defiant husband, who also had been accused, inaccurately, of plotting an attempt to assassinate Lincoln.

Davis was taken to Fort Monroe, then the most powerful fort in the country, to prevent escape or rescue attempts. On May 23, 1865, he was placed in solitary confinement in a cell in Casemate No. 2 (a stone walled chamber), creating a painful incident which almost cost him his life and may well have provided the cause for the periodic spectral return of Varina Davis to Fort Monroe during the past century.

A day after his imprisonment, Davis was ordered to be shackled. When a blacksmith knelt down to rivet the ankle irons in place, the angered Davis knocked him to the floor. He sprang to his feet, raised his hammer, and was about to crush the Southerner's skull when the officer of the day, Captain Jerome Titlow, threw himself between the two men. Thereafter, it took four Union soldiers to subdue Davis long enough for the irons to be secured.

The next day, Dr. John J. Craven, chief medical officer at Fort Monroe, examined the prisoner and was shocked at his sickly appearance. He quickly recommended that the shackles be removed and they were a few days later. Meanwhile, the determined Varina fought hard for more humane treatment of her husband, and eventually she and Dr. Craven were successful. Davis was moved to better quarters in Carroll Hall. In May 1866, Varina got permission from President Andrew Johnson to join Davis at the fort, and she brought along their young daughter, Winnie. Jefferson Davis was released from captivity on May 13, 1867, travelled extensively in Europe, and later retired to Beauvoir, a mansion in Biloxi, Mississippi. He died in 1889 at the age of 81 and today is buried in Hollywood Cemetery in Richmond.

It is supposedly the apparition of the iron-willed Varina who has been seen on occasion at the fort, appearing late at night through the second floor window of quarters directly across from the casemate where her husband had been so harshly shackled. A number of residents have reported seeing her. One awoke early one morning to glimpse the figures of both "a plumpish woman and a young girl peering through the window." She got out of bed and walked toward them, but when she reached out to touch the woman's billowing skirt, the figures disappeared.

A wide range of psychic phenomena has been experienced in a splendid old plantation-style house facing the east sallyport that is known as Old Quarters Number One. Manifestations have included the clumping of boots, the rustling of silken skirts, the sounds of distant laughter and the strange shredding of fresh flower petals in mid-winter.

It is here, appropriately enough in the Lincoln Room, where the image of Honest Abe himself has been seen clad in a dressing gown standing by the fireplace appearing to be deep in thought. According to Jane Keane Polonsky and Joan McFarland Drum, who in 1972 published a book on the ghosts of Fort Monroe, other residents of the house have told of seeing Lafayette, Grant and Chief Black Hawk wandering about. All of them stayed at Old Quarters Number One during their lifetimes.

"Ghost Alley," a lane that runs behind a set of quarters long known as the "Tuileries," is the setting for one of the oldest and saddest stories of the supernatural at Fort Monroe. It is here, always under the cloak of darkness, that the fabled "White Lady" has been seen searching for her long lost lover. In the versions that have been handed down for a century and a quarter, she was a beautiful young woman who once lived in a Tuileries unit with a much older husband, a captain, who has been described by authors Polonsky and Drum as being "stodgy and plodding."

Being of a flirtatious nature, she inevitably, and as it turned out, tragically, attracted the attentions of a dashing younger officer, and their obvious longings for each other soon became apparent to all but the unimaginative captain. And when he left on a trip, the young lovers consummated their relationship. The captain, however, returned unexpectedly early one evening and caught the lovers in bed. In a fit of rage, he shot his wife. And ever since, she has been sighted fleetingly in a luminescent form roaming the dark alley looking for her handsome companion in hopes of rekindling their once-fervent romance.

Undoubtedly the most famous enlisted man ever to serve at Fort Monroe, even if it was only for a brief four months, was a 19-year-old named Edgar Allan Poe. He arrived at Old Point Comfort on December 15, 1828 and almost immediately sought help to get out of the army so he could pursue a career in writing. He was successful, and was discharged at Fort Monroe on April 15, 1829. He is known to have returned to the area once, 20 years later, when he recited some of his now-famous poetry at the old Hygeia Hotel on September 9, 1849, just four weeks before his death in Baltimore.

It is the spectral image of Poe, many have speculated, that was seen during the late 1960s at housing quarters on Bernard Road which, by coincidence, also backs onto Ghost Alley. It was here that a lady tenant of the house heard a mysterious tapping coming from the rear of a downstairs room one night in May 1968. Upon investigation she saw the figure of a man dressed in a white shirt with puffed sleeves, a red vest, and dark pants. She couldn't see his face in the shadows, even when he turned to give her a disdainful look. In an instant, he vanished in a gray mist through a window. Oddly, it was the same window in which the woman's son, a year early, had reported seeing a white mist float toward and go out. The shadowy figure was sighted once more in 1969, in a "bentover, crouching position" moving down a hallway, where he was said to have gone through a closet door without opening the door!

In other parts of Fort Monroe playful and noisy ghosts, sometimes known as poltergeists, have both frightened and amused, but most often bewildered, residents. At the Old Slave Quarters, for example, officers, their wives and children have been subjected to series of strange shenanigans over the years. Several tenants have found their downstairs furniture rearranged or shoved into the middle of the room overnight with no rational explanation for how it was done. One couple locked their pet cat in the kitchen at night in hopes it would rid the room of mice. Inexplicably, they would find the cat outside at the back door the next day, meowing to get back in.

At a two-story house next to the chapel, occupants found a heavy chest had been moved during the night and fireplace andirons were rearranged. On other occasions footsteps heard in the night ceased each time a light was turned on, drawers seemed to be opened and shut by unseen hands, doors slammed, and loud bangings and hammerings occurred. Even the post commander's quarters has been affected. There, such items as a pedestal cake stand and a Dresden figurine have been discovered broken overnight with no apparent cause.

The stories do abound at Fort Monroe! There is even an instance of a colonel who told of sighting a "monster" swimming about in the moat which encircles the fort. It is 60 to 150 feet wide and eight feet deep at high tide. The colonel said whatever he saw was pretty big. He followed it to an old footbridge where it disappeared.

The thing about all these happenings at the fort, aside from the sheer number of them, is the consistency with which they have been told and retold over the years in most cases by more than one person, and in some cases by many. The other thing is the durability of the incidents. Some are alleged to have occurred decades or

"Ghost Alley"

even a century or more ago. Others are far more recent. The ghostly episodes continue even to this day.

Workers at the Casemate Museum, which is well worth a tour in itself, tell of the relatively recent visit of the obviously shaken wife of an officer. She had heard of the many ghostly tales at the fort and wanted to share her own unnerving experience. She had been in a bedroom with her two teenagers watching television one night while her husband was in the basement. Before their startled eyes, a bedside table lifted up and flew across the bedroom, smashing into the fireplace, shattering the marble top. She and the children screamed, and their dog went wild, pawing at the floor. Oddly, a Waterford crystal lamp that had been on the table remained unscratched.

And finally there was the officer and his wife who were living in the quarters where Robert E. Lee was once housed. The husband was in the kitchen one night when a wet dish cloth sailed across the room and smacked him soundly in the face. He yelled at his wife, asking her why she had done that. She didn't answer. He discovered later she was outside the house at the time.

The playful poltergeists at Fort Monroe apparently were at it again.

A Case of Crisis Apparition

(Norfolk)

t is a shaded, secluded "isle of serenity" amidst the hustle and bustle of downtown Norfolk. It has been that way for 350 years. In fact, the first church built on the site of the present-day St. Paul's was known as "Ye Chappell of Ease." It was erected in 1641 as part of the Elizabeth River Parish. Norfolk became a borough in 1736, and the present church, known as the Borough Church, was built in 1739.

The church was struck and partially burned by the British on January 1, 1776, when Norfolk was bombarded and destroyed. The building was serving as a shelter for women and children during the attack. In the Civil War, Federal forces occupied the church from 1862 to 1865. The one and three-quarter acre church yard is very similar to the old yards of England. There are 274 listed graves here, the oldest of which is that of Dorothy Farrell, who died on January 18, 1673. Some of the stone markers bear a skull and crossbones, which signified death, not the resting place of a pirate.

Wedged into the far northeast corner of the church yard is an above ground tombstone with a strange quotation carved into it.

"Yes," says a church spokesman when asked, "that was a tragic case. The poor man lost his whole family. It is our only ghost story."

It also was, apparently, a case of "crisis apparition." This occurs when a person — the "receiver" — suddenly becomes aware that another person — the "transmitter" is undergoing a crisis. This may be in the form of pain, shock, emotion or death, even though the transmitter may be some distance away; in some cases thousands of miles. The most common examples of such phenomena occur in times of war, when a mother, for example, may report seeing or hearing her son at the moment he is wounded, often at the instant of his death. The theory is that the pain and shock trigger off involuntary telepathic contact between son and mother, or transmitter and receiver.

David Duncan's crisis apparition occurred in 1823. Three years earlier he had married Martha Shirley, the daughter of a widow who operated the Norfolk boarding house where he often stayed. Duncan was captain of the cargo schooner *Sea Witch*, and he took his bride on a honeymoon voyage to several Mediterranean ports. Afterwards, they settled in Norfolk and she gave birth to twins, Davis and Ann. Early in 1823, Duncan set sail again on a merchant voyage, carrying a cargo of lumber and animal hides.

On the night of May 12, the *Sea Witch* was anchored in the harbor of Genoa, Italy. Most of the crew had gone ashore to unwind, but master Duncan had stayed behind, reading in his cabin from the 18th century poet Edward Young's "Night Thoughts on Life, Death and Immortality." It was eerily apropos.

Thousands of miles away, a fire broke out in the bakery

beneath the Duncan's rooms. Martha desperately tried to escape with her infants, but a rickety staircase collapsed, and they perished in the flames. At that precise instant David Duncan was reading the poet's lines describing Death and an "insatiate archer" when he envisioned a fire at the foot of the main mast. He ran from his cabin and when he reached the deck the fire seemed to blossom. In the midst of the flames he clearly saw the wraith-like form of his wife frantically clutching their son and daughter.

Her screams pierced the silence in the harbor. "David! David! Save us!" she cried. And then, in a flash she was gone, as was the fire. Although crazed with anxiety, it was not until sometime later, when his ship finally docked at Norfolk, that Duncan learned the awful horror of his illusion was real.

And so, he placed a horizontal, raised tombstone, inscribed with Martha's name and the date of death over the single grave site in St. Paul's churchyard. To this, he had the stonemaker carve the two lines of verse he had been reading when his loved ones died: "Insatiate archer, could not one suffice? Thy shaft flew thrice and thrice my peace was slain."

CHAPTER 12

The Girl Who Was "Born To See"

(Portsmouth)

She was," says Gabrielle Bielenstein, "'Born to see'. Isn't that a marvelous expression? It means, of course, that a person is psychic. Some people are born with perfect pitch, and some can play the piano by ear. She was 'born to see.'"

Gabrielle is talking — in the darkened, high-ceilinged parlor of her magnificent Art Nouveau home at 328 Court Street in Olde Towne Portsmouth — about the teenage black girl who worked for Gabrielle's mother nearly half a century ago.

It is called the Maupin House, the family name, and it was built in 1885 because Gabrielle's grandmother, Edmonia, wanted to live on Court Street since it was the most fashionable section of the city. And it was erected on the last available lot in that section of Portsmouth, over a creek bed. The house has "20-odd rooms, including six bathrooms," a beautiful spiral staircase, exquisite wood paneling throughout, and was built at a cost of the then-princely sum of $7,000. Behind it was a splendid walled garden which was a showpiece of the area.

Gabrielle and her identical twin sister, Florence Mary Maupin, grew up in these fashionable surroundings, and the young girl came to work there in the early 1940s, during World War II, when most of the other servants had gone to work in the Norfolk Naval Shipyard nearby.

Almost immediately, she began to "see" things others didn't.

"There had been some strange occurrences in the house before," says Gabrielle, "but we had never paid much attention to them. One would hear tales. Some of the other servants would talk occasionally about a rocking chair rocking on the front porch. We would hear noises that sounded like someone descending the staircase. Things like that."

But the new young girl, whose name escapes Gabrielle, saw, felt, and sensed presences in and around the house almost from the day she began work there. And, with uncanny accuracy, they perfectly fit descriptions of past residents, both animal and human.

Consider, for example, the instances of the buried pit bulls. "My

328 Court Street, Portsmouth

Gabrielle Bielenstein with Portrait of Miss Edmonia

mother, Florence, had about given up on having any children, before my sister and I came along, so she had a number of pit bull dogs," Gabrielle says. "Now you have to understand, this was at a time when those dogs were very rare. Few people knew what they looked like. They hadn't got all the notice they have in recent years.

"But my mother didn't have much luck with them. Most of them died very young, and they were all buried in little pine coffins in a corner of the yard. When the young girl came to work for us, there hadn't been any pit bulls around for years, and I don't believe she had any way of knowing what they looked like. Yet, she told us she saw the dogs playing in the yard. When she was asked to describe what they looked like, she said they were just like Miss

Julia's dog. Miss Julia was a neighbor who had a Boston Terrier, which closely resembles the pit bull. How did she know what those dogs looked like unless she saw them?"

The girl also saw the apparition of Miles Portlock. Born a slave before the Civil War, he had been a servant to Gabrielle's great grandmother. "We considered him a part of the family, and as a child, I can remember him sitting at the kitchen table and drinking ice tea. Someone had given him a gold or silver-headed cane and he used to use it to dig out the grass that grew between bricks. When I was a little girl, he was so old then that this was about all he could do."

Gabrielle says he died about 1939 or 1940 somewhere around the age of 90, well before the girl came to Maupin House to work. Yet she said she saw him in the garden with his cane, and she described him perfectly, too.

And then there were the sightings of Miss Edmonia, Gabrielle's grandmother. The girl said she saw an "old woman" on the staircase at times. "We had a lot of photos in the house in those days," Gabrielle notes, "but there were no recent photos of Edmonia before her death, because she refused to have any taken after she reached middle age. She had been a beautiful woman.

"We took the girl around to view all the photos, and she immediately picked out an earlier portrait of Edmonia, and said that was who she saw. She said it was the same person, only she was much older now. How did she know? How did she pick that one picture out of all the ones in the house. She had no way of knowing what Edmonia looked like. I can't explain it, other than she was born to see!"

The girl only worked at the house for a short period. Her psychic ability unnerved the other servants and they demanded that she leave. In the intervening years there have been a few other haunting occurrences. Gabrielle's husband, Hans, a native of Estonia who now teaches Chinese at Columbia University in New York, once woke up in an upstairs bedroom and saw the apparition of a woman appear at an open door.

"They're still here," says current house sitter Emily Mossberger of the ghosts. "They are friendly, but strange things go on." Her daughter was taking a nap one day in a room on the third floor when she was awakened by "something" that was moving her bed. It kept moving as she sat up.

The Maupin House is one of the most popular ones on the annual Olde Town Ghost Walk at Halloween. Either an actor or a local resident usually plays the part of old Miles Portlock and tells the story of the ghostly legends, and the young girl who was "born to see."

The Incredible Feats of "Old Crump"

(Virginia Beach)

he saga began one night in 1898 when young Henry Stone, who had recently been blinded in a hunting accident, came to spend the night with his friend, Eugene Burroughs at an old farmhouse in Sigma, near the present area of Pungo in Virginia Beach.

They were each about eight years old, and because the house was crowded with guests, the boys slept on a pallet on the parlor floor. Burroughs was roused when his pillow "slid away from under his head." He blamed Stone, who claimed innocence. Then Stone's pillow sailed across the floor, and they got into a fight which subsequently was broken up by Burroughs' father. When they told him what had happened, he laughed and said it was just the spirit of "Old Crump" — a man named Crump Bonney who had died in the house a century before. After Mr. Burroughs left, the boys said "things, like cats," kept walking across their feet, and chairs and other pieces of furniture seemed to "parade in a circle around the room." Frightened, but unharmed, they finally nodded off to sleep.

For the next 40-plus years, whenever Stone and Burroughs got together, an invisible force inexplicably moved objects about. And not just small objects. Pot-bellied stoves, bunk beds and chests of drawers slid across rooms, and in several instances, men and women were jostled about. "I cannot explain it," Burroughs said years later, "but that's the way it has been ever since Henry and I were boys." Such incidents were witnessed, documented and written about by scores of investigators, including doctors, scientists, newspaper reporters and lawyers. In fact, as time went on, and the story of the awesome phenomena got around, hundreds of people from all over the country came to see special seances Stone and Burroughs held, and they were rarely disappointed.

Two of the most expert witnesses were Edgar Cayce, the famous psychic, and his son, Hugh Lynn. Hugh Lynn sat in on a number of meetings with Stone and Burroughs and commented that the force was not very active when he was present. Once, however, a manifestation did occur that he could not explain. "It was pitch dark," he wrote later, "and I sat between Burroughs and Stone, with one foot on one of Stone's feet, and my hand and other foot on Burroughs. A picture came off the wall. I got up and put it back, winding the wire about the nail to make it more secure. Then I insisted that Burroughs and Stone stand in the middle of the room. Again, the picture came off the wall. This I can't explain."

As the boys grew older, the "happenings" grew stronger and more varied. Burroughs, for example, recorded the following in a privately published family chronicle: "We went to bed early; hardly had we put the light out and gotten into bed before our pillows left the bed and the covering followed. We decided to let the invisible force take everything it wanted and not try to get anything back, but the force threw everything back on the bed.

"Just then a big old-fashioned rocking chair hopped on the bed. It only felt as heavy as an ordinary chair when it first landed, but the longer it stayed the heavier it got. We thought it best to put it on the floor, and that is when the wrestle started. It took 30 minutes to get out from under the chair. We held a little conference and decided to put the chair, pillows and covering out of the room, which we did, the pillows in a big wood chest in the hall and the chair near the chest. We came back and fastened the door with an old-fashioned night latch. We got back in bed and the pillows from the hall were already there! Again, before we had time to do any investigating, the chair was on the bed."

Crump, Burroughs said, made objects, heavy or light, even people, go sailing about, irrespective of gravity, thick walls "or the personal wishes of those present." Particularly disturbing events occurred during the winter of 1906. Burroughs' parents were away from home for a few days, so Henry and another boy, Joe Walters, came over to stay with him. The first night the pillows and blankets "acted up again," so the next evening they hatched a plan to "catch" the invisible force.

Remembered Burroughs: "After locking all windows and doors, we knew there was only one place where Crump could enter — through the stove pipe hole in the chimney. Henry agreed to sit by the chimney. When we were sure Crump was in the room, he was to put heavy cardboard over the hole. Then it would be up to Joe and me to catch Old Crump.

"Joe and I went to bed. It wasn't long before Henry yelled, 'He's got my hand!' Joe and I rushed to him, but he had been dragged under the bed! The cardboard had been torn in two. We were very frightened. We decided to keep the lamp burning and to sit up the rest of the night." That was enough for Walters. He went home.

Two nights later, with Stone and Boyd Beecham there to spend the evening, the manifestations continued. Said Burroughs: "After a half hour, our shoes fell heavily into the bed. The covers crept away. I thought that Crump would never work in the light, and, since we were in no mood to go without blankets that night, we lit a lamp. I'd scarcely gotten into bed when the lamp flew over from the dresser, about 15 feet away, and nudged me. It was still burning. I returned it to the dresser and wearily crawled back into bed. The lamp sailed right back and was on us again.

"We got a lantern and a piece of rope from the barn, but now the lantern jumped onto the bed. I tied the lantern to the bedpost with the rope, whereupon the lantern began to rattle. 'You can jump as much as you please,' I told the lantern, 'but you can't get on the bed this time.' With that, the bed turned bottom up."

After that harrowing experience, Stone and Burroughs did not get together again for two years. In April 1908, they both were working for the Stephens and Easter Fish Company at their packing house in Virginia Beach. Dog-tired after a hard day's work, they both decided to spend the night in the company's bunk house. After all, Crump had only shown up in Burroughs' home. Burroughs shakenly recalled what happened next: "During the night a terrible crash shattered the quiet. The pipes of the kitchen cookstove at the far end of the house had fallen. The stove came sailing 25 feet in mid-air — to stop by our beds. I jumped out of the window and the stove crashed to the floor.

"The next night several fellows from the other camp saw shoes, clothing, fishing gear — everything, thrown onto the bunks — except the stove. After the men returned to their camp, we went to bed with the lantern lit. It landed on us still lighted. Harry Flanagan, the plant engineer, came by and suggested we tie the lantern. With us, he saw the lantern rattle and jerk from its lashing.

It sat on us; then, after five minutes, flew back to the floor and sat. When the lantern came back to us, we grabbed it. The upper frame stayed in our hands, but the bottom section and chimney fell to the floor." At this point, Burroughs left to spend the rest of the night in another camp, and nothing else happened.

As the years passed, curiosity seekers came from all over, besieging the two men to make the mystery force appear. On one such occasion Burroughs' sister-in-law brought a group of women to the old farmhouse in Sigma. Burroughs told about it in the family publication. "The force seemed to take pleasure in entertaining everybody," he wrote. "It inevitably began throwing pictures around the room, very much to the amusement of our guests. For awhile it had everybody excited. It changed from throwing pictures to pillows.

"Everybody began to relax. Just then we could hear a noise in the next room. In came an automatic shotgun loaded with five shells. When everybody found just what it was, we all came near fainting. We moved very carefully and took our time extracting the shells from the gun. The gun was put out of the room and then, as everybody was jabbering, Mr. Stone, Burroughs, and several others were thrown to the middle of the floor, their chairs on top of them.

"It was a scramble to try to get on your feet and place yourself where you were, seeing how easily the invisible force handled all those people. Fear began to come into the room and everyone was tense. Finally, they settled down again, but not for long. There came a crash and in came our coats. They had been put in the adjoining room on a bed. We decided it was time to go home, but a few stayed to see what else would happen.

"Soon a little noise was heard in the bedroom. Just then, in came a quilt, then came the mattress. Another loud crash — one that sounded as if the door was coming down between the living room and the bedroom. We investigated and found the bedspread jammed in the door leading to the living room. Everyone went home after that."

Through all the "visitations," Burroughs maintained that neither he nor Stone had any control over what might happen when they got together. He recalled one special incident which seemed to bear him out. "Once," he said, "Stone and I met unexpectedly on a street in Norfolk. Immediately, stones, bottles and other things began rolling toward us. We had to get off the street before we alarmed passersby."

But there was one unconfirmed story that suggested they

could, on occasion, "will" the spirit. Charles Thomas Cayce said he heard that once one of the two, either Stone or Burroughs, owed some money to a country grocer in the Pungo area and they got in an argument over it. Cayce said that one day all the grocer's stock "moved" from the shelves to outside the store, bewildering the grocer. "It was never clear just how much control they had over the force, or if they had any control at all," Cayce noted. "Maybe the force just moved things at random."

One person who had first hand knowledge of "the Stone and Burroughs show" is Mrs. Thelma LaBarrer who still lives in Virginia Beach. She remembers a time when her late husband and a friend stayed with the two men one night, sitting on their bed to hold the covers on. The covers kept coming down anyway. She said things would come off the wall and fly around the room whenever Stone and Burroughs got together.

In 1925, Dr. J. Malcolm Byrd, from the prestigious *Scientific American Magazine* came to Virginia to investigate the force. He told Burroughs that they should try communicating with the spirit by means of tapping. "The first time we tried to talk to Crump," Burroughs said, "was at 12:30 the night of July 5th, 1925. We went out to the barn so as not to disturb Mrs. Stone. After about five minutes in the inky blackness, Crump threw some sticks into my lap.

"I said, 'Invisible Force, I have been informed that you will talk to us. If so, speak.' No response. 'How about talking to you in code?' I said. 'One knock for yes, two knocks for no, three knocks for I don't know. If this is satisfactory, knock once.' We heard one really loud knock. My stomach contracted with fear. I had a thousand questions to ask him and all of them left me. I did manage to ask, 'Who are you?' He replied 'Uncle Billy.' He was my mother's uncle who I had known as a small boy and who died only a few years prior to the beginning of the poltergeist activity. We still called him Old Crump." Later, Burroughs added, they talked to the invisible force many times and he often replied, with the best results coming when the moon was full.

Dr. Byrd warned the men not ever to make the force mad. "You don't know what you're dealing with nor how much harm it may do you," he said. "We've never made the force mad as far as we know," Burroughs said. "No one was ever hurt by it — except a few who have hurt themselves in their haste to get away from a seance."

Burroughs said Old Crump could create all kinds of physical noises, including, for example, the "rip" of stitches being torn apart, or the grinding of the hole being bored through a wall, or even music from a piano. Once, when Burroughs' uncle came to Sigma for a visit, "a lot of toilet articles came into the room. He told his nephew that he bet nothing else would move in the room when he propped himself against the door. "At that moment we heard a boring sound as of an auger boring a hole through the wall," Burroughs said. "Then a Coca-Cola bottle appeared in Uncle Jerome's hand. He marked it to identify it and put it in another part of the room. It returned to him as mysteriously as before."

Burroughs said some persons experienced a cold rush of air on their cheek, or the feeling of being rapped on their legs, or having ice put down their back. "Once a pillow in my hands began to breathe like a living thing! I beat on the pillow to make it stop, but it jumped out of my arms and slid across the room," he continued.

One of the most terrifying of all "force" experiences took place when Stone and Burroughs were talked into giving a special seance during a vaudeville-type show. They had stopped giving seances because they felt they could not control the spirit, but on this occasion they relented. The event drew headlines in the local paper, and so many people tried to wedge their way into Girkins Hall in Norfolk, that Stone and Burroughs had to have a police escort to get there.

The force apparently had temporary stagefright that night, because the men sat on the stage for nearly an hour and nothing happened. With the audience getting restless, Burroughs appealed to some of his spiritualist friends to see if they knew something that would "hurry things up." About 25 people joined hands and said a prayer.

Burroughs picks up the story from there. "In a few minutes, a young lady opposite me rose to her feet. She put her hands out and in a moment sailed over to me. She traveled a distance of 12 feet after swaying a moment there in her place. Fortunately, I was able to catch her. I gave her a hard push and let go. She stretched out in a horizontal position about two feet above the floor, her arms still straight in the air. She was lowered slowly to the floor during a period of about five minutes.

"I then tried to stand her up straight, but she was completely rigid. We called a doctor. He checked her and whispered in my ear, 'Burroughs, she's dead! She has no heart beat nor pulse.' I asked him how she could become rigid in so short a time. I was alarmed. A friend of mine, Captain Ford, helped the doctor and me to stand her on her feet. She was so stiff you could have broken her fingers like match sticks. The Randalls (professional magicians also performing that night) told me to tell her she was all right.

"I did that. I kept repeating it and after 10 minutes, she drew a long breath. She came to relax and we were able to sit her on a chair. I asked her to explain to the audience that she was not a part of the show and to tell us what had happened to her. She said she didn't remember anything after joining hands."

Burroughs said he, too, had been suspended in mid-air "many times." Other persons were transported about the room during such sittings. "I never had attributed this power to myself," Burroughs said, "but always to the Invisible Force. Certainly, I was not conscious of any will to transport myself or any one else."

Another time, Stone and Burroughs and two friends were approaching a barn when a corn planter, with no one in it, headed directly toward them. They stopped it and tried to take it back to the barn, but it "rolled out in the yard for some distance and fell over." Inside the barn a grass scythe, hanging on a wall, "came down from its hook" and fell across one of the men's laps. Burroughs also said that many times people tried to "trick" the force, or to catch it, never with any success, and often with unnerving results. One photographer who had brought his camera to take pictures one night was, according to Burroughs, "heaved, camera and all, out the door."

Throughout their lives, Henry Stone and Eugene Burroughs never really found out what caused the psychic invisible force. "I keep hoping I'll understand some day about the strange powers that Henry and I possess," Burroughs once said. "We have discovered that our sons also engender the Force when they meet. Is it inherited?" Indeed, the younger Burroughs said in 1968 that he "had witnessed the events brought about by his father's association with Stone, and that he himself also had been the victim of similar happenings when in the presence of Stone's son. It has been many years since anything has happened. We were young teenagers the last time the force manifested itself."

"Is the Force part of our subconscious minds?" The elder Burroughs once asked. "Is it mischievous spirits that enjoy our amazement at their pranks? Or is it really Uncle Billy Cox?"

Whatever it was, it was very real. Said Hugh Lynn Cayce many years ago: "I have talked to many honest, intelligent people who certainly believe they heard and saw all manner of poltergeist activity. I cannot explain it."

CHAPTER 14

In visions of the dark

night I have dreamed of

joy departed

(A Dream)

An Obsession Named Melanie

(Virginia Beach)

 ary Bowman is a vivacious, red-haired, admitted workaholic who, along with her partner, Kay Buchanan, ran a successful interior design business called "Mary and Me" in Virginia Beach.

Mary Bowman also is, in her words, "metaphysical."

There are, of course, many definitions for this. One is supernatural. Another is relating to the transcendent or supersensitive, or, if you prefer, a division of philosophy that includes ontology and cosmology. Ontology, in turn, is a branch of metaphysics relating to the nature and relations of being. It also is a particular theory about the nature of being or the kinds of existence. Cosmology is a branch of metaphysics that deals with the universe as an orderly system.

To Mary, however, metaphysical simply means "open." "If

you are open," she says, "you go beyond the five senses, which are earth-bound." The lay person would probably call Mary psychic, and she probably would not disagree. She has had a special sensitivity since childhood. When she was 10, for instance, she had a vivid dream in which her grandfather died. She awoke and told her parents. They told her to go back to sleep. An hour later the telephone rang and the family was informed of the grandfather's death. She also once was "visited" by her grandson, in the form of an apparition, a year before he was born!

"Oh yes, I've had some experiences over the years," Mary smiles. But nothing in the conscious world of the metaphysical prepared her for what happened in the fall of 1985. After working late at her office one night, which was most often the case, she got in her car and headed home. As she was driving past the old John B. Dey farm on Greatneck Road, she felt a sensation. "There was a voice," she remembers. "It was a girl's voice, and it was crying out for help."

It was not unusual for Mary to receive such a message. She often "reads" the troubled thoughts of others in daily contacts with people, and has had to learn how to turn off such waves. "Otherwise you would be depressed all the time, and I have enough troubles of my own. I can't take on the burdens of the world," she says. But the girl's voice was different. It sounded urgent, and it seemed like she had singled out Mary for a specific purpose.

As time went on, the sensation grew stronger. Each time she drove past that section of the city, she would hear the voice calling out. Mary began to form a mental image. "It scared me at first," she says, "because she looked so much like my own daughter. I saw a picture of a young girl, maybe 18 or 19, or perhaps a little older. She had long blonde hair. She was lying down, as if she were in a coffin. She appeared to be wearing Colonial-era clothes. She had billowing sleeves, and I got the feeling that she lived 200 years ago."

There were other distinct features in Mary's picture. She envisioned a big, meandering farm house with a large porch in white lattice work, part of which was broken. And very distinct in the image was a brick wall. Somehow, Mary felt, all these things were connected. "I became obsessed with it," Mary says. "I took off from my work in the middle of the day and would drive around looking for the house and brick wall. Things got crazy. I had to find out about the girl. Who was she? What did she want? Why was she calling to me? I became a nervous wreck."

Mary went to a well-known psychic counselor in Virginia Beach, but that proved inconclusive. She then was referred to Kay Buchanan who also was psychically gifted. "Kay immediately identified with me," Mary says. "She saw the same thing I did. We felt the name of the girl was Melanie, and that she might have been a school teacher. She had an affair with a married man and had gotten pregnant. We sensed that her lover had killed her, and hastily buried her in an unmarked grave."

It was at this point that Mary says she had to let go. "I wanted to help, but it had become so overpowering I was afraid the search for Melanie would consume me." For the next several months, Mary went about her life, blocking out the vision.

Then one day, as she was out in the area of the old Dey farm on a business call, she saw it. The wall. The brick wall just as she had visualized it. It surrounded the farm house, separating it from the rows of new houses that were being developed all around.

Mary went up to the door of the farmhouse and knocked. When the owner answered, she told him the story of her obsessive dream from start to finish, including the brick wall. "I was afraid he would think I had escaped from the mental ward, but he hardly seemed surprised. In fact, he just said, 'I've got something to show you.' He led me into the garage and there was a pile of human bones. He said the developers had unearthed about three or four unmarked graves in their diggings, and he had rescued the remains and was going to have them reburied.

"Everything became clear to me all of a sudden. *That* was why Melanie had been calling to me for help," Mary says. "Her resting place had been disturbed. She had been trying to tell me that. Kay and I believe she might even have been worried that people would find out she was pregnant. I don't know for sure."

She must have found peace at last with her reburial. And with it, Mary, too, felt a tremendous relief. The vision and the voice disappeared.

CHAPTER 1 5

He might not sing

so wildly well

A mortal melody

(Israfel)

A Haunting Love Story
(Virginia Beach)

The house in the Laurel Cove section of Virginia Beach has been a hotbed of psychic activity ever since Bee and her husband moved into it in 1972. For personal reasons soon to be evident, the woman's full name, and the names of others involved here have been abbreviated.

A great range of manifestations have occurred, and still do. In fact, says Bee today, "the house is absolutely alive with ghosts. I've heard the sound of footfalls on the stairs. There are moaning voices, and a woman giggling. You sometimes hear someone humming. There is a distinct noise of a rustling skirt. Doors open and close with no one there. An expensive jade vase was knocked off the mantel, and pictures have fallen off the walls."

Bee is not alone in having experienced the occurrences. Her husband, and a number of her friends have also witnessed the spectral happenings. "Our bed has been shaken and slapped on occasion," she continues. "Once we heard the sounds of a gala party going on downstairs at 2 a.m. When we went down to investigate, all was quiet. Another time, we had our own New Year's

Eve party to beat all New Year's Eve parties! A meatball leaped four feet in the air out of its chafing dish. And a guest had his plate of food whisked from his lap. It fell on the floor but no food was spilled. At a card party once, one of my guests had her tea cup stand on its own at a 90 degree angle, yet no tea spilled."

Some of the strangest events have involved the many mirrors Bee has placed throughout the house. Once she awoke to find the distinct handprints and footprints of a baby clearly outlined on a large mirror. One of the footprints had six toes! A newsman photographed the images, and although the results are blurred and inconclusive, he himself had no doubts of what he had seen.

At various times the house has been filled with odd odors, including those of fudge cooking, and of tomato sauce. Bee also has seen the apparition of a small girl, "with long hair and a protuberant stomach," looking at her clothes in the bedroom closet. The ghostly phenomena have been so consistently prevalent that several newspaper and magazine articles have been written about them.

Bee, who says she has been "intuitive" all her life, believes the manifestations are directly related to the history of the area. The development is built on the site of the Eastwood Plantation, which dates back to 1637. "There are a number of desecrated graves right in this vicinity," she points out. "There are at least six graves and one tombstone just across the street. There may be more directly under the house."

But as interesting and as unusual as all that has gone on in the house has been, it merely serves as a prelude to the incredible story of Bee's long-term life and death relationship with a gentleman we shall call Bill.

He was tall — about six foot five — charming, debonair, generous and charismatic. He seemed to have been everywhere and done everything. He had been a friend of Al Capone. He had been involved in the development of fuel for diesel engines. He had been in the silent movies. He had married a millionairess. He was the epitome of social grace and courtly manners. He had an imposing personality. Everyone liked him.

From the moment Bee met him, she was mesmerized. And Bill fell immediately and irretrievably in love with her. The problem was, each still had a spouse. Bill nevertheless openly professed his love to Bee, and then even to her husband. Bee told Bill she would not leave her husband. Bill then decided that the next best thing would be to spend as much time in Bee's company as possible.

From then on, for the next two or three years, the four of them

— Bee and her husband, and Bill and his wife — were almost inseparable. Then Bill got cancer. As his condition worsened, Bee spent more and more time with him. They talked endlessly about life, death and the hereafter. He told her that he believed the mind goes on living even after the body expires. He said he called it the mind. Some people called it the soul. He told her that if there was any way for him to communicate with her after he died, he would find it. "We shed our astral bodies," he said, "but our minds go on." Bee told him she would try to be receptive. He died in October 1982.

Some time later — Bee doesn't remember exactly when — she

began writing down details of their relationship in long-hand. She felt that Bill was so colorful, and their love had been so special, that it would make a good book, and possibly a movie. One day she was reading her rough notes onto a tape recorder, trying to dictate them in paragraph form. She finished one passage and then hesitated, trying to recall just what had happened next. There was a pause on the tape. Then she went on.

In playing back the tape, when she got to the part where she had paused, she gasped. On the tape was a man's deep voice filling in the blanks in her memory. It was Bill's voice! Frightened, Bee grabbed her car keys and ran out the front door. She didn't come back for hours.

Later, she had the tape analyzed by experts. They couldn't explain it. In time, Bill's voice began appearing on other tapes. Once Bee was singing at the piano with her sister. Bee had long ago been a singer at a French nightclub on Long Island. When she played that tape back, Bill's voice came through loud, if not clear, singing "There Is A Place For Us." Bee and her sister were astonished. The male voice is deep and raspy, and it sounds like a record that is being played at half speed. The voice kind of drags and shakes. It is, to say the least, an eerie sound.

There are other manifestations of Bill's return, too. "He used to smoke expensive, imported cigars," Bee says. "They had a marvelous aroma about them. I used to love them. That's one way I know he's around today. I can smell the same aroma." Another way she can sense his presence is through her tiny dog, Brandy — half Chihuahua and half Beagle. "He sees Bill," she says. "I see Brandy's eyes follow him across the living room until he sits down in his favorite chair."

At other times, Bee has had her hair stroked by a mystery hand. "Once I looked in the mirror when this happened, and I could see my hair move," she says. At one point, she called a psychic couple and had them visit her in the house to offer advice. The woman saw Bill's vision sitting in his chair. She described him perfectly to Bee although she had no prior knowledge of what he looked like. The woman's husband advised Bee to establish a set means of communicating with Bill. He suggested having the ghost turn the light switch to one room on and off as a signal. Bee says this is how she knows Bill is around now.

"I feel like we are soul mates," she says. "He had so much empathy, so much feeling and sensitivity for me. He loved me so much he wanted to share it in life after death."

Is all that we see or seem

But a dream within a

dream?

(A Dream Within A Dream)

The Psychic Search for Chief Black Foot

(Virginia Beach)

(Author's note: After hearing of, reading about, listening to, and otherwise personally investigating literally hundreds of ghost stories over the past dozen years or so, there are times when I get the feeling that I have been doing this too long; that maybe I have heard it all. How many footsteps in the attic can one write about? But fortunately, each time this has happened, along comes an incredible tale that jolts the psyche and defies belief.

Such is the real-life saga of Victoria Mauricio, a Virginia Beach psychic-healer. I first learned of her through another psychic, a friend of mine, Kay Buchanan, who told me about a woman who found "the bones of a great Indian Chief." Her name was "Victoria something," Kay had said. I was intrigued. After some asking around, I found Mrs. Mauricio, now a widow in her sixties, who was gracious enough to grant me an extended interview.

She is, she told me, a psychic from a family of psychics which runs back 1,000 years! "I had a strange birth. It took a week. I was born with hair almost six feet long. Long, thin strands. Isn't that odd? And I weighed only two pounds," she says. She was born in South Wales. "For all my life I have been involved with psychic phenomena. My mother, grandmother and aunt were all psychic." She married an American after World War II, had a son, and moved to this country in 1952, eventually settling in Princess Anne County.

What is doubly remarkable about the extraordinary experience she had, which began in 1975, climaxed in 1978, and continues today, is that it has been so well documented. When her story became known in 1978, NBC television filmed it; the former network program, "That's Incredible," did two segments on it; a local station did a "P.M. Magazine" piece for TV; *Fate Magazine*, the national publication on psychic phenomena, did a cover story; *National Enquirer* ran a large feature; and scores of other newspapers and radio stations, large and small, from Norfolk to Cody, Wyoming, and Billings, Montana, all covered it extensively. Wilford Kale, writing in the *Richmond Times-Dispatch*, called it an episode "straight out of the Twilight Zone." Victoria herself wrote a book on her adventures called "The Return of Chief Black Foot." It is a fascinating account which, unfortunately, is today out of print, although there is a copy at the Virginia Beach library.

And now, here is Victoria's story)

It all began one night in September 1975, when she was asleep in her bed with her husband. She was suddenly awakened by a distinct — and loud — sound of drums beating. "And I can tell you this," she emphasizes today, years later, "it was not a dream. It was real." She awoke to find the bedroom ceiling and roof of her house had disappeared and she was staring straight up at a darkened sky pierced only by shafts of moonlight.

She tried to sit up, but then realized, to her horror, that she was buried in prairie dirt up to her neck. Blades of grass tickled her cheeks. As the drumming grew more intense, Victoria says, "a group of Indians in war paint came into view. They glared at me menacingly, then began to dance and chant. I was terrified." She was afraid she was about to be scalped. "I said to myself, let it be fast so I won't suffer," she recalls.

She tried desperately to scream, but no sound came from her

throat. As her fears mounted, a huge Indian, standing six feet five inches tall and brandishing a large tomahawk, approached. He had coal black hair, braided and hanging nearly to his waist, and he was wearing buckskin pants and a breech cloth. At his appearance, the other Indians fell into an awed silence. He raised his hands to the sky and yelled, "Peace, brothers, not war." With that, the band of warriors quickly dispersed.

The great Indian then walked over to Victoria, who feared his tomahawk would soon be embedded in her head. Instead, he told her not to be afraid. "I am your Indian guide," he announced. "I am the spiritual one you have asked for. I am Black Foot of the Crow. I will protect you." He then pointed to his weapon and added, "This will be a sign between you and me. I shall be back to talk to you." He then disappeared, and Victoria felt no more fear. "Almost immediately I saw the room spin and there I was in my bedroom," she says.

This was the bizarre beginning of an unusual loving relationship that has lasted through the years and changed Victoria's life. Over the next several months Black Foot "visited" her regularly in her home in Virginia Beach. "I always saw him as you would see another person standing before you. He was just there, although I never knew how he came or went," she says. They often talked about psychic things, and Victoria had the feeling she was somehow being tested. Her attempts to question him as to why he was there were ignored.

In the spring of 1976 he came to her and said her patience had been good. He told her he wanted her to go to the "room of many books," which she interpreted as the library, and he said, "There, you will find a picture of me. Look in the book of the Plains Indians. I shall be holding a tomahawk." After hours of poring over books at the library, Victoria finally found a photo of five Crow Indians. Black Foot, clasping his tomahawk, was the second on the left.

The next day he appeared before her again and told her, "You must contact my people." When she asked him what she should say to them," he just smiled and then was gone again. "I sensed that his communication had more than ordinary significance," she later said. His cryptic comment led her on a zig-zagging chase to track down the Crow Indians. Eventually, she contacted a woman named Clara Turner, whose Indian name was Clara Whitehip. She worked for the Bureau of Indian Affairs on the Crow Reservation near Billings, Montana. When Victoria explained her mission — to

Victoria Mauricio

find out about Black Foot — Clara told her she had never heard of him, but she would check with tribal historians.

Some time later Clara called back and told Victoria that Black Foot, indeed, had been a very famous Crow. He had been a chief of chiefs. She had not recognized the name earlier because the Crow had referred to him as "Chief Sits-in-the-Middle-of-the-Land." She sent Victoria a packet of information on the chief and the history of the Crows.

Over the next two years, Victoria continued to have encounters with the chief, but still there was no inkling as to what he wanted. In the meantime, she developed a friendship by long distance with the Crow people in Montana. When they learned that she was a psychic healer they began asking for her assistance. When one Indian disappeared from the reservation, some thought he was dead, but Victoria assured them he wasn't. She told them he was an epileptic and had left temporarily because he was angry over a family fight. (She was right.) Another time a child was missing overnight and Victoria was called. Black Foot told her the child was dead, then, through Victoria, he gave details of where her body could be found, which also proved unerringly accurate.

Meanwhile, Black Foot began prodding Victoria to go to the Crow people in Montana. One evening while she was in a trance state, he said, "You are to go to the mountains as soon as possible. The time is right for you to go now." By this time Victoria's relationship with Clara and the Crow people had developed into a warm personal one, through the many telephone conversations they had, and through the long-distance healings.

And so, on July 11, 1978, Victoria and her friend from Virginia Beach, Barbara Neilson, boarded a plane and headed west. They were welcomed on the reservation as honored guests, were treated royally, and were showered with Indian gifts. On July 15, as Victoria prepared to go to a sun dance ceremony, Black Foot came to her and, at last, told her what he wanted. He said, "I want to be brought back to the reservation. I am in white man's land and I want to come home."

By now, after considerable research, Victoria knew a lot about Black Foot, and his message made sense to her. He was born about 1795 near or in the Absaroka Mountains of the western Big Horn Basin — a time when there were no white men present. He had grown up hunting the abundant buffalo, elk, mountain sheep, bear, deer, antelope, small game, birds and fish. He became a great Crow leader — a chief of chiefs — who headed the Indian representatives when the important Treaty of Fort Laramie was signed in 1868, which established the Crow reservation boundary and included a provision allowing Crows to hunt on unoccupied federal lands. It was Black Foot who decreed, ahead of his time, that all decisions of the tribe should be made by the majority and not just by the chiefs.

After the Crow reservation boundary was established by the Treaty of Fort Laramie, Chief Black Foot said to his people, "So long as there is one living Crow Indian, he will have a place to come home to. The earth of the reservation is your mother...your second mother, and she will shelter and protect you..."

In 1877, when the majestic chief was in his eighties, he and his wife went off the reservation, in the direction of northern Wyoming, on a hunting trip. They are believed to have caught pneumonia and to have died within a day of each other. Their remains had never been found although the Crow had been searching for them for more than 100 years.

This is why, Victoria believed then, he had come to her. She was a psychic. Through her, Black Foot would lead the Crow to his burial grounds so that he could be taken from the "white man's land," and be reinterred among his own people.

"Now," said Victoria, "my mission was clear."

Soon after, the chief made it known that he wanted to speak to his people through Victoria. She was advised to hold a seance in the home of a Crow medicine man, or shaman. Arrangements were made for the seance at shaman Francis Stewart's house. There was to be only a small group attending, but word of the event had leaked out and when Victoria arrived, the house was jammed with Crows. Reluctantly, she proceeded. It was agreed that Black Foot's presence would be determined by the "swaying and flaring up" of a candle.

Victoria went into a trance. In a few minutes the candle swung violently from side to side, then flamed high in the air. When Black Foot made his presence known, Barbara Neilson said Victoria's face "took on the features of the chief. Her cheekbones got high and a blue streak appeared from her mouth down her neck." The chief told the audience that he wanted them to bring his remains back home, and then, speaking in Crow to the shaman, he said when that happened, his people would prosper.

Later, shaman Stewart cried. He told Victoria that this was the culmination of the prophecy made in Crow history more than a century earlier: that a great chief would be brought back and "miracle" healings would come from an outsider.

For the remainder of her stay in Montana, Victoria led a series of healing sessions, "and the cures were many." Before she left to come back to Virginia, she told historian Joe Medicine Crow that Black Foot had often said something like "Tse Tse." It had no meaning to her, but Joe was immediately shaken. He told her there was a town across the Wyoming border called Meeteetse. "That must be where he is buried," Joe exclaimed. Previously, the Crows had suspected Black Foot's remains were somewhere near Cody, Wyoming, about 75 miles to the west, halfway to the Yellowstone National Park.

The Crows were excited by this news and began to organize a search party. Just before Victoria left, Black Foot appeared to her and said, "Tell them to start the search. I will direct them through you to where I am." She then returned to Virginia Beach on July 25, 1978.

From that point on, the clues from the chief and the transmittal

of them by phone from Victoria to the Crow in Montana came fast and furious. Over a period of the next four weeks she relayed the following signals:
• A pitchfork would somehow enter the picture.
• Seven white women would "appear" before they found the chief.
• There would be three odd-shaped rocks, and a tree "like a finger."
• The hooting of an owl would be heard in the daytime.
• The ground would glisten.
• An animal's scratching would be heard.

None of this made any sense to Victoria at the time, but she passed on the messages anyway. Several of the Crows went on the search on weekends in July and August. They were joined by Bob Edgar, a Cody historian and archeologist. It was tedious, exhausting work, but the party began drawing nearer to their quest. In an area near Meeteetse, above the Greybull River and 100 miles south of Billings, the clues seemed to be falling in place. They came upon the Pitchfork Ranch. It was owned by a woman who had seven

Chief Black Foot

77

heirs — all of them women. They heard an owl hooting — another key sign. They were getting closer. They called Victoria. She told them to go through a gate and look for the highest ridge. There would be three outstanding rocks and a big pine tree to the right of the opening of a cave. She said they would hear scratching sounds when they were near where the chief was lying, and that there would be a glitter when the sun hit the rock.

The search party found the rocks, the tree and the ridge precisely as described. They also heard scratching sounds, and, as darkness fell, there was another omen that hadn't been described. One of the Crows saw "what looked like a person" disappear behind a pine tree, move toward a rock, and then vanish! In the enveloping gloom, a flashlight beam hit a rock and "the whole area was a glitter."

The team had to call it a night and return home, convinced they had located the general area of the sacred site. The last weekend in August they returned and climbed the ridge. Once again, as they did, Victoria was awakened in her home by Black Foot. He told her he would be found that day. High on the side of the ridge, above the Greybull River, 17-year-old searcher Willie Plainfeather entered a sandstone cave. Apprehensive, he looked around and then started to leave when a strange incident happened. He felt a "thing" grab his shoulder and then literally throw him into the interior of the cave. It is best told in Willie's own words: "I couldn't explain what it was," he said. "I went into the cave and had a funny feeling, as though someone was there with me. This scared me and I wanted to get out of there. When I turned to go I felt someone grab my shoulder and throw me in. All of a sudden I saw this bone, like it came up through the floor of the cave. It was the weirdest thing I ever saw. And then I saw the buffalo hide and a lot of other things so I went to get the others." As he did, he excitedly yelled, "I found it. I found it."

What they saw, near the east wall of the cave, was the end of a human arm bone protruding from the cave floor. There, half buried in the sand, was the skeleton of a very large man, surrounded by black, white and blue beads — all the trappings of a great chief laid to rest. Strangely, there were no signs of the chief's wife's bones.

Bob Edgar, the archeologist, said all the pieces of the puzzle fit Black Foot. The wear on the teeth, he noted, indicated an old man, and the length of the bones showed that he was very tall. Black Foot was six foot five and in his eighties when he died. The beads found with the remains were made before 1850, Edgar added. Another expert said the beads were of extremely valuable crystal "of a type worn only by Indian chiefs."

When Victoria was called with the news later in the day, before they told her, she said, "I know. You've found him!" After the remains were carried down from the cave, a special ceremony was performed. A blanket was laid out on the ground and the bones and beads were placed at one end. A braid of sweet grass was then lit, and the smoke was circulated around the bones. Everyone rubbed their skin with sage, to cleanse themselves for the ceremony. Then shaman Francis Stewart took out his long pipe, pointed it directly at the bones, and gave a long prayer in the Crow language. The pipe was lit and passed around the circle of searchers.

Chief Black Foot, again through Victoria, arranged his own "proper" funeral. He told her when he wanted to be buried — October 4th, 1978 — and where, close to the Bureau of Indian Affairs Office near the Crow Reservation. Victoria flew out for the event, which was a glorious affair attended by about 2,000 Crows and others including a host of television crews and newspeople. The story had been front page news throughout the West.

Victoria was invited to take part in a dance around the grave site. Then she was asked to speak. As she stood up to address the crowd, she saw Chief Black Foot, "standing by his coffin, in all his dignity. He nodded approval to me," she said. During her talk a large bald eagle flew overhead at treetop level, and when she ended her speech, the eagle screamed and flew off. "The Indian friends there were amazed to see this phenomenon," Victoria said. "To most of them, it was the ultimate proof that Chief Black Foot was there...A genuine psychic event had taken place. The great Chief was an eagle shaman and always worked with the birds, using their feathers. He wore the largest eagle feather in his hair and it was legendary."

A monument was built with the following inscription: "He that sits in the middle of the land. Chief of all chiefs of the Crow nation. Founder of the Constitution and the Crow Reservation..."

When most of the crowd had left, Victoria, alone, walked back to the grave site wondering now, at last, if the chief was satisfied. He appeared before her once again and nodded. Then he spoke. "Yes!" he said. "Now I am with them (the Crow), and I can do the work that was unfinished when I died."

"I felt great satisfaction with his reply," Victoria Mauricio said. The Crows gave her some of the beads that had been found with the chief's remains in the cave. She treasures them. They have also accepted her as one of their own, and have bestowed many honors upon her.

"You and my people are now one," Black Foot told her.

* * * * *

It seems somewhat anti-climactic to add footnotes to this incredible story, but there are two of a very curious and interesting nature. The first is an experience which happened to Victoria on her first visit to Montana in July 1978. It has not been recorded in the thousands of words written about Chief Black Foot's return in the media, but Victoria noted it in her book.

She was taking a bath one day when the chief appeared to her. "No one will ever hurt my woman," he said. She asked him who his woman was, and he told her *she* was. Later, she asked one of her Indian friends what this meant. "It means you were his wife," the friend said. "Why would this great chief go all those thousands of miles, also to a strange country, to seek her out unless she was his wife during his lifetime?"

Victoria said this answer seemed to open "a gate of awareness" for her…"It explained many things to me and I sat in a sea of memories…What do you do when you realize the spiritual love had been that of a physical nature?…

"I knew the tallness and gentle nature of this formidable man, how he liked to walk naked in the tepee, have his skin rubbed with scented oil, his chest so huge and his figure tapered to slim hips; how his giant hands had caressed my hair, and how he smiled on me lovingly; and how my face had reached just about his chest as he held me in a warm embrace. He never spoke harshly to me. We sat by the fire together and his love always protected me, as he protected me now."

* * * * *

The second strange occurrence came some time after the chief's remains had been found. Back in Virginia Beach, one of the area television stations wanted to film an interview with Victoria, to fit into a segment of a syndicated program called "P.M. Magazine." She agreed, and arrangements were made to do the shooting in a friend's house. The crew — producer, interviewer, cameraman and technicians arrived and set up their equipment. Nothing worked.

So they packed everything up and left, setting another date for the filming. This time they brought a lot of backup equipment, but again nothing happened.

Said producer Bob Field: "We went out two times. We got in there the first time and we couldn't get any picture, and we had problems with the recorder. It just wouldn't respond. We were not getting anything. We took it back to the shop, and the engineers started it up — no problem. We rescheduled and came back out, and again this time there wasn't any picture. It was spooky. The crew had used the machine at other times between the first and second shootings. The third time we went out, we didn't use our own equipment. We borrowed some from the station. We plugged it in and had trouble with that."

At this point the totally frustrated producer told Victoria that she looked uncomfortable, which she wasn't, but he suggested that she go out in the kitchen and fix some coffee. She did. In the kitchen, the vision of Chief Black Foot appeared to her. He was very angry. "I won't allow you to do this filming," he told her. "Why not?" she asked. "I just won't allow it," he repeated. "But that's not fair," she retorted. "A lot of people have gone to a lot of trouble to do this. It could be a very good thing for your people and for me. Why don't you want us to film this?"

"Because," Black Foot ranted, "Yellow Hair is here!" "Who?" Victoria asked. "Yellow Hair, the evil one." "Do you mean General (George) Custer?" Victoria queried. "Yes!" Victoria was incredulous. She knew that Black Foot, the Crow, and other Indian tribes all hated Custer, and also that, oddly, the Custer Battlefield was less than 50 miles from the Crow reservation in Montana. But what on earth did Black Foot mean?

"Go tell the producer why this can't be done," Black Foot demanded. Victoria went back into the other room and told the producer that Black Foot was here and he wouldn't allow the filming to take place because "Custer" was present. She thought the producer would think she was nuts, but instead he got a puzzled look on his face and replied, "how did he know that?" Now Victoria was bewildered. "What do you mean?" she asked. The producer turned to one of the cameramen in the room and said, "He's a direct blood descendent of General Custer!" Victoria looked at the young man and was amazed. Not only was he related, but he looked exactly like Custer's pictures, yellow hair and all! And further, his name was Phillip Armstrong McCutchen. His middle name was even the same as that of his famous ancestor!

"That's astounding," Victoria mumbled.

She went back to Black Foot and explained that this man wasn't really General Custer, but merely a descendent, and that he shouldn't stop the filming because of such a strange coincidence. Black Foot frowned, but then, reluctantly, gave his approval for the interview to take place. Victoria told the crew their equipment would now work, and when they tried it, it did. The filming then took place without further incident.

"It really happened," Field said. "It was all kind of weird."

A Host of
Haunting Hounds

I sprang to my feet, my inert hand grasping my pistol, my mind paralyzed by the dreadful shape which had sprung out upon us from the shadows of the fog. A hound it was, an enormous coal-black hound, but not such a hound as mortal eyes have ever seen. Fire burst from its open mouth, its eyes glowed with a smoldering glare, its muzzle, hackles and dewlap were outlined in flickering flame.

"Never in the delirious dream of a disordered brain could anything more savage, more appalling, more hellish be conceived than that dark form and savage face which broke upon us out of the wall of fog.

"With long bounds the huge black creature was leaping down the track, following hard upon the footsteps of our friend. So paralyzed were we by the apparition that we allowed him to pass before we had recovered our nerve...Far away on the path we saw Sir Henry looking back, his face white in the moonlight, his hands raised in horror, glaring helplessly at the frightful thing which was hunting him down...."

This is how, nearly 100 years ago, Sir Arthur Conan Doyle described the great black beast — "gaunt, savage, and as large as a small lioness" — in his classic Sherlock Holmes' thriller, "The Hound of the Baskervilles." In this story the crime is built around a legend which holds that a gigantic hound appeared on the moors before the death of a member of the Baskerville family. While this story was, of course, fiction, there are a number of deadly serious psychic encounters with animals, most notably dogs, on record in Virginia. Herewith is a small sampling:

THE GHOST DOGS OF NORTHERN NECK

olorful folklorian tales, which once thrived in the Northern Neck section of Virginia, east of Fredericksburg, have been all but lost in the unblinking glare and clutter of modern day television. One story that has survived, however, involves the periodic sightings — generally in creek pond "bottoms" from which mists often arose about the marshes — of a headless dog. The accounts of its appearances, although always sketchy, nevertheless held children enraptured when recounted around the breakfast or dinner tables. And they were always sworn to with a solemnness that defied challenge.

The headless dog seemed to roam mostly in the lower section of the Neck, where he, or she, was occasionally joined by — take your choice — a white mule...a headless man...and another dog, this one with a head featuring "glaring red eyes." Scores of witnesses, young and old reported seeing this dog and their descriptions all were remarkably similar. The animal was as large as a calf, brown in color with patches of gray around its mouth. A large chain encircled its neck and dragged on the ground and rattled as the dog moved. And it moved only at night and only between Cockrell's Neck and Heathsville. Lastly, according to the long-held legend, it only was sighted just before or after the death of a local resident!

* * * * *

THE SPECTRAL CANINE OF GOOCHLAND

ldtimers still talk about the big black dog in Goochland County. They say it was the size of a young calf. It roamed about the county and claimed sightings of it were made near the State Farm, at the entrance to Thorncliff and at Chestnut Hill Bottom. He often appeared out of nowhere to trot alongside someone walking, on horseback, or riding a buggy.

Despite its grotesque size and appearance, the dog seemed harmless.

One person who experienced such company was a prominent lawyer named P. A. L. Smith, Sr. He used to walk from his home to the State Farm to get the train to Richmond, and on many evenings when he returned and walked back home in the dark, the big dog joined him.

There was a woman, too, who lived near the State Farm, and she told quite an extraordinary story of the dog. She claimed it entered her house one night by opening the screen door. It then walked over to her old-fashioned ice box, unfastened the door, helped itself to some food, and then, carefully, closed the door and left the house. It should be added that other strange events took place in this particular house. In fact, when it was vacant, people came to "see and hear the windows and doors rock and rattle."

Many people didn't seem inclined to discount the woman's narrative, because there were even more peculiar dog "anecdotes." Some of the local citizens didn't take kindly to having the dog accompany them, and on more than one occasion they shot the beast with their pistols. Eerily, the bullets passed through the dog's body and he kept right on trotting beside them. Needless to say, this abruptly changed their annoyance into raw fright.

* * * * *

THE CAST IRON GUARDIAN OF
HOLLYWOOD CEMETERY
(Richmond)

nother story involves the statue of a cast iron dog, which stands in Richmond's Hollywood Cemetery. This dog once, in the 19th century, stood in front of a store on Broad Street in Richmond. And every day, a little girl would come by the store and pet the dog and talk to it soothingly. She loved it as if it were real. Then one day the little girl didn't come by anymore. She died in an epidemic in 1892. They buried her at Hollywood, and because she had such an affection for the cast iron dog, it was placed at her grave site.

There, some will tell you, it stands guard over her to this day, its iron jaws set to chase away any intruders who might bring harm to its little friend.

Interestingly, not far away is the tomb of famous Richmond writer Ellen Glasgow. When she died, her will stipulated that her two pet dogs, who had preceded her in death, be dug up from the backyard of her house and be buried with her. And there are those

The Cast Iron Guardian of Hollywood Cemetery

who say these dogs can be heard on occasion scampering about late at night.

And maybe a case can be made that the sounds heard at Hollywood in the wee hours of the morning may not be just the rustling of leaves, the whistling of the wind, and the gentle rush of the rapids. Could they also include the whines of canines — both real and artificial?

* * * * *

HIS MASTER'S HOUND OF THE BLUE RIDGE
(Botetourt County)

Sir Arthur Conan Doyle's "Hound of the Baskervilles," serves as an eerie prelude to the following account of a massive black spectral dog which, in the late 17th century, was reported to have roamed along Skyline Drive, southwest of Charlottesville. The spectacle was recorded by a Mrs. R. F. Herrick in the *Journal of American Folklore*, published in 1907. Following are excerpts from that account:

"In Botetourt County, there is a pass that was much travelled by people going to Bedford County and by visitors to mineral springs in the vicinity. In the year 1683 the report was spread that at the wildest part of the trail in this pass there appeared at sunset a great black dog, who, with majestic tread, walked in a listening attitude about 200 feet and then turned and walked back. Thus he passed back and forth like a sentinel on guard, always appearing at sunset to keep his nightly vigil and disappearing again at dawn. And so the whispering went with bated breath from one to another, until it had travelled from one end of the state to the other. Parties of young cavaliers were made up to watch for the black dog. Many saw him. Some believed him to be a veritable dog sent by some master to watch; others believed him to be a witch dog.

"A party decided to go through the pass at night, well armed, to see if the dog would molest them. Choosing a night when the moon was full, they mounted good horses and sallied forth. Each saw a great dog larger than any dog they had ever seen, and, clapping spurs to their horses, they rode forward. But they had not calculated on the fear of their steeds. When they approached the dog, the horses snorted with fear, and in spite of whip, spur, and rein, gave him a wide berth, while he marched on as serenely as if no one were near. The party were (sic) unable to force their horses to take the pass again until after daylight. They were laughed at by their comrades to whom they told their experiences.

"Thereupon they decided to lie in ambush, kill the dog, and bring in his hide. The next night found the young men well hidden

The Hound of the Blue Ridge

behind rocks and bushes with guns in hand. As the last ray of sunlight kissed the highest peak of the Blue Ridge, the black dog appeared at the lower end of his walk, seemingly unconscious of the presence of the hunters. Again and again they fired and still the dog walked his beat. And fear caught the hearts of the hunters, and they fled wildly away to their companions, and the black dog held the pass at night unmolested.

"Time passed, and year after year went by, until seven years had come and gone, when a beautiful woman came over from the old country, trying to find her husband who, eight years before, had come to make a home for her in the new land. She traced him to Bedford County and from there all trace of him was lost. Many remembered the tall, handsome man and his dog. Then there came to her ear the tale of the vigil of the great dog of the mountain pass, and she pleaded with the people to take her to see him, saying that if he was her husband's dog he would know her.

"A party was made up and before night they arrived at the gap. The lady dismounted, and walked up to the place where the nightly watch was kept. As the shadows grew long, the party fell back on the trail, leaving the lady alone, and as the sun sank into his purple bed of splendor, the great dog appeared. Walking to the lady, he laid his great head in her lap for a moment, then turning, he walked a short way from the trail, looking back to see that she was following. He led her until he paused by a large rock, where he gently scratched the ground, gave a long, low wail, then disappeared.

"The lady called the party to her and asked them to dig. As they had no implements, and she refused to leave, one of them rode back for help. When they dug below the surface they found the skeleton of a man and the hair and bones of a great dog. They found a seal ring on the hand of the man and a heraldic embroidery in silk that the wife recognized. She removed the bones for proper burial and returned to her old home. It was never known who had killed the man. But from that time to this, the great dog, having finished his faithful work, has never appeared again."

CHAPTER 1 8

The Resplendent Ruins
of Rosewell

(Gloucester County)

osewell!
Today, more than two and a half centuries after its construction began just off the northern shores of the York River in Gloucester County, the name Rosewell still evokes excitement, even though it has stood in ruins since being gutted in a 1916 fire.

The accolades of its once-magnificent presence continue to ring true. Says Claude Lanciano, Jr., author of "Rosewell, Garland of Virginia": "The masterpiece called Rosewell at the height of its glory, in mid-eighteenth century, knew few rivals and has been called by many the finest example of colonial architecture in America."

Construction on this palatial brick masterpiece began in 1725 under its land owner, Mann Page. Built in the style of a Georgian town house which slightly resembled the Governor's Palace in Williamsburg, it stood four stories high with white marble casements and two turrets on the roof, inside of which were little rooms. These turrets had windows on all four sides which made excellent lookouts. A pitched roof supported massive chimneys. From the lantern windows, one was treated to a superb panorama of meadowland, low hills, and the misty reaches of the York River and of Carter's Creek. The interior plan of Rosewell showed five large rooms on the first floor. On the second was a huge apartment used as a ballroom. In all, the house consisted of 35 rooms, three wide halls and nine passageways. It was full of beautifully carved staircases, mantels, and paneling that is said to have been exquisite beyond description. The entrance hall had full-height pilasters, and the immensely high stairwell extended from the first floor to the rooftop. It could be ascended by eight people abreast. The balustrade of the stairs was elegantly carved with designs of baskets of fruit and flowers.

Mann Page never lived to see his great house finished. His son, Mann Page II, completed it in 1744. A generation later Thomas Jefferson spent a great deal of time at Rosewell as the guest of his friend John Page. There are some who say Jefferson even penned a draft of the Declaration of Independence at Rosewell, but this is unsubstantiated.

In its time, Rosewell was known throughout Virginia and the east coast for the lavish parties and balls that were thrown there, attended by aristocratic gentlemen and hoop-skirted, velvet dressed Southern Belles. Cases of the finest French wines, and magnums of champagne were brought in by boat to wash down gourmet meals fit for a king. Scores of garlands of flowers, especially roses, richly decorated every room, and dances lasted till nearly dawn. It was a grand time.

But Rosewell had a dark side, too. Parke Rouse said the plantation was "ill-starred." In retrospect, it could be compared in a way with the fictional Tara of Margaret Mitchell's "Gone With The Wind." There is even a Scarlett O'Hara type character associated with Rosewell, and therein lies a haunting tale well worth the retelling.

It occurred sometime during the period of occupancy by Mann Page II, probably about the middle of the 18th century. Anne Page, the renowned hostess at Rosewell, announced a ball. It was the talk of Gloucester for weeks in advance. Amid the society gossip was the speculation as to whether or not Letitia Dalton would attend. Letitia was the "Scarlett" of that day who lived with her husband, Fairfax, at nearby Paynton Plantation. Two days prior to the ball, her sister, Caro, had died under the most mysterious circumstances.

Letitia had commanded her to go outside the house to fetch her some grapes in the midst of a ferocious storm. Caro never returned to the house that night. They found her body the next morning. Some said a tree limb crushed her skull. Others contended she had stumbled into a pile of cut glass, severed arteries, and bled to death. Whatever, it was widely known that Letitia and

Caro hated each other, and often had raging arguments. There was talk that Letitia had somehow engineered her sister's death.

And so it came with some surprise, and considerable indignation among the guests, that Letitia not only showed up for the ball, but as Scarlett did on so many occasions, she stole the show. Just before dinner, long after everyone had gathered downstairs, she made her flamboyant entrance, descending the staircase in a wide-hooped gown of rose-pink satin with panniers of rose-lattice lace. Her powdered hair was massed with roses and plumes of rose color in the Versailles style.

Not only had she captivated the men at the ball, at the expense and disdain of their ladies, which mattered not the least to Letitia, but she spent a good part of the evening ignoring her husband and flirting with a handsome Englishman, Captain Godfrey Chandos, heir to a dukedom. Her behavior was, in a word, scandalous. She rejoiced in it.

Nor was it any secret that she made Fairfax's life miserable, often driving him from the house in total frustration with her merciless, deceitful harangues. He, in fact, spent much of his time in consolation with his good friends, the Pages, at Rosewell.

No sooner had the talk of Caro's untimely death died down when tragedy struck again at Paynton. Fairfax Dalton had retired to his bedroom one evening when it was reported that he heard a soft voice calling from the bottom of the stair well. "Fairfax. Here. Fairfax, I am here," he heard faintly. Sensing a note of fear and urgency, he went to the top of the staircase and peered downward into the lurking darkness. "Here I am. Look over here," he heard. As he leaned hard on the balustrade, the wooden railing collapsed and he plummeted head first down two stories onto the marble floor. He died of a broken neck. There were no witnesses. Letitia claimed to have been asleep in her own room, but opinion was rampant that she had been the one who called Fairfax to his death.

Letitia was labeled a murderess, but ironically, she was never called to answer any charges. She died of natural causes in her bed. Her gruesome legacy, however, lived on. For years afterward, guests at Paynton Hall told of seeing a small, shadowy figure of a woman passing through darkened halls. As she went by, they felt a sudden push or a tripping of their feet. One lady saved herself from hurtling down the stairs by grasping a newel post.

Others heard horrible cries ring through the house late at night, and there were oft-told stories of blood on the marble floor impossible to rub clean. In 1840, it was reported, slaves refused to stay in the huts near the old stud cabin, saying they had seen a Negro woman, crouched on the floor of the cabin wailing over a young girl who was covered with blood. The superintendent told of hearing sobs of terrible anguish coming from the cabin late at night.

And, years after her tragic death, a story surfaced explaining what happened to Caro. It was widely surmised that Letitia had, in fact, gone out earlier in the night, as a fierce storm was brewing, and had piled shards of glass above a spot where the finest grapes hung in clusters. The roof was shored by rickety planks, and she had wrenched them loose. Then, she placed a loose board in such a position that anyone stumbling over it would send the shoring, glass and all, showering down on them. Then, later in the evening, when the wind was howling at its worst, she had sent Caro upon her fatal mission.

At last, Paynton Hall was burned to the ground during the Civil War battle of York Plains Ford. Nothing but grass grown foundations remain. The voices, cries of anguish and apparitions, too, have disappeared.

But others have surfaced at nearby Rosewell. Many Gloucester natives have told stories of strange sightings and noises emanating from the rose-red brick foundation ruins. Some claim to have seen young boy servants standing beside the great pedimented doorway at night, lighting the way for arriving distinguished guests who vanish ascending the Corinthian pilastered stair well. Others swear they heard violin and harpsichord music rising above the towering chimneys.

Ronnie Miles, an office worker in Williamsburg and a native of Mathews County, had two psychic experiences at Rosewell about 20 years ago. Once, he and his friend were exploring the ruins at night when they stumbled onto what may have been an entrance to a wine cellar. Miles' friend lit a match to see better, only to have a flung brick knock the match out of his hand. He never went back to Rosewell, even in daylight. "I have to admit, it scared the hell out of us," Miles said. "We had always heard a slave had been buried in the walls."

On the second occasion, Miles and another friend and two girls were walking through the old Rosewell cemetery at night, as teenagers sometimes do for kicks. Miles and his friend saw what appeared to be a light coming from the house ruins. Not wanting to scare the girls, they walked back to the site alone to investigate. "As we reached the perimeter of the ruins," said Miles, "we both

Rosewell Ruins

were overcome by the most all-powerful stench I have ever smelled. It was potent. I have never smelled anything like it in my life. It literally drove us away."

Another chilling instance was experienced by Tom Gulbranson, an amateur psychic investigator, his sister, and some friends. As a hobby, Gulbranson and his brother, John, check out ghost stories, complete with sophisticated camera and tape recorder equipment. While in the Gloucester area one night several years ago, they decided to go look at the Rosewell ruins.

They drove down to the edge of two cornfields near the entrance road and got out there because the road had been chained to discourage visitors. They had two guard dogs with them, but the dogs immediately began howling wildly and refused to budge. "We tried to pull them, but we couldn't move them an inch," Tom says. Previously, the dogs had never exhibited fear.

The dogs were tied to a tree and the group walked through the cornfields and down the entrance road. A couple of the young men swore they heard the sounds of a drummer coming from the Rosewell site, but when they got there, they found nothing. They then retraced their steps back to the car and everyone got in. Just as they did the dogs began barking furiously at the back window and the hair on their backs stiffened.

Tom and the others looked out the window, and a few yards away they all clearly saw a black man suspended four or five feet above the ground. Tom's sister, Carol, began screaming hysterically, and they drove off, spinning their tires in the dirt.

They had the distinct feeling, the man, or whatever it was, was following them, so they sped so fast on the rough surface, their heads bumped against the roof of the car.

A mile or so down the road they stopped, got out and looked back. The man was gone. There was one small tree, only about an inch in diameter at the side of the road, which leaned out over the lane. Without warning, the tree began shaking violently, but they could see no cause for it.

Again, they jumped into the car and raced away. This time they didn't stop until they got back to civilization, and they pulled up under a street light. They got out and walked around the car. It was covered with dew. One of the group called the others to the rear of the car. There, in the dew, were the crystal-clear impressions of a baby's hand and a man's hand with a missing index finger!

But perhaps the most frightening phenomenon of all at Rosewell was experienced by Raymond West, a maintenance worker at a fiber plant in James City County. He and a friend were out joyriding with two young ladies when they decided to go visit the Rosewell ruins. It was about two in the morning and the story is best told in West's own words. "There was an old dirt road that ran for about half a mile leading up to the place," he recalls. "As we made the last turn to the left, there before us was an old black car with 1930s license plates blocking the driveway. It had one half moon window in the back and was facing away from us. It stunned us. I slammed on the brakes, and a big dust cloud rose up then cleared, so you could see the car real well in the headlight beams. It was eerie.

"Then, as we sat there in silence, we saw the head of a woman rise up in the rear window and she stared at us. She had coal black hair and an ashen-white face. We panicked. I tried to get the car in reverse, but the gears kept sticking, and all the time that woman kept looking at us, unblinking. Finally, I got the car in gear and we burned rubber getting out of there. We pulled back a few hundred yards and then stopped. We were plenty scared, but we decided to wait until daylight and check things out. There was no other way out of there, no other roads, paths or anything. If that car left, it had to go right past us.

"At daybreak, we drove back down the driveway to the spot where we had seen it, and there was nothing there! The car and the woman had disappeared. There were no tracks or anything. We looked everywhere but could find nothing. I tell you, I never believed in ghosts or anything like that, but to this day I can't explain what we saw or why."

Could they have seen a manifestation of Letitia Dalton, returning to seek the attentions of the handsome British Captain who escaped her flirtations in life? Could that also explain one of the most common psychic sightings over the years at Rosewell — that of the figure of a woman in a red cloak running toward the grove where the roses once bloomed?

Could that possibly explain why the artist James Reynolds once wrote: "Certainly tremendous doings took place within the fire-riven walls of Rosewell...And what stories one hears of hauntings! All I hear seems in keeping with the magnificence and stature of this baronial, deserted house."

*They weep: — from off
their delicate stems
Perennial tears descend
in gems*

(The Valley of Unrest)

Tragic Teardrops in the Snow

(Gloucester)

I f sad stories disturb you, perhaps it would be best to skip the following chapter, because this melancholy saga is definitely a two-or-three hanky affair. It begins with a broken heart, includes such grisly details as a premature burial, grave robbing, and a severed finger, and ends with a tragic plea for help that was drowned out in a blinding snowstorm. In the world of the macabre it exceeds even the feverish imagination of Edgar Allan Poe. There is also an intriguing epilogue involving the lush seasonal growth of violets "watered by the tears of a dying girl."

If however, the above has piqued your interest, and you have the heart, read on.

The setting is Church Hill in Gloucester, where a large frame house stands today on an elevation just above the Ware River. In

1650, a grant of 1,174 acres was given to Mordecai Cooke, who later became a member of the House of Burgesses, and who once served as sheriff of Gloucester. In 1658 a brick house was built at this site and was known as "Mordecai's Mount." In the 1700s, the main part of the house burned, leaving a brick wing. Later, this, too, burned and an entirely new frame house was constructed on the old foundations and became known as Church Hill.

The Cooke property passed in a direct line to descendants named Throckmorton. Then one of the two heiresses of the house married William Taliaferro, and when she died, her sister married the widower. Both the Throckmortons and the Taliaferros produced a number of distinguished citizens in Colonial days.

One of the Throckmortons had a beautiful daughter named Elizabeth, which is somewhat strange in itself, because one writer reported there is no record of an Elizabeth Throckmorton at Church Hill. Whatever her name was, her father took her for a visit to London where she met a handsome young English gentleman, with whom she fell deeply in love. They both declared eternal faithfulness to each other and arranged to complete plans for their wedding by correspondence. Elizabeth's father, however, was staunchly against the match, and intercepted the letters, so neither ever heard again from the other after Elizabeth had returned to Gloucester.

In time, as Elizabeth longed for her lost love, she fell ill and, apparently, died. Friends contended she had lost the will to live, and "pined away." On a blustery November afternoon near sunset, they buried her in the graveyard at the foot of the garden.

According to one account, an evil butler, angered at some slight accorded him by the family, dug up her gravesite that night and opened the coffin to steal valuable jewelry that had been buried with Elizabeth. One particular ring would not slip off her finger, and in his haste, the servant severed the finger.

To his horror, however, he found the girl was not dead! She had lapsed into a cataleptic coma and had been presumed dead. The shock of having her finger cut off roused her, and the terrified butler ran off into the night never to be heard from again.

Somehow, the frail girl, barefoot and thinly dressed managed to climb out of the grave, crawl past the last dead stalks of the garden, and drag herself through a driving snowstorm — the first snow of the season — to the house. There, in a weakened condition, she scratched feebly at the door. If her father, sitting inside before a roaring fire, heard her, he dismissed it as one of the dogs

Church Hill

trying to come in out of the storm, and, lost in his grief, ignored the sound.

The next morning, Elizabeth's body was found at the doorstep beneath a blanket of snow. She had frozen to death. There was a trail of bloody footprints leading from the garden.

For years afterward, succeeding generations of Throckmortons and Taliaferros swore that manifestations of Elizabeth were present in the house. Whenever the first snow fell, each year, there would be sounds of a rustling skirt ascending the staircase, followed by the distinct placing of logs in fireplaces and the crackle of a hearty fire in various rooms. Investigations would find no such logs and no fires. There also would be traces of blood in the snow following the route Elizabeth had taken from the graveyard to the house. Such sounds and sights were experienced not once, but many times, and were attested to by various members of the family and their servants.

On one noteworthy occasion, generations later, in 1879, Professor Warner Taliaferro, then head of the house, left home one evening to spend the night at a friend's home. Neighbors reported, that in the midst of a fierce storm, they saw Church Hill ablaze with lights. Junius Browne Jr., passing by on horseback, rode up to the house to see if his sisters, visiting in the neighborhood, had sought shelter from the storm there. There was no one home. Servants living in their quarters on the property, also saw the lights and had assumed Mr. Taliaferro had returned. He had not. This mystery was never explained.

But the most telling phenomenon concerns the violets, which grow in lush profusion near the steps to Church Hill. They are finer and more beautiful here than those in other parts of the grounds. It is said they were watered by the tears of a dying girl seeking refuge from the season's first snow!

And Thou, a ghost,

amid the entombing

trees Didst glide away

(To Helen)

The Multiple Haunts of Old House Woods

(Mathews County)

 f all the ghostly tales of Tidewater, perhaps none is more widely known, or has been told, retold, written and rewritten more often than Old House Woods, also called Old Haunted Woods, near the tiny crossroads town of Diggs in Mathews County, northeast of Gloucester.

And for good reason. The colorful stories that have been passed down from generation to generation for more than 200 years about this 50 acre patch of pine woods and marshlands near the Chesapeake Bay contain some of the most bizarre and unusual psychic phenomena ever recorded. They are, in fact, so strange that one tends to lend some credence to them, because even the most fertile imagination would have difficulty dreaming them up.

They include all the elements of the creative thrillers of Robert Louis Stevenson and Edgar Allan Poe combined! Consider for example: swashbuckling pirates burying stolen gold; retreating British soldiers hiding colonial treasure during the Revolutionary War; a full-rigged Spanish galleon which vanishes in thin air; skeletons in knights' armor wielding threatening swords; mysterious groups of shovelers digging furiously late at night; ghost horses and cows which appear and disappear before one's eyes.

"Yes, it's true. All those stories and more have come out of Old House Woods," says Olivia Davis, a lifelong resident. She should know, as well as anyone still alive. Her great-great-grandfather, James Forrest, bought this land in 1838 and it was kept in the family and farmed for more than 100 years. She still has the original, handwritten deed.

Old House Woods got its name, simply enough, from a large frame house, once known as the Fannie Knight house, which had a wood-covered plaster chimney, and stood in the midst of the forest in the late 1700s. Later, after being abandoned for years, it fell into disrepair, and thereafter became known as "the Old House."

"What you have to remember is that in the days before television and even radio, telling tales was a popular pastime, particularly in this area," Olivia says. "Old timers used to gather in the woods on Sundays and swap yarns. The best story teller was the one who could best hold your interest. I can well recall my grandfather, Silas Forrest talking about ghosts and it was spellbinding."

Does she believe they were true? "I consider them just exactly what they are — stories."

But there are scores of others, residents and visitors to the area alike, who swear by them. And then there are those who have personally experienced the phenomena in one form or another. There is no way they will ever be shaken from their beliefs. They were there. They saw for themselves. And they never forgot, carrying their terrifying memories to the grave.

There are, allegedly, three reasons why Old House Woods are haunted. According to one legend, the crew of a pirate ship came ashore here in the 17th century, buried their treasure somewhere deep in the woods, then returned to sea where they perished in a furious storm. That explains, say proponents of this theory, why mysterious figures have been seen digging feverishly in the woods on dark nights by the lights of tin lanterns. They are the pirate ghosts returning to claim their lost loot.

Another version of this was recorded by *Richmond Times-Dispatch* staff writer Bill McKelway in 1973. "Some say," he wrote, "Blackbeard, the infamous Edward Teach, intercepted the treasure and then murdered the men who were hiding it. At any rate, legend has it that those murdered men still haunt the woods today, preying on those who dare to trespass the blood-stained earth in search of the lost treasures."

A second possible reason may also have occurred in the second half of the 17th century. After being defeated at the Battle of Worcester in 1651, Charles II of England was said to have considered coming to Virginia. In preparation for this trip, a group of his followers dispatched several chests of money, plate and jewels to the colony by ship. However, for some unexplained reason, the riches never reached Jamestown. Instead, the ship sailed up the Chesapeake Bay and anchored in waters at the mouth of White's Creek near Old House Woods. There, the treasure was offloaded. But before it could be safely hidden, the Royalists were attacked and murdered by a gang of renegade indentured servants. In their rush to escape, these bondsmen took only part of the loot, planning to come back later for the rest. But they, too, ran afoul of the elements. A sudden storm struck the bay and all hands on board drowned when the ship capsized.

It may well be that the storm, which took the lives of both the pirates and the renegades, account for one of the many Old House Woods ghost stories — that of the "Storm Woman." She has been described by those who claim to have seen her as "a wraith of a woman in a long nightgown, her long, fair hair flying back from her shoulders." Reportedly, whenever black clouds gather over this section of the bay, foretelling a coming gale, her figure rises above the tops of towering pine trees, and she wails loudly to warn watermen and fishermen to take cover.

The third theory about the hauntings supposedly happened in late 1781, just before Lord Cornwallis' army was defeated at Yorktown. Tradition has it that two British officers and four soldiers were entrusted by their superiors with a huge amount of money and treasure. They slipped through enemy lines and headed north, hoping to find a British ship on the Chesapeake Bay. They managed to bury their riches in Old House Woods before they were found and killed by a unit of American cavalry. Thus, it may be their ghosts who still hover over the site in eternal guard.

Whether or not one subscribes to one or more of these reasons, or to none at all, they do offer some possible insight into why certain sights have appeared to a host of people in the area over the years.

And the sightings have been prolific and explicit, however far fetched they may sound today. One of the most celebrated is attributed to Jesse Hudgins, described as a respectable merchant of unquestioned integrity, who ran a store in the town of Mathews Court House in the 1920s. Hudgins told his story to a *Baltimore Sun* newspaper reporter in 1926, and to anyone else who would listen, and he swore to its authenticity.

"I do not care whether I am believed or not," he often said. "I am not apologetic nor ashamed to say I have seen ghosts (in Old House Woods). I have seen ghosts not once, but a dozen times. I was 17 when I first actually saw a ghost, or spirit. One October night I sat by the lamp reading. A neighbor whose child was very ill came asking me to drive to Mathews for the doctor. We had no telephone in those days. I hitched up and started for town. The night was gusty, clouds drifting now and then over the moon, but I could see perfectly, and whistled as I drove along.

"Nearing Old House itself, I saw a light about 50 yards ahead moving along the road in the direction I was going. My horse, usually afraid of nothing, cowered and trembled violently. I felt rather uneasy myself. I have seen lights on the road at night, shining lanterns carried by men, but this light was different. There was something unearthly about it. The rays seemed to come from nowhere, and yet they moved with the bearer."

Hudgins continued, "I gained on the traveler, and as I stand here before you, what I saw was a big man wearing a suit of armor. Over his shoulder was a gun, the muzzle end of which looked like a fish horn. As he strode, or floated along, he made no noise. My horse stopped still, I was weak with terror and horror. I wasn't 20 feet from the thing, whatever it was, when it, too, stopped and faced me.

"At the same time, the woods about 100 feet from the wayfarer became alive with lights and moving forms. Some carried guns like the one borne by the man or thing in the road, others carried shovels of an outlandish type, while still others dug furiously near a dead pine tree.

"As my gaze returned to the first shadowy figure, what I saw was not a man in armor, but a skeleton, and every bone of it was visible through the iron of the armor, as though it were made of glass. The skull, which seemed to be illuminated from within, grinned at me horribly. Then, raising aloft a sword, which I had not hitherto noticed, the awful specter started towards me menacingly.

"I could stand no more. Reason left me. When I came to, it was

103

broad daylight and I lay upon my bed at home. Members of my family said the horse had run away. They found me at the turn of the road beyond Old House Woods. They thought I had fallen asleep. The best proof that this was not so was we could not even lead Tom (the horse) by the Old House Woods for months afterwards, and to the day he died, whenever he approached the woods, he would tremble violently and cower. It was pitiful to see that fine animal become such a victim of terror."

Hudgins' story, strange as it may seem, was corroborated some years later, according to newspaper reports at the time. One account said: "A Richmond youth had tire trouble at a lonely spot along the road near the haunted woods one night, very late. As he knelt in the road a voice behind him asked: 'Is this the King's highway? I've lost my ship.' When the youth turned to look, he beheld a skeleton in armor within a few paces of him. Yelling like a maniac, the frightened motorist ran from the spot in terror and did not return for his car until the next day."

Perhaps the most unusual phenomenon sighted in Old House Woods is the legendary ghost ship. It allegedly has been seen by many, some from a far distance, some from frightening close range. One of the most descriptive accounts was given more than 60 years ago by Ben Ferbee (or Ferebee) a fisherman who lived along the Chesapeake Bay shore early in the 20th century.

His vivid recollection, also told to a newspaper reporter, in 1926, is as follows: "One starry night I was fishing off the mouth of White's Creek well out in the bay. As the flood tide would not set in for some time, I decided to get the good fishing and come home with the early moon. It must have been after midnight when, as I turned to bait up a line in the stern of my boat, I saw a full-rigged ship in the bay, standing pretty well in. I was quite surprised, I tell you. Full-rigged ships were mighty scarce then; besides that, I knew I was in for it if she kept that course. On the ship came, with lights at every masthead and spar, and I was scared.

"They'll run me down and sink me, I thought. I shouted to sailors leaning over her rails forward, but they paid no heed to me. Just as I thought she would strike me, the helmsman put her hard aport and she passed so close that I was almost swamped by the wash. She was a beautiful ship, but different from any I had ever seen. There are no ships like her on any ocean. She made no noise at all, and when she had gone by, the most beautiful harp and organ music I ever heard came back to me.

"The ship sailed right up to the beach and never stopped, but kept right on. Over the sandy beach she swept, floating through the air and up to the Bay Shore road, her keel about 20 feet from the ground. I could still hear the music. But I was scared out of my wits. I knew it was not a real ship. It was a ghost ship!

"Well, sir, I pulled up my anchor and started for home up White's Creek. I could see that ship hanging over Old House Woods, just as though she was anchored in the sea. And running down to the woods was a rope ladder, lined with the forms of men carrying tools and other contraptions.

"When I got home my wife was up, but had no supper for me. Instead, she and the children were praying. I knew what was the matter. Without speaking a word she pointed to Old House Woods, a scared look on her face. She and the children had seen the ship standing over the woods. I didn't need to ask her — I started praying too."

Soon after, Ferbee and his family moved from the area.

Many others claim to have sighted the fabled ghost ship. One was a 14-year-old Mathews County boy who related his experience this way: "A friend of mine and I were taking a boat from Mathews Yacht Club over to Moon post office. You go up Stutts Creek and then over the Billups Creek. It was just after sunset and everything was sort of misty. Then about a half mile from the mouth of the creek, we saw it. We both saw it, but couldn't believe it. I'd never seen anything like it before.

"There was a big sailing ship floating in the marsh. It had two or three masts and was made of wood. There's only a foot of water there but it looked like it was floating. It was the kind of ship the pirates used. We watched for about a hundred yards more and then it just disappeared. I went home and told my mother, but she just laughed. She said everyone knew of the stories about the ghosts in Old House Woods."

Another who saw the phantom galleon, and many other things too, was Harry Forrest, a farmer-fisherman who lived only 600 yards from the edge of the woods. "There are more strange things in there than I could relate in a whole day," he once said before his death in the 1950s. "I've seen armies of marching British redcoats. I've seen the 'Storm Woman' and heard her dismal wailings, and my mother and I have sat here all hours of the night and seen lights in the woods. We have sat here on our porch overlooking Chesapeake Bay and seen ships anchor off the beach and boats put into shore, and forms of men go into the woods. I would see lights over there and hear the sound of digging."

House at Edge of Old House Woods

Forrest told of his ship sighting this way: "I was out fishing right off the beach one day in broad daylight when I saw a full-rigged ship headed straight for me, just 100 yards away. I rowed to shore as fast as I could, and just as I got on the beach, she started drifting, and she lifted and sailed straight to the Old House Woods, and you heard the anchor chain clank."

On another occasion, Forrest recalled: "Tom and Jack Diggs and I were going through the woods one night when one of those ships must have been just about to land. There was a terrible racket right close to the Old Cow Hole as she dropped anchor, and then she drifted off with that blaze of light running right along through the hawsepipe. I've seen many a one, and they all go off that way. It's the chain running out too fast through the hawsepipe that starts the blaze. And such bumping you never heard. Most of 'em are square riggers."

The Old Cow Hole, it should be explained, is where Forrest believed treasure was buried. It is somewhere near the center of the woods. He once took a newsman to the site. The reporter described it as being a "small, circular pool of gray water, which seemed to swirl, and yet it was dead still."

"This is where they buried the money," Forrest told him. "I think they must have killed a pirate and put him with it. There's everything in there. You hear chains rattle sometimes. I've seen everything on earth a man could see in these woods — not so much in the day-time, but it's bad enough then."

While Forrest claimed he was not afraid of the dead, even though he believed the dead come back, one experience he told of even shook him to the marrow. "Once I went out one brilliant November night to shoot black ducks," he recalled. "I found a flock asleep on a little inlet where the pine trees came down to the edge of the water. As I raised my gun to fire, instead of them being ducks, I saw they were soldiers of the olden time. Headed by an officer, company after company of them formed and marched out of the water.

"Recovering from my astonishment and bewilderment, I ran to my skiff, tied up on the other side of the point. Arriving there, I found a man in uniform, his red coat showing brilliantly in the bright moonlight, sitting upright and very rigid in the stern. I was scared, but mad, too. So I yelled to him 'Get out of that skiff or I'll shoot.'

" 'Shoot and the devil's curse to you and your traitor's breed,' he answered, and made as if to strike me with the sword he carried. Then I threw my gun on him and pulled. It didn't go off. I pulled the trigger again. No better result. I dropped the gun and ran for home, and I'm not ashamed to say I swam the creek in doing it, too."

Forrest also used to tell of seeing a white ox lying in his cornfield one night. "I went out to drive him away," he said. "When I reached the spot where the animal was lying, I saw it was a coffin covered with a sheet and borne along by invisible hands, just at the height pallbearers would carry a corpse. I followed until it entered the woods. The sheet only partly covered the coffin.

"Well, sir, the following Wednesday they brought the body of Harry Davis ashore from Wolf Trap lightship. Harry was killed when the boiler blew up aboard the lightship. As the men carried him up the beach to the waiting hearse, I recognized instantly the coffin I had seen borne into Old House Woods. The men were carrying it in the selfsame manner in every particular, a somewhat clumsy, swaying motion I had observed in my cornfield."

Still another tale that has been printed in both books and newspapers involved a farmer's wife who lived adjacent to the haunted woods. One evening at dusk she went into a pasture to bring home their work horses. She drove them down a lane towards the barn. Arriving at the gate, she called to her husband to open it. He did not respond at once, and she opened it herself. As she did so, her husband came out of the barn and laughed at her, saying he had put the team in the stable two hours before.

"Don't be foolish," she said. When she turned to let the team pass through the gate, instead of two horses standing there, she saw two headless black dogs scampering off towards Old House Woods! "That woman," says Olivia Davis today, "was my great grandmother." Over the years there also have been numerous reported sightings of headless cattle wandering aimlessly in the woods.

Through the decades there have been many mysterious disappearances in the area, involving both humans and animals. None has been satisfactorily explained to this date. In 1951, Harry Forrest told of one. "It was near about 100 years ago that Lock Owens and Pidge Morgan came through these woods with their steer, on the way back from a cattle auction, and nothing's been seen of 'em since. Steer, carts and everything disappeared in there. Lock had a little black dog and the only thing that ever was found of it was a little bunch of hair off of that dog's tail.

"There used to be a lot of cattle down on these points, but they got to wandering in here and never came out," Forrest said. "Everything that comes in here heads for the Old Cow Hole and disappears. It's very strange. One night that Old Cow Hole will be covered with water, the next it's dry. Some night it'll be light enough to pick up a pin in these woods, and black and storming outside. And sometimes, you'll come in here and it'll be pouring down. You get wringing, soaking wet, you can wipe the water off you. And then you come out and you'll be perfectly dry."

And finally, there is the tragic tale of Tom Pipkin, a local fisherman who lived in the vicinity around 1880. Fired up by the age-old stories of buried or sunken gold, he took his small boat into the woods, following an old channel some say was originally cut by pirates two centuries earlier, and headed for Old Cow Hole.

Several days later his boat was found in the bay. Inside the boat were two gold coins of unknown age, and a battered silver cup covered with slime and mud. One coin bore a Roman head, and the letters "I V V S" were distinguishable. No one would take Pipkin's boat and it rotted away on nearby Gwynn's Island. He was never heard from again.

"A thousand people have been in here after that money, but

they'll never get it," Harry Forrest once said of Old House Woods. "The trees start bending double and howling. It storms. And they get scared and take off...The woods is haunted, that's what it is."

A Hair Raising Encounter in Deltaville

(Deltaville)

I
t would be one thing to wake up from a deep sleep and see the wispy apparition of, say, a gnarled old woman standing at the foot of your bed. You likely would rub your eyes, shake your head, and look again to see if your "dream" had concluded. If the transparent figure was still there, it surely would be a scary situation. But even then, in all probability, the wraith would disappear within a matter of seconds. Such has been the experience of most people who have had such supernatural visions.

But it would be altogether another thing to wake — realize fully that you are awake and not dreaming — and turn over to see another *person*, or apparent person, in bed with you. And rubbing your shoulder with an icy hand on top of that!

Yet this is exactly what happened to a young man named Fred — he prefers not to give his last name — at an old 19th century house he had recently moved into in Deltaville, out on the eastern tip of Virginia in Middlesex County just north of Gwynn's Island. It is a very small town, noted for its seafood, that has one main street, Lover's Lane, lined with picturesque Victorian mansions.

Fred called the author one night early in 1993, sounding a little unnerved. "I heard that you have written a lot about ghosts," he said, "and I don't know if you can help me or not. I never really believed in that sort of thing, but now I'm not so sure." After telling him that I was not an expert on psychic phenomena, but I would be glad to listen, I asked him to continue. "Well," he replied, "a lot of very strange things have been going on in the house ever since I moved in, and others have told me things happened here well before that."

"Like what?" I inquired. "Did you ever get the feeling that someone or something was staring at you?" Fred asked. "I get that feeling often when I come into the house, and I know there is no one else here but me. There are times when I feel a definite presence here. Mostly, it's either in my bedroom, which is on the first floor, or in the kitchen. It's just a feeling, but it's a very real feeling. It's like there is someone else here. There are noises. Sometimes there are footsteps. Other times, I hear like someone coughing. Friends of mine have seen door knobs turning, and there is a woman renter upstairs who has seen blinds go up and down on their own."

"Go on," I said. "There have been times when I have heard a guttural-type growling sound. I have no idea where it is coming from or what is causing it, but I can tell you it's a little unnerving to say the least," Fred said. "And then there is my radio. I turn it on every night when I go to bed, so it will wake me up in the morning. But in the morning it is always turned off. How does that happen? Like I say, most of what happens, most of the feelings I get, occur in my bedroom. There are some definite cold spots in that room. You can step into them and it's like an icy chill. I have a Himalayan cat, and he will not go into my bedroom for anything. I've carried him in the room a few times, and he goes crazy. He shoots out of there like a dart.

"But the real reason I'm calling is what happened to me last Sunday," Fred said. "It was about 2:30 in the morning. I had been asleep for some time, when I woke up suddenly. I felt something cold on my shoulder, and I looked across the bed, and there was a man laying there. He was not transparent and translucent, at least not from the waist up, which is all I could see. He was a young man, probably in his 30s, with brown hair. And he was calling my name!"

"What did you do?" I asked. "I was petrified," Fred said. "I was literally speechless. I sat up in bed and tried to scream, but nothing would come out of my mouth, not even a whisper. I don't know how long I sat there, but I think I scared 'him' as much as he scared me. Finally, I was able to move, and I yanked the covers off the bed and leaped out of it and bolted across the room. I looked up, and 'he' was standing by the chimney now, and then he just kind of, I don't quite know how to put it, he kind of dematerialized. His form became misty-like and then it just vaporized. It wasn't there anymore. At last, I was able to yell, and my roommate came running in from the other room. I lost it. I couldn't move for about 30 minutes afterwards. Like I said, I never really believed in any of this stuff before, but now I don't know. How do you explain this? It was a very real experience. What should I do about this?" Fred asked. "I have been startled."

I told Fred that some of the people I had talked with who have had similar experiences and wanted to do something about it, usually did one of two things. Many of them, simply, would sit down and talk with their ghost, telling it that they lived here now, and even if the house had belonged to the ghost in past times, the two of them would now have to learn to peacefully co-exist. Surprisingly, this has seemed to work with some degree of success. The other thing, I told Fred, would be to call in a psychic to sense the presence of whatever spirit was in the house. Sometimes such psychics could even direct the ghost onto whatever road they should be on anyway.

And then I told Fred about a friend of mine, Tom Gulbranson of Virginia Beach, who is a student of paranormal behavior and a sort of amateur ghostbuster. I suggested that I have Tom get in touch with Fred and possibly bring his photography and recording equipment out to the house. Fred agreed, and Tom and his wife, Karen, went out to Deltaville about a week later. Tom called me the following week.

"There is definitely a strong presence in that house," he said. "Has anything new happened since I talked to him?" I inquired. "Yes. Both Fred and his roommate have heard footsteps in a room that no one ever goes in. It scared the hell out of both of them. Fred also said he would come into the house some evenings and see shadows darting out of the corners of his eyes. He would turn and see just a flash or a wisp of something and then it would be gone.

"What about you, Tom. Did you see or feel anything?"

"Yes. There was an oppressive feeling when I walked into Fred's bedroom. It was a tangible feeling. There was a significant cold spot in the room, and when you stepped in it, it was at least 20 degrees or more colder than the rest of the room. And when I say oppressive, I mean it was like I felt a weight on my chest when I was in the room. I could feel the hair on the back of my neck tingle."

"Did you learn anything more about the person or apparition

or whatever it was that Fred saw in his bed?"

"Well, maybe," Tom replied. "Fred told me that even though the man appeared to be young, his face was lined, weathered and deeply tanned. Fred described it as being a face that had been out in the elements a lot. And then he told me that he had been doing some research on the history of the house, and he thinks he may have found an answer to the mystery."

"What?" I asked.

"He learned that sometime in the 1800s a fisherman died in the house — he thinks in his bedroom — of a high fever. The fisherman was 28 years old!"

CHAPTER 22

The Mystery of the Bloody Millstone

(Eastern Shore)

 h, she's still around. We still hear from her every once in a while. We find things out of place, you know, where they shouldn't be. And the stain still appears on the stone every time it rains. She's still a part of her family."

Sam Nock is talking about the resident ghost at Warwick, the ancestral home of the Upshur family in the small town of Quinby in Accomack County on the Eastern Shore. Sam is a teacher at Nandua High School there. The ghost is that of Rachel Upshur who died a terrible and tragic death on Christmas Day nearly 250 years ago.

Sam says Rachel married Abel Upshur sometime around 1725, and they had five children. Abel was the grandson of Arthur Upshur, who had arrived on the Eastern Shore as a cabin boy sometime during the first half of the 17th century and rose to become one of the leading citizens in the area. Abel and Rachel moved to Warwick, one of the earliest brick houses still standing in the country, in 1738.

Eleven years later, on a bitter, blustery and rainy winter night, the couple was awakened by a loud commotion in their chicken house. Although he was ill at the time, Abel got up to check on the noise, although Rachel begged him not to go. She told him she had a terrifying nightmare in which a "white-shrouded, grinning skeleton with upraised arms had solemnly warned her not to venture out of the house that evening." If she did, she would "meet death in some horrible manner!" Abel reassured her that everything was all right, and for her to stay in bed.

But when he didn't return within a reasonable time, she became worried, hastily threw a coat over her nightgown, and ventured, Sam Nock believed barefooted, outside to find out what had happened. She found Abel standing in the cold and wetness. The chickens were still making a racket, but he had not discovered why. She implored him to get back in the house.

As they walked toward the door, Rachel stepped up on an old millstone that was embedded in the ground at the foot of the steps. As she did, a fox raced out from under the steps and sank its teeth into one of her heels. Blood spurted out on the millstone as she limped inside.

The fox was rabid, and a few days later Rachel contracted hydrophobia. There was no known cure at the time for this horrid ailment which viciously attacks the nervous system causing a victim great pain, suffering and madness. Family members, with no choice but to put her out of her misery, smothered her to death between two feather mattresses. It was Christmas Day 1749. She was buried in the family plot at Warwick.

The old millstone is still there today. It is a solid gray, well-worn stone. Curiously, Nock declared, whenever it rains and the stone gets wet, a large, dark red stain appears on the identical spot where Rachel bled when the fox bit her so many years ago.

Blithe Spirits
at Bell House

(Colonial Beach)

n a book on the history of Colonial Beach, a 35 minute drive due east of Fredericksburg, the town is called "a rare period piece, an example of the small waterside resort. In its oldest sections the density and variety of its blocks of Edwardian cottages creates a sunwashed impression unique in Westmoreland, if not all of tidewater Virginia north of the James."

Colonial Beach "prospered" on tourist trade, steamboat excursions, summer housing and its attractive business and residential establishments. Writing in the monthly journal "American Genius," in 1882, Frederick Tilp captured the interesting spirit of growth in the area. He paints a vivid, if somewhat prejudicial picture of a bygone era, as follows:

"There has been a steady increase for the past few years in summer trips to the salt waters of the Potomac. As the capital (Washington) grows, so will the desire to find healthful recreations, and summer residences on this most interesting part of the river."

The excursion boats, of course, have long passed from the scene, and many other east coast stretches of shoreline are favored by today's summer tourists, although Colonial Beach still draws a loyal clientele.

Many of the old houses still stand along this strand of the Potomac, visual reminders of an arguably grander era. One of the most famous, along historic Irving Avenue, is known as the Bell House — named either for Alexander Graham Bell, inventor of the telephone, among many other things, or his father, Alexander Melville Bell, renowned himself as the creator of "Visible Speech." Or perhaps it was named for both Bells.

This beautiful Victorian edifice originally was named "Burnside Cottage," after its builder, Colonel Burnside, paymaster in the Union army and the son of General Ambrose Burnside of Civil War note, who also is said to have coined the word "sideburns." The Colonel built the house for his bride to be, but ran into financial problems with the government, and the house was sold at auction, as a summer home, to Melville Bell in 1886.

Complete with roofed balconies, tower, wraparound veranda and such "period delights" as heavily corbelled chimney caps, polychromed glass overlights and decorative cross saw work, the Bell house has been declared a Virginia Landmark. A noted elocutionist and an astute businessman, the elder Bell's Visible Speech became an internationally-accepted system by which those who had lost their hearing from disease, could speak and understand the words of others. That he enjoyed his later years at this pleasant mansion at Colonial Beach was well expressed by one of his close friends, who once wrote: "To see him ensconced in his chair on the well shaded vine-clad veranda of his riverside home, at times reading and smoking, or watching the brooding, ever chattering sparrows he had encouraged to build their nests along the inner eaves, was to see incarnated content upon his countenance."

A frequent visitor in the early 1900s was Bell's famous son who inherited the house when his father died in 1905. Oddly, no mention of the summer resort was made in Alexander Graham Bell biographies. It has been noted, however, that Melville Bell conducted many experiments while living here, including the sailing of paper kites and "other paper contraptions" from the second floor balcony. Some of this effort led to the discovery of the tetrahedron, a three-sided pyramid design, described as the ideal space flight frame.

The house eventually passed from the Bells through several owners, and at times sat idle. Such neglect may in part explain why it slowly developed a local reputation as being haunted.

Current owners are Judy and Bob Warsing, a professional couple who work in Fredericksburg, commuting to and from Colonial Beach daily. "We had heard stories about the house being haunted even before we bought it," Judy says. "Kids in the area told of seeing faces in the front windows, although the house was vacant for two years before we moved in." And once the Warsings moved in, it didn't take them long to personally experience psychic manifestations, some conventional, some otherwise.

"There are plenty of strange noises in the house," Judy says, "but we pretty much have gotten use to them. Most of them you could probably explain anyway. It's an old house." Nevertheless, incidents kept occurring that were much more difficult to understand. Bob, for example, had two scary encounters. "Once he was going up the stairs from the first to the second floor, when he said he felt something 'swoosh' past him," Judy continues. "He said the air moved as if someone was passing him on the stairs. He was white as a sheet."

The other time, Bob got up in the middle of the night to go to the bathroom. He flipped on a light switch to avoid stepping on the family cat. As he was ready to get back into bed, he flipped the switch off, and in the flash before the room darkened, he glimpsed a wispy figure leaning out of the bathroom. But when he went to investigate it, there was nothing there.

Bell House

Judy, too, has had "brushes" with the inexplicable. "There have been times when I have been in the kitchen, and it is difficult to hear anyone upstairs. I have heard someone or something calling my name, 'Judy.' But each time I went to the foot of the stairs and asked Bob what he wanted, he said he hadn't called me. He heard my name also."

One of the strangest and most uncommon forms of the phenomena concerns hairpins. "We have found them all over the house," Judy says. "I have vacuumed the floors thoroughly, only to find hair pins afterward. And these are not tiny pins. They are about two inches long. Old fashioned wire hairpins. Once, we sanded, varnished, waxed and vacuumed the floor with a heavy duty vacuum to suck up wood shavings. Even then, I found hairpins afterward. Another time, I walked through the house passing over the light colored carpet in the front. When I came back through the hallway, there was a hairpin on the carpet. I can swear to you it was not there the first time I walked over the carpet!

"I can tell you, it was a little unnerving. We believe the pins are left behind by Bertha." Bertha Bryon was the previous house owner and lived in the house for about 50 years, the last 20 or so by herself, after her husband died. "She loved the house," Judy says. "Her father had been friends with the Bells, and she often visited the house as a little girl. She was a piano teacher, and served tea to guests. She was very refined. Bob and I think she is pleased with what we have done with the house. We've taken good care of it without really changing anything dramatically." Judy doesn't know why Bertha leaves hairpins around. Perhaps it is some sort of signal to let the Warsings know she approves of them living there.

"I have never felt afraid or threatened here," Judy says. Still, she once had a priest come out and bless the house. She also paid a visit to the well-known Fredericksburg psychic, Beverly Newton. She took a picture of the house with her and asked if there were any spirits there. "She looked at the picture and told me she smelled grapes. She said good wine had been made in the house," Judy says. "I found that fascinating, because there is a grape arbor in the back of the house and beautiful concord grapes grow there. We learned, too, that Bertha did make wine in the house. Beverly told us she felt spirits in the house, and she told us to cleanse it with pine chips. If there are still spirits here, I think we have convinced them we can peacefully coexist. There hasn't been much activity in the past year or two."

Of all the phenomena associated with the Bell house, however, possibly the strangest manifested before the Warsings moved in. "The house was completely empty then," Judy notes. "There was no furniture, no curtains, nothing. I bought a couple of plants and put them on the front porch. A friend of ours took a photograph of the house, and we didn't notice anything out of the ordinary then. But about a year later, we were showing some photos in an album to some friends, when we took a closer look at that picture again. In the front window, you could see clearly the image of a man standing at the window peering out. It was white and wispy, but you could distinguish features. The man had white hair and a white beard." Judy says the man was identical in appearance to that of a man taken in a photograph decades ago and published in an area newspaper.

That man was Melville Bell!

Caring Katina of Fall Hill

(Fredericksburg)

rs. Lynn W. Franklin, born February 28, 1899, is both a delightful and a remarkable person. Although in her nineties, she is today still an active woman with a lucid, sharp mind who can rattle off historic dates, names and places with the rapidity and accuracy of a serious student in American history prepping for final exams. She is a direct descendent of Alexander Spotswood's wife (he was a highly respected colonial Virginia governor), and she has lived in the magnificent hilltop plantation called Fall Hill near Fredericksburg since 1908.

She has lived there these past eight decades, she says, with a long-time resident ghost. But she harbors no fear. "I doubt that you would ever find a more friendly spirit than the one we have here," Mrs. Franklin smiles. "In a way, it's actually a comfort to have her here. This house is surrounded by 100 acres of woods, and it's good to have a ghost with me so no mortals bother us."

Exactly when the house, or rather houses, at Fall Hill were built is still somewhat debatable. "Oh, I guess there's an argument about that," Mrs. Franklin says. It is, however, generally accepted that ever since the first Francis Thornton arrived in this country from England in 1673, his descendants have lived within thousands of acres of scenic land at the site with a majestic view overlooking the picturesque Rappahannock River on the outskirts of Fredericksburg.

One account says he built an "interesting old house" about

1680, and named it "The Falls," since the falls of the river thundered nearby. A later Francis Thornton — there were a number of them in a direct line of descendance — put up a "cottage" or summer residence somewhere in the 1738 to 1740 time frame.

According to the Virginia Landmarks Register, the present house, which includes eight rooms and, says the current owner, "an enormous attic and basement," probably was built for Francis Thornton V sometime around 1790. Mrs. Franklin disagrees. "The house certainly was here before 1790, she contends. "I believe it was started in 1763."

The legend of the benevolent spirit which sometimes surfaces at Fall Hill had its origins in Williamsburg, when a young Indian girl — some have said she was a Sioux princess — was captured and given to then-governor Spotswood. Her name was Katina. When this venerable gentleman retired from active public life in 1720, and moved to his palace in the wilderness at Germanna, near Fredericksburg, he took the Indian maiden with him, and she became the nurse, or nanny, for his four children. Her services were excellent, and she was treated like one of the family. William Byrd was so impressed with her during a visit, it is said he gave her the "largest tip" ever received by a servant.

After Spotswood died in 1740, Katina went to work for the Thorntons at Fall Hill, where she helped raise three generations of children. "But she was much more than a servant," says Mrs. Franklin. She was "the essence of dedication and devotion to the young ones she loved, and they loved her." Recalled as being small, dark and lithesome, Katina taught the young Thorntons the ways of the Indian, and how best to appreciate nature's most beautiful secrets.

She died in 1777, and was buried in the garden, "beside a little stream, with great boulders of granite gathered from her native hills marking the spot...this Indian sleeps her last sleep beneath a tree, up and over which climbs a wild grape vine..."

"When I first came to Fall Hill to live, I was nine years old," Mrs. Franklin says. "My grandfather took me by the hand one day and told me, quite solemnly, 'I'm going to show you the grave of our old family nurse, Katina.' We knelt beside a little grave covered by a granite stone. But nothing was written on it. Katina was a slave and the family was very careful not to discriminate or show partiality by engraving her stone.

"My grandfather then told me that when his great-grandfather lived, she brought him up and taught him to speak Indian. She was a very old woman then, and when she died, he was inconsolable. He wept and said he'd lost his best friend."

Exactly when Katina first reappeared at Fall Hill, allegedly to make sure that young descendants of the Thornton family were being properly cared for, is not certain, though recorded reports of her sightings go back to the early years of this century. When Mrs. Bessie Taylor Robinson lived in the house in the 1920s, she said that "many persons…have spoken of seeing her walking about the plantation as though looking for her companions of long ago."

Mrs. Franklin says one of the first occurrences she remembers was when two boys were home from school on vacation and were sleeping in the nursery. The next morning one of the youngsters came downstairs, "appearing quite pale," and asked Mrs. Robinson if she had come in their room the previous night to cover them. She told them no, and inquired why he asked. He told her that "an old woman with long black braids" had come in during the night and then disappeared through the wall at the head of the bed!

Mrs. Franklin says that in 1938 a New York journalist named Alice Dickson came to Fall Hill as a guest of her mother. "One afternoon she was taking a nap upstairs. She awoke around five

Mrs. Lynn W. Franklin at Fall Hill

o'clock and started to get up when, she said, a young boy dressed in knee britches walked through the open door. He had his hair tied back and was attired in colonial period clothes. Then she said that behind him followed a little Indian woman with long black braided hair."

Mrs. Franklin says the woman thought the children in the house had dressed up to amuse her. But when she addressed them, they didn't answer. They just disappeared! "There were no children in the house at the time. She'd seen the ghost of Katina!"

In 1969, a newspaper reporter named Linda Raymond was invited to spend a night at Fall Hill by Mrs. Franklin. She wanted to do an article on Katina. She started her resulting story by saying, "She'd been dead for more than 200 years (actually 192), but she was there that night close beside me, as near and thick a presence as fog in a river bottom." Ms. Raymond also said, "I could feel the ghost's presence all around us. The only thing that seemed strange was that we couldn't see her when she was so close."

On yet another occasion, Mrs. Robinson saw the apparition. She came home late one night from a meeting in town and as she stood in the downstairs hall, she witnessed "a figure" come out of the room where her younger son was sleeping. Upon examination, Mrs. Robinson found every other member of the family sound asleep and all the doors and windows were locked shut. She told friends she had no doubt had seen Katina, still checking on the youngsters in the house.

And, finally, a few years ago, Mrs. Franklin herself had an ethereal experience in her bedroom. "I had been away for awhile and I was in bed, wide awake, reading. I had my little grand-daughter in the house with me. We'd just recently lost her father, and it was a period of considerable stress, as you can imagine.

"I had never seen a ghost of any description before, although, of course, I was well aware of the stories about Katina. I never thought I would see her, and to be truthful, I was never quite convinced that anyone had ever seen her. Imagination can do a lot of things, you know. But I definitely wasn't dreaming. I was alert. Then, at the foot of my bed there appeared this darkly beautiful face. She just looked at me with those dark Indian eyes. Her expression never changed, but it seemed like she had a look of great concern. I interpreted it to mean that I had better take good care of my granddaughter. She was there just for an instant, and then she was gone. But I have no question that she was real."

There is a curious footnote to the appearances and disappearances of Katina over the years at Fall Hill. Mrs. Franklin says that those who claimed to have seen the Indian ghost say that she most often has been seen near the top of the stairs, where she vanishes from sight by apparently walking through a bedroom wall.

"Years ago, we stripped off the old wallpaper in that room," Mrs. Franklin notes. "We discovered that during the 1800s there were some alterations made in the house. At the spot where Katina appears to walk through the wall, there was, under the wallpaper, an old sealed-up doorway. It was a second door to that bedroom. I believe it was once the nursery!"

Terror in the
Aquia Belfry

(Stafford County, near Fredericksburg)

hat is it about an old house or building reputed to be haunted that fascinates people? Elmwood in Essex County near Tappahannock quickly comes to mind. When newspaper accounts of haunting activities were published more than a half a century ago, hundreds of people tramped through the woods every time the moon was full to see for themselves what eerie happenings might unfold in the then-vacant mansion. Literally thousands of curious onlookers have braved many a cold and damp night on the railroad tracks near West Point to catch a glimpse of the mysterious train light that is said to appear and disappear on occasion. And in Portsmouth, years ago, so many people clustered around a small frame house after it was reported there was a resident poltergeist inside, that the police had to barricade the place to protect its mortal occupants.

Aquia Church in Stafford County, about 20 miles north of Fredericksburg is such a place. It has held generations of area youngsters spellbound with the oft-told tales of its haunting past. In fact, this venerable, two-and-one-half century old structure has to be guarded around the clock every Halloween because so many teenagers otherwise would descend upon it, as they did in years past, occasionally rendering it harm.

Could it be the element of danger that is so intriguing, particularly in the case of Aquia Church? One must wonder about the sanity of those who want to explore its ghostly interior to prove their manhood, so to speak, because it was on just such a venture, a long time ago, that a young man allegedly lost his life!

The church itself, according to the Virginia Landmarks Register, is a "good illustration of rural Virginia's use of ecclesiastical architecture endowed with urbanity and sophistication." The Register adds that its "elegant classicism contrasts with its isolated woodland setting." Is that not a perfect setting for ethereal happenings?

Ill winds swirled about the church even before its completion. Begun in 1751, it was seriously damaged by fire on February 17, 1754 — three days before construction was to be finished! It was rebuilt within the walls over the next three years.

The hauntings at Aquia stem from a night of horror in the church more than 200 years ago, probably during the time of the American Revolution. A young woman was murdered in the chapel by a highwayman or men, apparently after a violent struggle. Her body was hidden in the belfry, and, as the church was not in use during this period, it was years later before her skeletal remains were found, with her golden hair still intact.

It is said, too, that the blood stains from where the woman was slain were clearly visible for more than 100 years, until early in the 20th century when a new cement floor was laid. Not only was this physical evidence present, but there also has been, through the years, a continuous stream of scary psychic phenomena, so much so, in fact, that reportedly, through most of the 18th century, even the parishioners were afraid to go into Aquia Church at night.

The most prominent and persistent manifestations are said to be re-created by the victim. They include, with only slight variations, the sound of feet running up and down the stairs to the belfry, heavy noises of a struggle, and the apparition of a terrified woman standing at one of the windows.

While this oft-repeated phenomenon is the most common occurrence, it is by no means the only one. There is, for example, the popular tale of the prominent socialite who spent her summers in Stafford County in the 1920s, and who became interested in the church through the spectral stories related to her by her maids. She decided to see the spirits herself, but couldn't get any of the strapping men in the area to accompany her. They all politely, but forcefully backed off when they learned she was going at night. Undaunted, she recruited two "scientists" — likely early 20th century ghost-busters — from Washington. They entered Aquia

Church on a dark night, led by the determined socialite. But just after she walked through the door, an unseen hand slapped her sharply across the face. The two men ran inside and searched everywhere, but they found nothing, and had no rational explanation for what happened. But that it did happen was evident in the fact that the mark on the lady's face remained for several days!

There is, too, a time-honored story of a "whistling spirit" at Aquia who saved the lives of two Confederate soldiers during the Civil War. It has been passed along for generations. The originator was a William Fitzhugh, who during a scouting mission in 1862 or '63, stopped off in the church with a comrade to rest. They had heard about the hauntings there, but they were too tired to care. They promptly went to sleep in the square pews.

Sometime during the night they were roused by what Fitzhugh described as "unmistakable footsteps at the rear of the church on some stone flagging." Then they heard someone or something whistling the tune, "The Campbells are Coming." Frightened out of their wits, they jumped up and struck a light, but saw nothing. Then they went to the door and looked out. A troop of Yankee soldiers was advancing along the road heading directly for the church. They raced to the back of the building, leaped out of a window and escaped. Fitzhugh later attributed the whistling ghost to saving his and his friend's lives.

Was it the spirit of the murdered girl? Or is it her apparition that Robert Frazier and his son have seen flitting among the tombstones in the Aquia cemetery? Frazier, a former caretaker there, told two reporters about 15 years ago that he has often sighted "things" running through the graveyards. He said they appeared "blurred and fuzzy." He added that they were white but not transparent. He couldn't see through them. The sightings were all at night, and when Frazier and his son went over to see what or who it was that was darting about, the figures disappeared. "They just fade away, kinda slow like," he told the journalists. He said he couldn't tell if they were men or women because they were too blurry. But he was convinced he knew what they were. "Everybody says there's ghosts up here. Me and my son seen 'em. They're here!"

The death caused by the ghost or ghosts of Aquia Church supposedly occurred more than 100 years ago. Supposedly, because while the story has been told and retold with relish and enthusiasm enough so as to defy disbelief, there is no documented record of who the victim was or when the event took place.

Aquia Church

What is told is that in the days when everyone was afraid to approach the church at night, one young man — perhaps taunted by a dare — declared that no ghost could get the best of him. He said he would go inside, in the dark of night, and even climb to the haunted belfry. Those he made the boast to, however, were skeptical, so they gave him a hammer and a nail and told him to drive the nail into the wall, so they could tell for sure later whether or not he had lived up to his word.

Alone, he set out through the woods toward the old church. When the young man had not returned, hours later, his friends became worried and went to the church to find out what had happened. They found him in the belfry — dead! In the darkness, he had hammered the nail into the wall through his coat! When he turned to leave, he was held fast. Evidently thinking he was in the grasp of an evil spirit, it is said he died of fright!

CHAPTER 26

A Potpourri of Restaurant Revelers

(Danville, Fredericksburg, and Virginia Beach)

pparently, some ghosts get hungry. Or at least they seem to like the smell of good food cooking. In one case there was a spirit who loved the aroma and taste of fresh-brewed coffee. Perhaps these are some of the reasons that a number of Virginia restaurants have reported hauntings over the years. Read on:

THE UNEARTHLY EYES OF JOSEPHINE CORBIN

nfortunately, the restaurant is closed now. But when it was open, for a few years in the 1980s, it was a popular dining spot at 913 North Main Street in Danville. It is now the residence of Chuck Sublett and his wife. He believes the house was built around 1883 or 1884. It is an imposing, two story building with a sweeping front porch decorated with ironwork. When Chuck bought it some years ago it was, he says, structurally sound, but cosmetically a wreck.

This was the home, for more than 80 years, of an attractive woman named Josephine Corbin. Her father died in the late 19th century and her mother lived into the 1940s. After that, Josephine became somewhat of a recluse and chose to spend virtually all of her time in a small, dark, back bedroom of the house.

After renovations, this room became a semi-private dining area

Portrait of Josephine Corbin

when the restaurant first opened. Almost immediately, reports of strange happenings in that room began to surface. Employees told of hearing mysterious footsteps overhead when they were in the room alone. This was particularly odd because there was no flooring above the room. One waitress said she heard female laughter there, but found no one in the room. A snapshot taken there produced a "shadowy female figure" by the side of the fireplace. No one could explain it.

Apparently, Josephine, or whoever it was, had an aversion to bluegrass music, because every time it was played, the stereo speakers in that one room would not work. As soon as more soothing music was played, the speakers came back on. Despite the haunting occurrences, diners frequently requested tables in the back room, even if they had to wait. "People really got into the spirit of things," Chuck remembers. "But after they had a glass of wine or two, the stories seemed to get a little embellished. I'm not sure everything that was said to happen actually happened."

Still, the mystique grew. A Danville reporter noted: "There is a haunting air of the past about the ornate red-brick mansion that houses the Victorian. The atmosphere in the elegant restored house can be almost chilling, especially in the back dining room. For it is in that room that the willful ghost of Josephine Corbin is said to walk."

Chuck today admits that there were "things that were unexplained." "I don't know of any face to face sightings," he says, "but I've had some things happen to me." One evening, he recalls hearing a weird repetitive drumming sound coming from the room when he stood in it. But when he backed out of the room, the sound stopped. He then stepped on the threshold and the drumming picked up again.

Chuck's wife, too, has had "experiences." "She has felt a presence that seemed to brush past her at times," he says. "And then there is our cat. It acts sometimes as if it is staring at something. Oh, yes, I had a friend tell me once that he definitely saw something in that room. He wasn't sure what it was, and he said it kind of appeared in his vision at about a 45 degree angle. He couldn't make out what it was, but he declared blatantly that 'it weren't no shadow.'"

Of all the phenomena associated with the Victorian, none is more unnerving than the piercing eyes of Josephine Corbin. They are a vivid blue color in an oval oil portrait of her as a young woman which hangs in her room.

Many who have dined and visited there swear that the eyes follow them as they move about in the room. The Danville reporter wrote: "The eyes, a startling blue in the otherwise black and white likeness, seem to follow as the viewer shifts position."

"She lived her last few years in that back room almost exclusively," says Chuck. "Maybe that explains why her presence is so strong there."

* * * * *

THE MYSTERY MAN AT SMYTHE'S COTTAGE

f you are lucky — or if you are unlucky, depending upon how you view such things — there is a chance you can have dinner in Old Town Fredericksburg and possibly see or sense a ghost at the same time. But even if no spirits arise, you can enjoy a good old-fashioned home cooked meal and learn about the colorful history of Smythe's Cottage at 303 Fauquier Street, about half way between the Rising Sun Tavern and the Mary Washington house.

Owner-host Lonnie Williams and his crew will be happy to serve up a variety of soups, salads and sandwiches for lunch, and at dinner time it is, in his words, "a little bit of everything," including roast pork, Virginia ham, chicken pot pie and stuffed quail among other entrees.

It is not exactly certain when the cottage was built. Former owner Joyce Ackerman, who used to serve a mean turkey hash there, believes it dates back to the 1830s, and originally was a blacksmith shop, hence the name. Lonnie, however, says tax records on the building go back to the 1850s, and he's not sure beyond that. He has heard that it may even have served for a time as a bordello during Civil War days.

In any event, both Joyce and Lonnie have not only heard others tell of unusual activities in the cottage, but they have had experiences of their own. In addition, there is a ghostly legend associated with an old house directly across the street.

Joyce vividly remembers the day, a few years ago, when a tourist approached her and asked why the old lady in that house was so rude. He told her he had gone up to the front door and knocked, and said he could see an old woman through a window

Smythe's Cottage

just staring at him. She then turned away and started crawling up the stairs on her hands and knees. Joyce said she just laughed and told the tourist, "that's just Tootie. She's been dead a year and a half!"

The tourist had apparently seen the apparition of a woman named Tootie Ninde, an eccentric town character. "She had been ill when I first bought Smythe's Cottage in 1975," says Joyce. "I think she had cancer and emphysema. And she did have to crawl up the stairs. Her room faced my place and I used to see her light go out at night. Then a curious thing happened. About two years after she died, I saw the light on in her room and then it went out. I didn't think anything about it at the time, because I just thought a relative or someone was in the house. But when I saw one of her relatives later and asked about it, he or she said no. Another time I walked over to the front porch and I saw someone inside at the foot of the stairs. It was like a figure, and it just sort of drifted away."

Joyce Ackerman says similar happenings took place at Smythe's Cottage when she owned it. "I had a little office upstairs, and on more than one occasion when I was up there working, I would hear noises downstairs, annoying noises. It sounded like a group having a conversation, like they were holding a meeting. But when I walked down, there was never anyone there."

Equally mysterious at the cottage was the periodic appearance of a tall man in a long black jacket with long black hair and a loose, western-style tie. Joyce saw him at least twice on the outdoor patio and she spoke to him both times and said he just "drifted away." Once, after closing up for the night, Joyce's cook was getting in her truck when she saw the man and she admitted it scared her to death. On another occasion, one of the kitchen helpers saw the vision and went after it with a knife, but it disappeared.

"I personally have never seen him," says Lonnie Williams, "but we have had customers ask us who the strange man was on the patio. They had seen him. We have had some odd things hap-pen since we've been running the restaurant. I've seen the chairs moving now and then and heard voices and footsteps when no one else was around. We've found the water running when we opened up in the morning — things like that. We have an old clock that Joyce told us hadn't worked in years. It has started up on occasion, keeping the right time, as if someone had just wound it."

"I can tell you this," Lonnie adds, "we had a waiter here once who claimed he used to see a young girl upstairs. He made up a story about her, telling customers that she had been a prostitute in the house. Every time he told that story, the candle on the table would crack. I can't explain that.

"But I guess the strangest thing was the time two or three years ago when one of our waitresses said she heard the door open and she turned a corner and ran into somebody — who wasn't there! She said there was somebody there, but there wasn't anybody there. That's how she explained it. She screamed and ran and got me. I was only a couple of steps from the doorway and when I entered the room there was no one there. She was terrified. She ran out the front door and never came back!"

* * * * *

THE PLAYFUL PHANTOM AT RISING SUN TAVERN

I t is written that George Washington "knew the Rising Sun Tavern in Fredericksburg well," and that the establishment and the tavern post office were frequented by Light Horse Harry Lee, Charles Lee, young James Monroe, Charles Carter and other notables. One published account states that "it is a matter of undoubted record that these, and half a hundred other young men, whose names were to become synonymous with freedom, discussed at the Rising Sun Tavern the topics of the day, chief among which was the rights of the colonist."

And, according to this source, all the leading men of Virginia have passed in and out of the tavern's doorway. "The Rising Sun," she wrote, "has known the hand of Washington, Jefferson, Madison, Mason, Mercer, John Paul Jones, and the famous Lees."

In fact, a lot of famous Virginians graced its premises. It has been beautifully restored and today is open to the public. One can no longer stop off for a heady brew, but at least a glass of spiced tea can be served.

Downstairs there is a "great room" for the "landed gentry"; a "common man's" tap room; a ladies' "retiring room" and a tavern keeper's office. Upstairs are three sleeping rooms, an "L" storage room and one "common man's" room, with no fireplace. For no more than a farthing, this room could be rented by the poor in yesteryear to get out of the weather. Gracious hostesses, costumed in colonial style dress, show tourists around.

It is the general consensus that the Rising Sun is haunted! One

Linda Mix at the Rising Sun Tavern

tourist brochure states that the tavern is "still a lively historic attraction, and its ghostly inhabitant maintains the spirit of cheer and mischief that once thrived at the tavern."

And there is further agreement as to who the haunter is. Most people believe it is John Frazier, the last tavern keeper. "It's mostly harmless and fun things," says Linda Mix, current manager at the Rising Sun, of the psychic manifestations which occasionally occur. "There's definitely nothing malicious about what happens."

Well, maybe at least one guide at the tavern might take issue with that statement. Or at least perhaps "he" got a little too playful for her liking. A few years ago someone, or something, kept unplugging the lights in an upstairs room. The hostess, tired of reaching down to put the plug back in its socket, decided to mildly scold the ghost. "Come on now, stop it!" she demanded. Then as she turned to leave the room, the "force" or presence yanked the rug out from under her, sending her sprawling to the floor.

And then there was the time another hostess felt something tugging at the hem of her dress as she was descending the stairs early one morning. She looked to see if her colonial skirt had gotten snagged on something, but it hadn't. Yet, something was holding her. Knowing of all the tales associated with the tavern and its mischievous former proprietor, she said, "All right, John, let go!" At that instant she felt herself suddenly freed.

Others have had their mob caps pulled from their heads when no one within sight was around. Candles have inexplicably "moved" from their storage places, and once a candelabra on a wagon wheel crashed down in the front hall one day. What made this particular incident scary was that, as Linda Mix tells it, "Someone would have had to lift it over the bannister for it to fall that way."

Linda says a lot of little unexplained "things" happen at the Rising Sun. The front door has opened and closed on its own at times. "The opening we can understand," she says, "but how do you account for the closing right after its been opened? We couldn't. Sometimes you just have a feeling that someone else is in the tavern when you are in it by yourself. This is especially true in the winter when tourists are few and far between. You just feel a presence.

"You know," Linda continues, "like the expression goes, I'm from Missouri and you have to show me. I think some of the things can be explained. If a mob cap flies off, it could be that the elastic was too tight. But I have to admit, there have been a couple of specific incidents that are really mystifying." One took place when a team of professional photographers came in to shoot some tourist promotional pictures. "They were setting up their equipment in one room while shooting in another," she says. "A camera began smoking on its own. Also, they had started one roll of film by photographing another site. When the film was developed, the shots of the other site turned out fine, but the ones taken in the tavern were blank."

Linda describes the other incident: "One of the hostesses was by herself one evening. She had the assignment to close up, and then to come back the first thing in the morning to open the tavern. She says that when she was locking up, she distinctly noticed that there were three hats lined up on pegs on the wall. When she opened up the next morning — and there had been no signs of a break-in or anything like that — the three hats were stacked neatly on a chair in the hallway!"

Despite the continuing series of manifestations over the years, those who work in the tavern are unafraid. "I believe John was a jolly old barkeep in his day," Linda says. "You had to be affable to survive as a tavern owner." Maybe he still feels the urge to carry on his pranks, because it apparently is good for business. "We have people coming in here all the time asking about the ghost," she notes. "They want to hear all the anecdotes we know."

John Frazier probably beams every time that happens.

* * * * *

THE IMPISH PRANKSTER AT PINE TREE INN

he next time you're in the mood for a nice quiet candlelight dinner, with outstanding ambiance and service, and superb cuisine, you might want to try Tandom's Pine Tree Inn on Virginia Beach Boulevard. You may even catch a glimpse of a puckish female ghost who is said to have been seen in the ladies' rest room, the linen closet, the kitchen and elsewhere from time to time. Often, "she" seems to enjoy playing mischievous little tricks on waitresses and kitchen help, but on occasion she also has appeared to diners.

Tandom's is one of the older — and finer — restaurants in Virginia Beach. Its veal, chicken and seafood dishes all are expertly prepared and many people have eaten there regularly for years, the most telling testament of all. It has been operating since 1927, and was a roadside stopover before that. There are tales that, during prohibition, high stakes poker games took place in a back

The Pine Tree Inn

room; bring your own bottle. According to one of the legends, a fashionable lady held her own in the card games until one day when a gentleman, who either caught her cheating, or just couldn't stand being beaten by a woman, allegedly shot her.

Whether or not this really happened has been long lost in the mists of time. The episode could not be factually verified. Still, one might wonder about it when the experience of Whitney Elliot is considered. Whitney is a bright, young entrepreneur who runs her own marketing business in Virginia Beach. She dined with a friend of hers at the Pine Tree Inn one evening in the winter of 1989-1990. It was late and there were only a few people in the restaurant, when Whitney went to the powder room.

She tells what happened next: "There are three stalls, and I always look under the stalls before I enter one. I saw a woman's feet under one of them, but the strange thing was, she was wearing real old shoes. They were the high button type with laces all the way up, like, you know, from another era, maybe the 1920s. I also heard a rustling sound, like an old time skirt.

"Weird, I thought, but I went into a stall opposite from where I saw the shoes. Now, no one else came into the room while I was there, and I didn't hear any other noises, especially of the door to the outer room opening and closing. There was no water running, no flushing or anything. Yet when I left, there was no one in the room! I looked under the stalls again and the shoes were gone. I know that no one could have left without me hearing it.

"I went back to my table and told my friend. We called the waitress over and when I asked her if they had a ghost in the restaurant, I thought she would faint. She turned as white as a sheet. She told us we were not the first to have such an experience; that, in fact, many things have happened to her. She told us, for instance, that she had the late shift one night. They close at 10 p.m. on weekends, but if someone comes in just before 10, it can be around midnight before she leaves. One of the last things she has to do when closing up is blow out all the candles on the tables, maybe 25 or 30 of them.

"She said she blew out the candles and went into the kitchen. A few minutes later one of the managers came in and asked her why she hadn't blown out the candles. She went back into the dining room to look. They were all lit! She said the hair on the back of her neck and arms stood up. She also told us that whatever the presence was, it was often felt in the old linen closet and that she would never go in there by herself. She added that she could always tell when the ghost was there. She could feel it. She had gone into the kitchen earlier and told the cooks, but they said no, 'she' wasn't in the dining room, 'she' was out in the fish house, because the door there had been opening and closing by itself that night. 'She' apparently knows her way around quite well.

"I can tell you this," Whitney concludes. "I know what I saw, and it wasn't something alive!"

One person who is convinced something or someone roams through the restaurant in the night and early morning hours is Angie Reitzel who has baked fresh breads and served as a prep cook and in other roles for nearly 20 years. "I've heard plenty of stories of her the time I've been here — from waiters, waitresses, dishwashers, cooks, you name it. And I've had a number of things happen to me personally that I could not explain."

Take, for example, the incident of the missing coffee. Angie arrives in the morning very early to do her baking, often while it still is dark outside. On this particular day, one of the managers came in and she asked him if he wanted a cup of coffee. Sure. "I made a pot and poured two cups full on the counter," she remembers, as if it had happened yesterday. "Then I turned around and went to get some sugar and cream, maybe five or 10 feet away. When I went back the coffee was gone! I said to myself, 'Am I crazy? I thought I just poured two cups.' Then I looked into the bottom of the cups and there was still drops of coffee left in them. I had gotten the cups clean from the cupboard. They had been stacked upside down. And the manager wasn't even in the kitchen. How do you explain that?"

Another time, a few years ago, Angie and a friend of hers were in the restaurant one night when it was closed. They were preparing food for a Christmas party for Pine Tree Inn personnel which was being held at another location. "We took off our coats and started to work," she says. "Then we heard some pots and pans rattling, and we thought my friend's husband had come in to help us. We looked around, but there was no one there. We forgot about it.

"When we finished, we packed up the food, put on our coats and started to leave. The doorway had long plastic flaps hanging down, and as we approached it, the flaps parted. They opened up as if someone were holding them for us! My friend screamed. She said she wasn't going through there. I had to talk to her for a long time before I could get her to go through the doorway."

Angie says there have been many other manifestations over

the years. Lights that apparently burn out at night burn brightly the next morning. The dishwasher, a big commercial one with "all kinds of switches," occasionally turns on and off by itself. Once, a waiter brought a tray of drinks to a table, then put them down and turned to get a cup of coffee. When he turned back, the drinks had vanished. At other times, matches seem to fly about inexplicably.

Angie says a lot of psychic activity is associated with the linen closet. "The lights go on and off in there all the time. Employees turn out the lights when we are locking up, and then they just go on again. This has even happened to the managers. One night one of them turned out the lights in the linen closet. He was sure of it. Then, in the parking lot he saw the light on in there," she says.

Angie thinks the ghost could be the spirit of a young girl who once worked as a bus girl at the restaurant, but died a tragic death. "Maybe she enjoyed working there and just comes back to visit. Who knows?" Angie asks. "The first time you hear or see something, you don't want to believe it. You shrug it off. But then you begin to wonder. So many things have happened."

Angie even saw the ghost once. "It was early," she recalls, "about 7:30 in the morning. I was at a mixing bowl preparing muffins. There was just me and one cook there. I looked over and saw this person sorting silverware. I couldn't tell if it was a boy or girl. I only knew he or she was young and had short hair. I thought maybe it was the new dishwasher. He comes in at 8.

"I asked him to get me some trash cans, but there was no response. I said, 'This kid didn't hear me, or he or she just didn't want to get the cans.' I tried again and there was no reply. I could see the person through and around a big stack of glasses.

"So I went over to where he or she was standing and when I got there he or she had disappeared. I couldn't figure it out. I went into the kitchen and asked the cook where the dishwasher had gone. He said he hadn't seen anyone. So I went through the dining room. I looked in the storage room, the linen room and both bathrooms. There was no one anywhere. Finally, I went out back and opened the door. The guy who opens our oysters was out there and I asked him. He said he hadn't seen anyone come in or out. They all thought I was crazy! But I saw it and it definitely was a real person. It wasn't an indistinct image or anything like that."

And so the mystery remains unsolved. Angie and others say the spirit seems to come and go at random. Nothing will happen for weeks at a time, and then, suddenly, the visitor is back. Is it the young bus girl, or is it the lady with the high button shoes from a time long ago? Or is it both?

Whatever, it is not a hostile spirit, but one who apparently has a prankish sense of humor. It seems to add an extra dimension to dining at Tandom's Pine Tree Inn.

CHAPTER 27

The Ghostly Houses of Robert E. Lee

(Westmoreland County and Alexandria)

I f there was, or is, a Robert E. Lee ghost — and certainly there would be plenty of just cause for one, grieving over his lost or starving troops — one might suspect he would reappear somewhere in his beloved Virginia, perhaps at the Wilderness, Cold Harbor, Manassas or Petersburg. Would not it be arguable that his "presence" should be felt at the Lee Mansion in Arlington or possibly even out of state, say at Gettysburg?

But, at these sites at least, such is not the case. Nevertheless, it is interesting to note that there are recurring reports, well documented and witnessed by many, of strong psychic phenomena at two historic Old Dominion houses in which Lee lived, one as an infant and toddler, and the other as a young boy and teenager. And, at least at one of these locations, many believe it is the spirit of a very youthful and exuberant Robert who is heard, and sometimes sighted, romping about.

This most venerable and revered consummate gentleman was born at Stratford Hall Plantation, in Westmoreland County January 19, 1807, the third son of Light Horse Harry Lee.

Stratford Hall has been described as one of the great houses of American history. A brochure points out: "Its magnificent setting on a high bluff above the Potomac River and its bold architectural style set it apart from any other colonial house." As one Lee biographer wrote: "No picture of the mansion gives any adequate idea of its chateau-like massiveness." Fashioned of brick made on the site and timber cut from virgin forests, its fortress-like walls are two and two and a half feet thick, arranged in an "H" configuration. The brochure says, "The great hall in the center of the house, 29 feet square with an inverted tray ceiling 17 feet high, is elaborately paneled. It is one of the most architecturally significant rooms to survive from colonial America."

And yet, as imposing as the mansion and its surrounding 1,600 acre estate are, an even more impressive distinction arises from the prominence of the family which resided there for so many years. Indeed, the Lees of Virginia certainly were one of the — if not the most renowned families in the country. Richard Henry Lee, for instance, made the motion for independence in the Continental Congress. "Light Horse Harry" Lee was a hero of the Revolution and a favorite of George Washington.

At Stratford today, however, tour hostesses are mostly reluctant to mention the presence of any form of psychic phenomena. They prefer to dwell on the rich history and superb architecture and setting of the house and grounds, and well they should. The plantation's grandeur is more than enough in itself to warrant visits and revisits. It has been faithfully restored to its original elegance and contains many fine pieces of period furniture, family portraits, and other pieces of Lee memorabilia.

As with so many worthy old estates, there is ample justification for ghostly encounters at Stratford Hall, for along with its integrity and eloquence, the great house and some of the family members have had their share of tragic events. Late in his life, Light Horse Harry Lee and some of his friends were brutally beaten by an angry mob in Baltimore. They were "stuck with penknives and had hot wax poured into their eyes." Lee had part of his nose cut off and was permanently disfigured. Would not one speculate that "he" might return to his ancestral home, scene of much happier days? As we shall see, maybe he did.

There in the case of Henry Lee, Robert's older half brother, who got his wife's sister "in the family way." That unfortunate incident, plus the tragic death of their young daughter, undoubtedly contributed to the fact that Henry's wife, Ann, eventually became addicted to a powerful drug, and Henry earned the dubious sobriquet of "Black Horse Harry."

Mrs. Walker Allard, who has worked at Stratford Hall for more than 40 years as an historical interpreter and as custodian of historic buildings, says the only fragmentary account she ever came across concerning psychic energy was the reported sighting of a ghostly figure at a desk in the great house. "Yes," she says, "that happened some time ago. There was a young maid who said she did see a man's figure at the desk." The woman opened a door to the library and was to go in the room to clean it. She went in and came right out again. Her supervisor asked her what happened and she told her she "didn't want to disturb the gentleman in there." When they reentered the library, no one was there. Could it have been Light Horse Harry? The maid said the figure seemed to be checking over some papers, possibly inventories. "She became very frightened and ran from the house," Mrs. Allard says. "But like I say, she was very young, and probably very impressionable. I think just about every old house has a ghost if someone wants to see a ghost."

Stratford Hall, it appears, after conversations with a number of both current and retired employees, is no exception to this theory. There have been, in fact, numerous accounts of psychic activity. Margie McGrath, a former hostess, says she was taking a couple through the house one day, and as she stopped to answer questions near the end of the tour, she felt "a sharp tug" at her hoop under her full, period-costume skirt. "I kept talking, but I brushed my hand to the area where I felt the pull, and my skirt wasn't hiked or out of place or anything, and no one else was in the room" she recalls. "Then I felt the tug again. Something or someone had pulled on my skirt!"

Mrs. McGrath says that on another occasion a few years ago she escorted a psychic on a tour. "She apparently was well known and had been asked to visit a house in Fredericksburg," Mrs. McGrath remembers. "When we passed through the great hall on the second floor, she stopped and said, 'Oh, I have so many good impressions,' and she said she could see the room full of Lees, and that there was dancing and music and entertainment. At the end of the tour she came to me and said that the Lees were pleased with how the house was being taken care of. And then she told me she had seen more of the family playing croquet on the lawn as she had approached the main house. I was fascinated. I don't laugh at any of this."

Jo Ann Boyer, a former chief hostess at the mansion, now retired, also has heard some strange stories and had a chilling confrontation of her own. "I have heard that the gentleman who the maid said she saw in the library that day has also appeared in one of the outbuildings," she says. "He has been seen with a ledger in his hands. Those who saw him say he was dressed in black with a ruffled shirt and white stockings, much like the clothing worn in the 18th century."

Mrs. Boyer says her personal encounter occurred on a "dismal, dark winter afternoon." "It was late in the day when I took a group through the house," she recalls. "Toward the end of the tour, we were in the far upper west end, and I had my back to the door and the people were facing me. Suddenly, I saw a woman and a child in the room in colonial period costume. The woman had on a gray cape and the child a red cape, and their hoods were up. I just thought to myself, who was that child with Mrs. McGrath, who was another hostess on duty with me that day. She had remained downstairs when I went on the tour. She had grandchildren who occasionally come to the house, and I just assumed it was Mrs. McGrath and one of her grandchildren. But I couldn't figure out why she was upstairs, and why did they have hoods on?

"So when the tour was over, I went downstairs and asked Mrs. McGrath, and she looked at me like I was crazy or something. She said she hadn't left the room downstairs, and no one was with her. At first, I thought she was joking, but when she realized that I was serious, she lifted her hand and covered her mouth, and said that I had finally seen them. I had seen Ann Lee, the distraught and broken hearted wife of Black Horse Harry Lee, and their little daughter, Margaret, who had died in the house at age two after falling down the stairs. People have heard the woman calling the little girl, and the sound of the child running and then both of them laughing, as if they were playing together. We had talked about it, but it never dawned on me when I saw them that day, that it was Ann and Margaret Lee," Mrs. Boyer says. Little Margaret Lee died in 1820.

At least two of the Stratford Hall security officers have experienced various forms of psychic manifestations in recent years. They voluntarily recounted the events, but asked to remain anonymous. "A lot of things happen, sometimes in the great house, and often in the Southwest dependency building," one of them says. "We have heard all kinds of noises at night, but never found any physical reason for them. What kind of noises? I mean racket. Loud racket at times." Both of the officers have reported the sounds of heavy furniture being moved about, but investigations revealed nothing out of place. Both have heard distinct footsteps on the second floor of the house when it is closed to the public and no one is in it. And both say they have heard the sound of "stiff clothing" —

possibly rustling petticoats and skirts, rubbing against chairs and tables. "It's like a cloak, or a coat, or a stiff skirt, or something like that," one says. "But how can you hear something and you don't see anything? That's what I can't explain. How can you hear furniture being moved around, yet you don't see it. I have no idea."

One officer reports he has heard fiddle music on occasion and once heard a harp being played. "I've heard doors slamming at two or three in the morning, but I could never find any cause for it," he says. "Now, I know in an old house there are going to be a lot of sounds anyway. Floors creak. The house settles. But I'm talking about noises that aren't like settling sounds. I was in the dependency one night when I heard something that sounded like a cinder block hitting the cabinet right behind me.

"And I'll tell you something else," the officer continues. "I was sitting in a chair one night when something got hold of my sleeve and lifted it up. Lifted my arm straight up. How do you explain that? Another time I was reading a book one night when I put it down to make my rounds. When I came back the book was gone. No one else was on the grounds. I was alone. Did this scare me? At first, maybe it did. But I got used to it. Whatever it is, or was, it didn't cause me any harm. It didn't bother me. But it did frighten some others. We had one man who started to work one night — his first night on the job — and he quit after just one hour. He wouldn't even talk about what happened to him." Another time, one of the officers said he met a psychic from Hanover County who had just been through the house. "He seemed shook up, so I asked him what was the problem, and he told me, 'you won't believe it, but there are ghosts in that house.' I asked him how many, and he said 'five'!"

Perhaps of all the phenomena the two officers have been exposed to, the most interesting was the sighting of a young boy, about four years old. Both have seen the apparition, on separate occasions. "I saw him late one afternoon," one says. "He was standing by the fence on the road some distance from the gate. He was wearing dark purple britches and a light colored purple shirt, kind of like they did in colonial days. As I drove past him in my truck, he came out into the middle of the road, and then he motioned toward the cows in the pasture, as if he wanted them to come to him.

"Well, I thought he might be lost, so I stopped the truck down the road apiece and got out to ask him where his parents were. Now I could see in all directions for at least a quarter of a mile or so, but that boy had disappeared. He just vanished. I looked all around, but I never found him. I believe he was a spirit. If he wasn't, where did he go?"

The other officer saw the same young boy at least twice. Once he sighted him in the old slave quarters. The second time, he saw him in the dependency building. He walked across the room as if he had lost something and was looking for it. "He appeared to be white all over," the officer says. "He was a little boy as near as I could tell. I believed he was either a ghost or an angel. I called (the other officer) and asked him what I should do, and he said not to worry, that whatever it was I was seeing wouldn't hurt me. And then he disappeared."

Who was this mystery child? Here, historically, there is at least a clue. Phillip Ludwell Lee was the son of Thomas Lee, the founder of Stratford Hall. And he had a son also named Phillip. According to family tradition, this boy fell down the stairs in the great house one day in 1779 and died. He was to have been the heir to the estate.

He was four years old!

And, finally, there is the testimony of J. R. "Butch" Myers, who lives in Richmond. Myers was a craftsperson who had been at the mansion over a weekend in June 1989 demonstrating his skills with leather. He travels around the country re-creating how 18th century shoes are made. Myers had a frightening experience which drove him from the dependency building just south of the main house. Here is his account of what happened:

"We had completed the show Saturday evening, and a few of my fellow crafts people had gathered in the dependency where I was to spend the night alone just to talk over the day's activity and compare notes. The session broke up around 12:30 or 1:00 a.m. I had lit six candles in stands, as there was no electricity in the building. As I was getting ready to turn in, I had sort of an uncanny feeling. I can't quite describe it. But then I saw a couple of sawhorses and a heavy sheet of plywood in the corner of the room, and it struck me that this would make a good bed for the night, so I unrolled my bedroll on top of it.

"As I kicked my shoes off, I heard the approaching footsteps outside of the security guard making his rounds. I grabbed a cigarette and started toward the door to chat with him for a few minutes. It was a particularly hot evening, with the temperatures high in the 90s during the day, and it hadn't cooled off much that evening.

Stratford Hall

"I took about two steps toward the door when a sudden down draft of freezing cold air hit me, taking my breath away. I mean it was icy cold. It was like walking into a cold storage locker. I got goose bumps all over. And just as this happened, there was a thunderous noise in the chimney. It sounded like the whole building was going to collapse. I didn't find this out until later, but the chimney was sealed top and bottom. There was no way anything alive could be in it.

"If this wasn't scary enough — and believe me, it was — I turned around just in time to see the candles go out. And they just didn't go out at once, as if blown out by a down shaft of air. They went out one at a time, in sequence, as if someone was snuffing them out. So I said to myself, 'okay, who's playing funny?' Now, I have some relatives in the area, some cousins, and they had told me about how Stratford Hall was haunted, and all that. So I figured maybe one of them was playing a little joke on me. But I was sober as a judge, and I didn't see anybody in the room except myself. How could anyone have done that with the candles?

"I got to the door and told the security guard what had happened. He didn't seem particularly surprised. He just said, 'Oh, you've just met our friend.' He asked me if I had seen anyone, and I had to say no. In a little while, he walked on off to complete his rounds, and I went back inside the room and relit the candles.

"Now you can believe this or not, I don't care. But the icy coldness in the room hit me again, and the racket kicked up in the chimney, which really scared me now, because the guard had told me about it being sealed. There was no breeze, or wind at all in the room, but someone, or something, very methodically extinguished each candle again, in reverse order this time. And I knew now, for a fact, that no one else was in the room. At least no one living. I was by myself.

"But there definitely was something there, a presence or whatever you want to call it. And that was enough for me. I said, 'listen, you can have the room. Just let me get my pillow and blanket, and I'll get out of here.' And I did. I got out of there as quick as I could, and I went over to the dependency on the other side of the mansion, where the guard was, and I told him I was spending the night with him!

"The next morning, I went back to the room and everything was just as I had left it. It was cool inside, but the air wasn't freezing as it had been the night before. I gathered-up my stuff and left.

"I went back to Stratford in the summer of 1991, for another craft show, but I didn't stay in the dependency. No sir. I walked around to it one evening, and in front of the big house there was a nice gentle breeze blowing. But when I got to the front of the dependency, everything was deathly still. Nothing was stirring. It was an eerie feeling. I put my hand on the doorknob and it was like clutching an icicle. That's as far as I got. I wouldn't go back into that room. There was something in there that didn't want me inside. The guards told me it wouldn't hurt me, but that's easy for them to say. They didn't feel what I felt in that room. I'm not saying definitely that it was something evil, but I didn't want to stick around to find out for sure.

"It had made its point with me. I'm not psychic or anything, but I definitely believe there is something to ghosts and spirits, and there's a lot we don't understand about all that yet. But I can say for sure that I am certain there is something strange at Stratford Hall. There was something in that room. And one experience with whatever it was, or is, was enough for me!"

* * * * *

Young Robert E. Lee moved from Stratford Hall when he was but three and a half years old after his father more or less "lost" the great estate through a series of bad investments which eventually landed him in debtors' prison. Soon afterwards they settled in a still-standing house at 607 Oronoco Street, built in 1795 by John Potts. In the late 1790s George Washington often visited here.

Although his father was no longer present — he was convalescing on the island of Barbados and died before he could return home — Robert enjoyed much happiness here. So much so, in fact, that it is recorded that after his surrender at Appamattox in 1865, he rode his horse, Traveler, to Alexandria, "and leaped over the garden wall to see if the snowballs were in bloom the way he remembered them from his childhood."

It also is well chronicled that this house, like Stratford Hall, often has been the site of strange psychic phenomena, although the occurrences surfaced long after Lee himself died. Those who have witnessed and written about these encounters agree that the spirits present are, as one author put it: "Some of the friendliest ghosts you'll ever want to meet." Another writer added: "No one complains that the old Robert E. Lee mansion in Alexandria, is haunted, because its haunts are among the most delightful and inventive ever to be recorded."

Most of the manifestations apparently took place in the early 1960s, before the house was acquired by the Lee-Jackson Foundation of Charlottesville.

At the time the property was owned by an investment banker named Henry Koch, and his wife. They had a seven-year-old son, William. Things began popping the day they moved in, June 10, 1962. The couple reported hearing sounds of running and childish laughter upstairs. They assumed it was William, but later learned, to their amazement, that he had not been near the area where the sounds were coming from.

The laughter and patter of "little feet" continued in the weeks that followed, sometimes several times a day. Mrs. Koch was quoted as saying, "It sounded as if it were coming from a child about four years old. The laughter was at about the level of our knees." Sometimes the invisible giggler would seem to follow the Kochs as they walked through the house, especially in the front hall and up and down the stairway.

Mrs. Koch told Susy Smith, author of the book "Prominent American Ghosts," that the sounds were always "cheery." The laughter went on frequently for about six months, and then trailed off. That the Kochs weren't "hearing things," was supported one day when a milkman asked them if they had heard "the little Lees." Mrs. Koch told him that they had, and he smiled and said, "Well, if you don't bother them, they won't bother you."

Lee House in Alexandria

Another example of psychic phenomena sometimes flowed through the house on Oronoco Street in the form of musical strains from "some kind of stringed instrument." Once, Mr. Koch hosted a meeting at his house, and the men were serenaded by soft melodies floating down from upstairs. Koch assumed it was his teenage daughter playing her guitar, but he later learned that she had left her instrument at school. No one else was in the house at the time.

Mrs. Koch, too, encountered her share of inexplicable incidents. On one occasion, she had misplaced her cigarette lighter, and searched the house for it. As she walked from the living room to the dining room, the lighter mysteriously came flying from "somewhere" and landed on the floor at her feet. She immediately thought it might be her young son, Bill, playing a trick, but he was found in another part of the house. At other times an invisible finger would ring the front doorbell, but there was never anyone there. Curiously, two family friends, visiting the house for the first time, asked without prompting, if it was haunted. Author Smith, herself psychically sensitive, said she "got prickly sensations along my spine," followed by goose bumps, when she stood in the back part of the downstairs hall under the landing. Another writer added that while she didn't see the apparitions of laughing children, she "certainly felt a presence."

And then there was the apparitional black dog. It was frequently sighted romping across the garden, and was described as a "little black dog with a long body and a long tail." Over a considerable period of time, a number of people claimed they saw such a dog in the yard and garden, both of which were walled off. Yet, oddly, the Koch's two dogs, often outside when the spectral hound was seen, never acknowledged its presence in any way. It has been speculated that the little black dog may have been the pet of the giggling child or children.

Consider this: a few years ago Alexandria city archeologist Keith Barr was conducting an archeological dig in the garden area of the yard. One morning he arrived at the work site to find dog prints in the dig area, a pit several feet deep. The yard, he pointed out, was tightly and highly fenced. There was no way for a dog to get inside. But what really chilled Barr was the fact that there were no animal prints of any kind leading to the dig!

Perhaps the strangest happening of all reported at the Lee house took place one Sunday when a retired admiral and his wife, neighbors of the Kochs, came over for a visit. As they sat talking, the woman suddenly appeared to be in the midst of a swirling snowstorm! The others stared at her in wonderment. The scary scene went on for several minutes when she finally asked what on earth was happening? And it was not an apparitional effect. There were real "big, fat" flakes falling on the astonished woman from about a foot above her head. Someone suggested it might be dust, but the woman shook her head firmly. "No," she said, "because I am all wet!"

A quick inspection determined that there was nothing leaking from the ceiling, and it was neither snowing nor raining outside. Understandably, the shaken woman and her husband got up to leave, and the snowfall started all over again, descending upon her as she walked to the door. Once she left, it stopped.

No rational explanation was ever found, nor was it ever discovered who might be the otherworldly source for the childish giggles, the sound of little feet, or the appearances of the small black dog. Some have surmised it might be the spectral antics of a prankish young Robert E. Lee, although he was not known to have had a dog as a boy growing up in Alexandria. Others have mused that it could have been one of the Lee children, perhaps the child who had been killed falling down stairs at about the age of four. But he never lived in this house.

There has been more or less general agreement that whoever or whatever was the cause for such occurrences was a happy spirit or spirits, content and comfortable in such historic surroundings.

CHAPTER 28

Apparitions Aplenty in Old Alexandria

A GHASTLY OCCURRENCE AT GADSBY'S TAVERN

One of the highlight stops on a popular ghost tour of Old Town Alexandria is the richly historic Gadsby's Tavern at Royal and Cameron Streets. It has endured as a well-liked watering hole for more than 200 years. In its heyday — in the late 1700s — it hosted many of the most famous figures of the early Republic, including the man who seemed to get around to just about every place, George Washington.

The original house dates from 1770, and the large, three-story section, "the ultimate in elegance and comfort for its time," was opened by a man named John Wise in 1792. The building got its name from John Gadsby, who operated the tavern from 1796 until 1808. It was at this site that Washington, in 1775, presided at a meeting which led to the adoption of the first "assertion of colonial rights," the Fairfax Resolves. During the American Revolution many important meetings and discussions were held here by such gentlemen-patriots as John Paul Jones, Baron de Kalb, Lafayette, George Clinton, and Benjamin Franklin.

Under Gadsby's genial guidance — he had been an English pub keeper — the fame of his hospitality spread, it is said, from New York to New Orleans. Under such an auspicious background, it is little wonder then that the tavern's ballroom woodwork is now displayed at the Metropolitan Museum of Art in New York City.

The rest of the complex has survived pretty much intact, and has been handsomely restored.

Gadsby's is also the scene of the spectral return of a beautiful young woman, a woman of consummate mystery, who died there in 1816 under the most suspect of circumstances. Visitors have reported seeing her at a bedroom window holding a candle and looking out. Others have sighted her walking the halls, or standing by her tombstone nearby. Intrigue and legend over who she was

Gadsby's Tavern

and why she reappears have swirled around the tavern for more than 175 years.

The most common rendition is that when she and her husband sailed into the Alexandria port in October 1816, she already was deathly ill. She was taken to Gadsby's and treated by a doctor and several nurses. When it became evident she was not going to recover, her husband asked everyone involved to promise never to reveal the lady's identity. She died a few days later and was buried in St. Paul's Cemetery. A finely-carved tabletop tombstone read, simply: "In memory of the female stranger, died Oct. 14, 1816, age 23 years 8 months." Soon after, the husband inexplicably disappeared without paying his bills, including $1,500 for the tombstone.

Speculative theories about who the woman was abounded in the city for years. Some believed her to be the daughter of Aaron Burr, the man who shot Alexander Hamilton in a duel. Others subscribed to the tale that she was one of four orphaned children who were separated from each other at a young age. Many years later, she unknowingly married her own brother, and she didn't want the horrible secret to be known.

The more popular version, told by ghost tour guide Ed Michals, is that she was a ward of an English nobleman who had fallen in love with her. He was 75, and she but 23. She loved him too, but like a father. Michals tells tourists that the nobleman walked into the garden at an undisclosed location one day and found her in the arms of a British officer. The old man reacted violently, and when he attacked the lover, he was pushed hard, fell, hit his head and died. The frightened couple then got on a ship and sailed to Alexandria, although she took sick enroute and never recovered.

Her most notable appearance came one evening a few years ago when a man said he saw her in the tavern ballroom. He followed her upstairs to what had been her bedroom, where she disappeared. It was dark, but in the corner of the room was a lit candle in a hurricane lamp. He picked it up and searched the premises but found nothing. Then it dawned on him; what was a lit candle doing in the deserted room? He raced downstairs and got the tavern manager to go back up with him. When they got there, the candle was not only not lit, the wick was still white, as if it had *never* been lit! The manager thought the man was either seeing things, or had imbibed too much that night. As he left the room, the man who had witnessed the apparition felt the lamp. It burned his fingers!

THE TRAGEDY ATOP RED HILL

here are a number of other stories that Michals and his associates tell on their tours. They range from the return of a crazed killer, bloody razor still in hand, to a helpful spirit who allegedly makes coffee sometimes in the city's visitor center. There is, supposedly, a poltergeist named John Dixon roaming about the Michael Swope House at 210 Prince Street still causing disturbances more than 200 years after he was reportedly erroneously executed as being a spy for the Colonies during America's War for Independence. Many have "felt his presence" when they were alone in the house. A few have seen him dressed in Revolutionary-era clothes. And neighbors have told of hearing him playing the piano when no one was home.

There is an account also of an English lady who was inspecting the home in the 1930s with the intention of buying it. She was shown everything from the darkened root cellar to the rooms on the first and second floors. She liked what she had seen. But then, as she was ascending the stairs to the third floor master bedroom, where Dixon had slept, "a force" stopped her and refused to let her through. "I'd love to own this house, but something is preventing it," she later said. "I'm very psychic, and I can tell you that there is definitely a ghost in this house — one that, for one reason or another, does not like me." The reason, most think, is that she was British, and Dixon was still harboring a grudge more than two centuries old!

There is the tragic and purportedly true tale of a house called The Anchorage atop what was once Red Hill and is now known as Braddock Hill in Northeast Alexandria. There lived, in the late 18th century, a reclusive couple, a sea captain and his lady. When he was at home they were rarely seen in public, and, human nature being what it is, rumors spouted. Some even thought they were witch and warlock. It seemed difficult for anyone to believe that they were simply a couple deeply in love who cherished their solitude.

Whenever the captain sailed, usually for voyages far away which lasted several months, his wife would toil endlessly in her garden. Then as time neared for his return she would daily watch from the top of Red Hill for his ship to sail into harbor. On one mission, however, the captain was struck with a severe illness and had to stay over in Europe for a lengthy recovery. Another officer brought his ship home. And when the lady saw the ship dock, but did not see her husband disembark, she assumed the worst. When she saw someone from the ship approach the hill, coming toward her, she feared he would tell her the captain had died. Grief-stricken, she went into her beloved garden and shot herself before the messenger arrived.

In the 1920s a woman then living on the hill saw a woman she didn't know. She was tall, slender, had dark hair and "large lustrous eyes," and was wearing a cloak thrown carelessly over one shoulder. She called to the woman and invited her into her house. The figure vanished! Startled, she related the story to a friend, another woman who had lived in the area all her life. When she described what she had seen, her friend smiled and said, "you saw the ghost of the sea captain's wife."

* * * * *

THE HOUSE THAT ISN'T THERE!

t has been described as "probably the largest and most beautiful mansion ever erected in Alexandria." At one time it occupied the entire 1100 block of Oronoco Street. Built in 1785, its traditions were, in the words of Margaret DuPont Lee, "deeply rooted in the soil of Virginia, and its history lends atmosphere, romance and charm to the old town..." Writes Mrs. Betty Smoot, who owned the mansion in the mid-19th century, "The grounds included a whole square block and were enclosed with an ancient brick wall, ten feet in height." The remains of a "pretty old garden" flanked the Colonial-period house and there were airy rooms on either side. There also were impressive wings and various out-buildings. Cupboards and closets were "without number," and there were dark cubby holes in the attic. Some back stairways and narrow halls apparently led nowhere. Despite the architectural credentials, this house, curiously, is not even listed in the Virginia Landmarks Register. It is called Colross.

Tragedy shrouded the estate. It is documented that Thomson Mason, son of the Colonial patriot George Mason of Gunston Hall, won Colross in a game of cards. He is the one who built the high brick wall. It is known that a notorious bounty jumper by the name of Downey, and at least two Civil War deserters were shot in front of the wall. This probably explains the legends of the ghost of a soldier who haunts the wall. But he is not the principal spirit or rather spirits, of Colross.

In the 1850s, Mason lived at the estate with his wife and their two young children, William and Ann. One spring day, as they romped in the yard, a terrible storm whipped up suddenly. William took shelter in an old chicken coop. Gale-force wind gusts toppled the creaky old building and killed him instantly.

The house was in mourning for weeks, and none took it harder than young Ann. She walked about in a constant daze and seemed totally oblivious to reality. Soon after, she drowned in a bathtub. Both children were interred on the grounds in a small locked vault. The Masons, emotionally destroyed by the twin tragedies, moved away from Colross.

From that time on, new residents of the house, including Mrs. Smoot, often reported hearing the distinct sounds of children playing on the grounds — when no children were in the house! They were heard giggling, singing and talking sometimes on an almost daily basis. Their cheerful presence was so strong, in fact, that successive owners at Colross had great difficulty in retaining servants there. Many past residents and servants also reported seeing the apparitions of a young boy and girl. And while these sightings recurred over a period of 30 to 40 years, the children, always dressed in pre-Civil War clothing, never grew older!

There was one other psychic oddity here that was never satisfactorily explained. The door of the vault where the children had been buried was locked with a large iron lock. Strangely, while it was exposed to the harsh elements of the weather for more than 75 years, the lock never rusted. Even more unbelievable was the fact that the lock, of which there was only a single key that never left the house, would never stay locked more than three days in a row! Mrs. Smoot, among others, could not explain this peculiar phenomenon. "Father would lock it himself," she once said, "and open it would come! Never was the lock broken."

Was it the mischievous spirits of young William and Ann who regularly broke the iron bonds so they could play on the grounds where they once enjoyed such happiness? We may never know. For earlier this century Colross was *moved* to a site in New Jersey. That is why it is not included in the Virginia Register of historic homes. The vault, with its mysterious lock, was destroyed and the bodies of the two children were reinterred at a neighboring cemetery. There were no further reports of gleeful activity from unseen youngsters at the new location. William and Ann, children of the Old South, apparently had no desire to venture north.

* * * * *

THE STAMP COLLECTOR FROM BEYOND

few years ago, a stamp collector in Killeen, Texas, successfully bid on the "mystery lot" of a major auction house. It was a trunk full of stamps on album pages, small collections, loose stamps, covers, packet material, plate blocks and other items "guaranteed to provide lots of fun during the long winter evenings."

And, in fact, the purchaser did enjoy his "treasure." He spent months going through the trunk, sorting and cataloging his stamps, and had so many left over, he decided to sell them as a dealer. He placed small ads in stamp newspapers offering "300 stamps for one dollar."

One day he received a letter from a lady who lived in the North Ridge section of Alexandria. "You sent a package of stamps to my father," she wrote. "He was a stamp collector, but he passed away two years ago. Are you just now getting around to filling an order that he may have placed with you before his death?"

The man who had bought the trunk was thoroughly puzzled by the letter. He couldn't remember sending any packet to Alexandria. But he had all orders on file, and he went through his lists, but he could not find the gentleman the lady had mentioned, nor anyone else from Alexandria for that matter. So he wrote her back telling her it couldn't be an old order, because he had only been in business a short time, and he had no record of any order from her father. He couldn't explain what had happened, but he did tell her about the trunk and how he acquired it.

Shortly after that, he got a call from the lady. She asked him to describe the trunk he had bought. He did. "That was my father's trunk," she exclaimed. "And that was the auction house to which we consigned the stamps after his death."

So the man suggested that maybe the lady's father had left a slip of paper with his name and address in the trunk and it somehow got mixed up with his sales orders. The lady agreed that it might be a logical explanation. But the man knew otherwise. He knew that nothing like that had happened. He himself had been a brigade commander in the Army, and he had gained a reputation for his organization and his neatness.

In passing along this particular incident to a reporter, however, he offered his own explanation. "The lady's father was an accumulator," he said. "And a little thing like death was not going to stop him!"

* * * * *

THE VANISHING PITT STREET GHOST

(Author's note: The following account was taken from the July 20, 1885, issue of the *Alexandria Gazette*. It is so colorfully worded in the vernacular of the day that any editing would border on blasphemy.)

 year or two ago several individuals, at different times, were scared out of a seven years growth by catching glimpses, at night, of a somber clad tall figure, supposed to be of the feminine persuasion, whose way it was to glide noiselessly along the pavement in front of St. Paul's Church, or to suddenly emerge from either of the alleys on that thoroughfare and stand in front of some related pedestrian until each separate hair on the latter's cranium assumed a perpendicular position.

"From whence it came or whither it went — hades, the abode of the blessed, gehenna or sheol — none were able to tell. The spook, or whatever it may have been, rendered many credulous persons nervous, and caused others to go out of their way on more than one occasion rather than risk a sight of the supposed spirit by walking to their homes over the dreaded square.

"All sorts of suggestions intended to clear up the mystery were advanced, the generally-received theory being that the apparition was nothing more than a harmless colored woman, slightly demented, who was accustomed to leave her home in the witching hour of night and walk around that neighborhood.

"The sensation, however, like all mundane things, died out, until last Saturday night, when it was once more revived by the 'ghost' making its appearance to Mr. James Wood, who was on his way home at the time. Mr. Wood lives on the north side of Wolfe, between Pitt and St. Asaph streets. It was twelve midnight, that lonely hour when grave yards yawn, and lunar's gibbous form had just sunk behind the western hills, when this gentleman, with a box of fried oysters under each arm, started from the Opera House restaurant for his home.

"He had arrived at the southwest corner of Prince and Pitt streets, intending to pass over the square opposite St. Paul's church, when directly in front of him there suddenly appeared the irrespressible figure he oft had heard of — not in sable habiliments, however, but snowy white. Mr. W. claims to be no believer in ghosts, hobgoblins, fairies or spirits, so he determined to catch up with and carefully survey whoever or whatever it was that glided — not walked — so stealthly before him.

"Accordingly, he accelerated his gait to the utmost to overtake the specter, but despite his every exertion, he could get no nearer than five feet of the apparition. He smoked up vigorously on a cigar he had in his mouth, for the purpose of shedding as much light on the scene as possible, when, in the twinkling of an eye, the spook vanished as suddenly as a ring of smoke or a burst soap bubble!

"At this denouement, our hero, sultry as the weather was, felt a cold chill meandering down the spinal column which soon eventuated in a tremor throughout the frame, and concluding that he had had enough of that adventure, became panic stricken and beat a lively retreat back to the restaurant he had previously left, arriving at which he rushed up to the proprietor in such a disturbed state of mind that the latter imagined him to be in a bellicose humor and prepared himself to act upon the defensive.

"Mr. Wood, however, soon explained himself by giving a thrilling account of his adventure, which he closed by informing some of the bystanders that they would have to accompany him to his home, as he was completely unnerved. A 'committee' kindly volunteered for that purpose, and in the course of half an hour, Mr. W. was safe within his own domicile.

"His disbelief in visitants from the unseen world is not so strong now as formerly!"

The Last Tantrum of Thomson Mason

(Lorton)

George Mason, many historians will tell you, is one of the most underrated patriots of American Independence. A contemporary and friend of George Washington, he was a reluctant public servant who spent a considerable part of his life trying to avoid the spotlight of colonial politics only to be drafted into service time and again. Mason was sometimes called the "Pen of the Revolution," because he was the author of the Fairfax Resolves, the first Constitution of Virginia, and the Virginia Declaration of Rights, the latter of which, scholars say, was used as the model and inspiration for the American Bill of Rights.

Mason's Declaration of Rights declares that all men are created equal, free and independent; that all power is derived from the people; that government is instituted for the common benefit, protection and security of the people; that no man or set of men is entitled to exclusive or separate privileges; that all men having common interests in the community should have the right to vote; and that the freedom of the press should never be restricted. Not bad foresight. Little wonder this retiring farmer was so highly respected by his legendary peers — Washington, Jefferson, Madison, Henry, etc.

A Virginia travel brochure reads: "These builders of our nation also built beautiful houses. Mount Vernon, Monticello, and Stratford Hall are noted as much for their architectural beauty as for their historic associations. In this important company stands

Gunston Hall

Gunston Hall." This was the house Mason had built in 1755. It is sited 18 miles south of Washington, DC., on the Potomac at the town of Lorton. The Virginia Landmarks Register flatly calls Gunston Hall "one of the nation's most remarkable examples of colonial architecture." Although the house is relatively small by colonial plantation standards, it nevertheless draws superlatives, such as, "extraordinarily rich architectural detailing of the interior," and "masterful woodwork." Open to the public, the house, adds the Register, "and its extensive formal gardens, following the outline of the original landscaping, present one of the most elegant expressions of colonial taste."

However, as the travel brochure points out, "There is more to a visit to Gunston Hall than the discovery of a beautiful house and gardens. It is also an introduction to the *spirit* of a great American patriot." How prophetic, for it also apparently is haunted. In a 1990 newspaper article, Mary Lee Allen, assistant director at the site, said, "The real ghosts are shadowy images left on some of the 18th century Georgian mansion's walls that tell researchers where ornate carved decorations once hung."

But many, including both tour guides and visitors alike, contend there also are otherworldly spirits at "the Hall." Employees have reported hearing strange sounds in the house when no one is there. And tourists occasionally claim to have sighted "glimpses" of shadowy figures. These brief encounters generally have been attributable to former Mason family members who had occupied the house at one time or another.

And there is one fairly well known psychic happening which transpired late in the 19th century and was experienced by George Mason's great-granddaughter, Helen, when she was but seven years old. It has been included in Margaret DuPont Lee's collection of "Virginia Ghosts," and elsewhere.

Young Miss Mason was at Gunston Hall, when one evening about supper time, she peered out a window overlooking the garden and saw the apparent spirit of her grandfather, Thomson Mason, who lived at Hollin Hall, five miles away. The sighting appeared only to Helen, because she called her mother to the window and she saw nothing.

The incident was often recounted with relish by an old black servant known as Uncle Jasper, who also was just a small boy at the time, but was present when Thomson Mason died. With some paraphrasing for clarity, here, in essence, is what Uncle Jasper used to tell: "I must have been a little brat, not more than five or six years old... It was like this. Master Thomson was one of those fidgety folks, always flying into a tantrum, and he just naturally despised to shave. He wouldn't let anybody do it for him, but insisted on doing it himself... One day he put it off till tea time, and then he called for some hot water and then he had Alec (a servant) hold the mirror, and he got two others to hold up some lights so he could see.

"Alec got so tired of holding the mirror that it began to wobble in spite of everything, and the master cussed at him and told him to hold it still, and then Alec made faces at him from behind the mirror and I started laughing out loud. The master, he turned around with the razor in his hand, and he was raging mad...

"And right there, he fell down in a fit. Alec dropped the mirror and it broke in a thousand pieces... Old Ike, he grabbed him quick and they laid him on the sofa... He was stone dead."

It was at that precise moment, five miles away, that little Helen Mason saw her grandfather in the garden. When she called her mother to the window to see, she had exclaimed, "What is grandpa doing out there in the garden in the wet? And he's got his neckcloth off, and his knee buckles are undone. Why he must be shaving!"

The Multiple Haunts of Woodlawn

(Mount Vernon)

 t is, among the great plantations of Virginia, perhaps the least known. It also may be the most haunted!

In his introduction to a small, well done book, "Ghost Stories of Woodlawn Plantation," (EPM Publications, McLean, VA), Brian Taylor Goldstein writes: "...There is more than just a sense of history here. Even in the reassuring light of day, when the sun chases all the shadows into far corners, there is an other-world feeling. It exudes from each brick and stone, from the earth itself, as if voices were trying to make themselves heard from across the abyss of time and death: voices of sadness and joy, of experience and life, all bound for whatever reason to a single place, reaching out to those who visit here. At night, however, the voices, and the house itself, take on a more mysterious nature.

"In the moonlight, the trees cast eerie shadows against the dark facade of the mansion, and slender, bony branches reach like skeleton fingers from out of the Stygian realms and into the foreboding sky. Owls cry in the distance as the wind rustles the leaves like rattling chains along old brick pathways. Faint, flickering lights occasionally glow from behind wavy, ancient glass — then mysteriously go out. A crow cackles from the rooftop. Shutters creak on rusted hinges. A grandfather clock chimes from somewhere deep within. The grass on the front lawn sways like an endless dark sea. A fence surrounds the property. Is it there to keep people out or to keep some *thing* inside? A huge featureless behemoth against the evening sky, the house no longer sits on its hill with dignified reserve but looms on its perch over the civilized world below. With an invisible but ominous grin, it dares the curious to approach and discover its secrets."

This is Woodlawn!

The plantation was a wedding gift from George Washington to his foster daughter (and Martha Washington's granddaughter) Nelly Parke Custis, upon her marriage to Major Lawrence Lewis, Washington's favorite nephew. The generous gift included 2,000 acres adjacent to Mt. Vernon. The location was well chosen. It commands a breathtaking view of the surrounding countryside, including Mount Vernon, the Potomac River, and Maryland on the other side. GW, in fact, called it, "A most beautiful site for a gentleman's seat." Unfortunately, the first President died before construction on the house began. When completed, in 1805, it consisted of a large central block with north and south wings connected to it.

Designed for lavish entertaining, Woodlawn, in time, acquired a reputation throughout the state for outstanding hospitality. Many elegant parties on a grand scale were held here, and leading dignitaries of the day were feted. But the plantation has known more than its share of sadness as well. Of the Lewises' eight children, only three survived. Most died in infancy at the house.

In the 19th century, after Woodlawn was passed along to other owners, it suffered greatly from neglect. In 1896, it was severely damaged by a hurricane, and for the next six years was left, "abandoned, battered, and desolate." Two eccentric brothers moved in at the turn of the century, along with their aged mother and 67 cats! They helped restore the great mansion to its former glory. Today, Woodlawn is lovingly maintained by the National Trust for Historic Preservation.

There are two things "different" about the spirits which apparently haunt Woodlawn. The actual manifestations of psychic phenomena, which are commonly witnessed there, are not necessarily out of the ordinary. They run the gamut: footsteps; thumpings on floors and walls; furniture moving about in rooms, seemingly on its own; doors locking and unlocking with no one around; candles extinguishing themselves; glimpses of gauzy figures which seem to vanish before ones eyes; objects disappearing and reappearing without rational cause or explanation; sudden rushes of cold air in specific areas or rooms; inexplicable shadowy images appearing on photos taken in the house; apparitions of "see-through" colonial-clad men and women; and mysterious taps on shoulders by unseen fingers, among others.

What *is* different about the phenomena at Woodlawn is that they surface in virtually every nook and cranny of the place. Generally, psychic encounters are limited to a specific area of a house — the attic, the basement, a stairway, or a particular room. Here, things seem to happen everywhere: the Lafayette bedroom; the boy's bedroom; the master bedroom; hallways; the center hall; the attic; the gift shop; north wing; south wing; what have you!

The second unusual aspect about Woodlawn is the great number of people who experience sightings and sensings of the "presences" there. Past residents, tourists and staff members alike all have been involved, and over a long period of time. Normally, spectral beings are felt only by one family, or even a single member of a family. Rarely are the phenomena so widely shared by so

Woodlawn

many people as they are here at this plantation.

What are some of these experiences? Fortunately, many of them have been reported on and chronicled. Author Judy McElhaney wrote the book, "Ghost Stories of Woodlawn Plantation" (EPM Publications, McLean, VA). Area newspaper reporters have a field day covering spooky accounts every Halloween, and there are numerous other magazine articles and book excerpts about the hauntings.

Here are a few selected examples:

** Experts believe when a mortal being comes in contact with a visitor from the spirit world, there is a very real sense of a chilly, sometimes icy-cold sensation. If contact is made, a cold dampness is felt. Many people have either fainted or felt faint when this happened. Woodlawn employees have felt such "rushes" of cold air in the master bedroom. One woman, securing the room for the night, turned out a small lamp, and started for the door, only to hear a distinct click behind her. She wheeled around to see the lamp lit again. No one else was there. As she hurriedly headed for the door, she felt a rush of frigid air pass her. This happened in the middle of summer when the house was not air conditioned.

** Author McElhaney states that many people have reported sighting "smoky figures" and "circles of billowing light" dance and seemingly float down the halls and staircase in the South wing. Too, patches of "gray light" and "circles of grayish matter" have shown up on photos taken in this area. Both amateurs and professionals have reported such "appearances," but no one has yet found a reason for it.

** A guest staying in a south wing bedroom in 1978 said she was awakened long after midnight by an eerie feeling that she was not alone. She opened her eyes in the dark and saw, at the foot of her bed, "a smoky glowing figure of what appeared to be a man. He was wearing a mask or veil and said nothing. He just stared at her. After several minutes, he faded away. The woman could not sleep the rest of the night.

Two years later, another guest in the same room, said she was awakened and saw "something luminous, perhaps ectoplasm, hovering about four or five feet off the ground." This "pulsating mass" moved about for several minutes and then "slowly disappeared in the night." Other guests have told of similar occurrences. One saw the forms of two men neatly dressed in "suits of long ago." She was mesmerized by the figures before they evaporated.

** Residents of Woodlawn between 1905 and 1925 often told of hearing unusual footsteps in the house; unusual in the sense that they sounded like someone with a peg or wooden leg thumping up and down stairs at night. John Mason lived at the mansion in the middle of the 19th century. He had a wooden leg. Also, the original owner, Lawrence Lewis, suffered badly from arthritis and gout, and is believed to have used either a crutch or a cane.

** Multiple manifestations have unfolded in the Lafayette bedroom. Blown out candles seemingly relight themselves. Oriental rugs have been turned over when the room was empty. Chairs have rearranged themselves, and items have disappeared from the closet. In the early 1930s a woman living at Woodlawn said she took her infant daughter into the Lafayette bedroom one evening and placed her in her crib. The baby was only a few weeks old. Shortly afterward, the woman heard the baby screaming and ran to the room. *She found the child out of the crib and across the room lying on top of a tall dresser!* There was no one else in the house. This mystery was never solved, but the woman and her family abruptly moved out of the house.

** In her book, author McElhaney shares a story told her by a former employee about an encounter on the south wing's back stairs years ago. As the woman went up the stairs, she sensed someone or something there. "It was," she said, "as if you feel someone is looking at you. I looked up to see who was there and saw what I can only describe as an aura. It's hard to explain. There was some density to it." The woman lurched back in surprise, but then fought her fright and climbed the stairs. "The sense of someone was still there," she recalls. "It was that of an impish youngster, most likely a girl, six or seven years old... *I'd gone through her!*"

** According to legend, says Brian Goldstein, "homes built atop wells are inevitably haunted. This is because wells forge deep into the earth to connect with streams, and, for metaphysical, symbolic and mythical reasons, running water has long been associated with the spirit realm."

This may help explain why there is so much psychic activity at Woodlawn. There is an old well here, in the gift shop. It was built into the floor of the connecting hyphen between the main block of the house and the south wing, which housed the kitchen. It has been called the "Well of Souls."

Goldstein says a well "allows spirits a means to travel up from the water" and into a house. This is one reason, he adds, that in most historic homes, wells are found outside or in separate structures. "When a well is open, spirits can freely pass between the water and the house. When the well is closed, however, spirits supposedly become confused, disoriented, and occasionally angry and violent. This frustration causes them to materialize and search throughout the building for an alternative means of returning to their world."

Goldstein says more than half of the reported sightings of ghosts at Woodlawn have occurred when the well lid has been closed. Also, he notes, there have been numerous instances when the lid had been shut at night "only to be found open the next day."

This chapter covers only a portion of the plethora of unearthly activities which continue to occur at historic Woodlawn Plantation. It doesn't even mention the fact that many people have said they have seen the ghost of George Washington himself riding his horse around the carriage circle.

Says Goldstein: "The most compelling evidence for ghosts is their appearances and sightings, and of these, Woodlawn has many."

The House of Tragic Deaths

(Prince William County)

ot much is happening at old Rippon Lodge in Prince William County these days. All has been more or less quiet — at least supernaturally quiet — for the past 60 years or more. But before that, in the late 19th and early 20th centuries, quite the contrary was true. This venerable frame house, dating to the first quarter of the 18th century, had gained a dark reputation that scared off potential tenants for years, leaving it abandoned and decaying.

"Many tragic stories are told of Rippon Lodge," said the *Manassas Journal* in a feature article published May 19, 1911. "More than one murder is said to have been committed there. A victim of a fatal duel bled to death on the parlor floor. This house is said to be haunted in such a ghostly and sinister fashion that no one will occupy it, and the public road has changed its course to avoid the neighborhood."

Located between Occoquan and Dumfries, near Woodbridge, this small (by plantation standards) dwelling was built in the 1720s by Richard Blackburn, a colonial entrepreneur and public servant. He named it after his native Rippon, a cathedral town in England. Carefully sited on a hill with a view down Neabsco Creek to the Potomac River, the house, says the Virginia Landmarks Register, "has acquired a picturesque aspect with its numerous later additions, such as the columned veranda, but preserves much original fabric, including two fully paneled rooms." Blackburn was a successful architect and farmer and once helped Lawrence Washington enlarge the house at Mount Vernon. George and Martha Washington were frequent visitors to Rippon Lodge. On a nearby tombstone of Richard Blackburn, who "departed this life" in 1757, are inscribed the words: "He was a man of consummate prudence, frugality and indefatigable industry whereby he made a large fortune in a few years." At the time of his death, he farmed 21,000 acres of land.

His monument was dedicated to his memory by his friend John Baylis. Ironically, Baylis, who had married Blackburn's daughter, Jane, was possibly the first to die tragically at Rippon Lodge. He had fought a duel with a challenger named John Scott, and, for unexplained reasons, Scott's second (an aide) shot Baylis. He was brought to the house and bled to death a few hours later. In 1809, Bernard Hoe also was wounded in a duel in Maryland. He, too, was ferried across the river to Virginia and carried to the Lodge where he also expired.

The brooding reputation of this plantation was further enhanced some years later, the exact year is not known, through the rage of one of the Blackburn women. She had come from a well known Prince William County family who were called the "Rattlesnake Grahams," a name stemming from their famous fierce tempers. A visitor to the house one Christmas day noticed a slave waitress crying. When she asked the woman what the matter was, the slave told her that her child had gotten in Mrs. Blackburn's way one day, and the mistress, in a fit of anger, shoved the child, who fell against the stone jamb of a fireplace, causing head injuries, and died soon after. Mrs. Blackburn, it is said, became callous and indifferent, but in her later years suffered greatly from remorse.

It was after Mrs. Blackburn died, and was buried on the grounds, that stories of disturbing noises at night and hauntings began to surface. It was during this period that no one would live in the house. It was empty for years and fell into a bad state of repairs. At some point, two young campers from Alexandria wandered onto the scene. They came upon Rippon Lodge as night fell, and finding it deserted, decided to spend the night there.

Before they could fall off to sleep, however, they began to hear loud and frequent sounds. They got up and searched the premises, room by room, but found nothing. Then they heard shrieks and "peals of unearthly laughter!" Convinced they were not welcome guests, they left immediately, never to return.

CHAPTER 3 2

A Village Full of Spectral Visions

(Occoquan)

pleasant air of romantic intrigue seems to envelop the quaint town of Occoquan, which lies just off Interstate 95 near Dale City and a few miles south of Alexandria. Occoquan is an Indian word meaning "at the end of the water," and it is believed that the Dogue Indians chose this site for their home, centuries ago, because the nearby river offered plentiful fish and ease of travel. Early settlers liked it for the same reasons and a tobacco warehouse was built here as early as 1736. Over the next few years there was a mini-industrial boom in this area which included the erection of an iron furnace, a forge, two sawmills, and one of the nation's first gristmills.

In the year 1801, a sailor named John Davis, who, it is written, had "an ebullient flair for poetry and prose," arrived in town to tutor the children of a local landowner. "Occoquan," he penned, "consists of a house built on a rock, three others on the river side, and a half a dozen log huts scattered at some distance." He added that he found the little settlement, "romantic beyond conception."

By 1828, Occoquan boasted one of the first cotton mills in Virginia, and within a few years had added several mercantile stores and various mechanics. It is said that farmers and traders came from as far away as the Blue Ridge Mountains. Many stayed overnight at the Alton or the Hammill hotels, the latter of which still stands, and dined on the town's famous roasted canvasback ducks, which were served even for breakfast, and sold, uncooked for a "shilling sterling apiece."

Even after silt filled the river and large vessels could no longer reach the mills, Occoquan still seemed to thrive, in part due to its convenient location along major travel routes, and partly because of the warmth and charm of its residents and merchants; a charm which survives to this day. And it has persevered despite the river's clogging, a devastating fire which destroyed much of the town in 1916, and the ravaging winds and waters of Hurricane Agnes in 1972. Today, it has become a shopper's paradise, with a rich assortment of more than 120 shops, boutiques, artists' cooperatives, restaurants, and distinctive inns. Here, as a merchant's association brochure says, "you'll find a wonderful selection of specialty shops and restaurants filled with art and antiques, handcrafts and gifts, and the kind of warm Virginia hospitality you'd expect from an unusual community..." For once, such a publicity brochure is accurate.

There still are a number of old houses and buildings at Occoquan which have survived the damages of time and nature, and, in fact, the historic district is listed in the Virginia Landmarks Register. Also surviving, and quite active today, are a host of

Occoquan

ghosts from Occoquan's past, so many, in fact, that it almost seems there is a haunt of one kind or another in just about every other building. Each spirit, says another brochure, "is authenticated by local legend and town gossip. We invite you to enjoy these stories in a light-hearted — but not mocking — mood."

Ed and Valerie Miller, for example, owners and operators of Miller's Lighthouse a shop of unique and nautical gifts and video tapes, tell of the mischievous spectral man who likes to "play tricks" at times.

"I never really believed in ghosts until these things started happening, but now I do," said Ed. What things? "Oh, we've had things missing, all of a sudden turn up right under our noses. I can't explain how they got there or who put them there. They weren't there five minutes ago when I looked, and then suddenly they're there!" Ed emphasizes. "Sometimes 'he' plays around with the video tapes. We were making some copies one day when there was a sudden burst of music, and Valerie stomped her feet and told 'Steven' — that's what we call 'him' — to stop fooling around. Just at that precise instant every music box in the store began to play. It was pretty eerie.

"The other thing 'he' does," continues Ed Miller, "is with the dolls." The dolls? "Yes, we have some Amish dolls. They're about two feet high. Every once in a while, when we place two of them together, you know, like a boy and a girl, 'he' flings them apart; just throws them out on the floor or across the room. They really fly. 'He' did it one day when a customer was looking at the dolls and it scared her. She said she hadn't touched them, and, of course, we knew what was behind it, or who, or whatever you want to call it."

Valerie adds that sometimes they find sooty footprints leading around their shop when they open it in the morning. The prints are generally found in the part of the building that originally was a coal bin when the structure was built, about 1888. Sometimes they find locked display cases opened and in disarray. Nothing is missing, but it appears "someone" had been having a good time. The Millers say their "intruder" seems to appear for a while and then takes a rest for several days or weeks before he comes back again.

A couple of doors down from Miller's Lighthouse, is an unusual shop called Ebashae (it's not Indian and it really doesn't stand for anything in particular), which sells American fine crafts such as functional pottery, jewelry, wind chimes and watercolors. Both here and in the adjacent Undertaking Artists' Co-op, persistent mysterious footsteps have been heard over the years, though the source has never been found.

"We've had other things happen, too," says Annette Riley, manager of the store. "We've had pottery fall off the shelf when there were no trains or trucks going by and absolutely no wind or anything. I am a skeptic myself, but there are many people who have said that they have heard the footsteps, particularly late at night.

"This used to be a funeral home and they had a bad flood here once and it smashed through the store front and some of the coffins were washed down into the river and were floating downstream there. Maybe that adds to the atmosphere of the place. We did have a young man who worked for us a few years ago and it was his grandfather who was the undertaker. He said he heard footsteps going up the stairs one night and he went up to look and said he saw a man in dress trousers and a long coat. He was certain that it was his long dead grandfather. Maybe he comes back to check on his establishment."

A little further down Mill Street (of course, about everything in Occoquan is just down the street) is the Country Shop, which features quilting supplies, calico, smocking and handicrafts. Previously, this building served as a restaurant (twice) and as a hardware store. And before that, it was a residence. According to a publication by the Occoquan Merchants' Association, the spirit of an elderly woman keeps "an eye on things" here today. From a preferred seat in a corner, she allegedly checks out the customers at the antique counter, and also monitors the outside scene through "her" window. "This lady," says the pamphlet, "has a reputation for shooing the children off her pavement, and she can still be seen shaking a finger at passersby."

"Yes, that fits the pattern," confirms Susan Lehto, manager of the Country Shop and daughter of the owner. And apparently the woman has stood such guard for generations. "We think it is a lady who lived here years ago. There was such a person who would run to the door with a broom and chase children on roller skates away from the sidewalk. A lot of people who have lived in town for a long time have told us about her," Susan adds. "A couple of years ago there was a psychic convention here and several of the attendees came in the store. Everyone of them said they definitely felt a strong presence."

Down the block at Waterfront Antiques, owner Sandy Higham recalls one eventful winter afternoon when she heard the "clatter

Occoquan Inn

of footsteps" on the stairs to the front door, then the door opened. This was strange, because she was standing in front of the shop and there was no one inside. She went in and searched, saw no one, but found a single rose laid on the staircase. She never has discovered an explanation for that or for repeated occurrences of merchandise being moved about by unseen hands, or the appearance of more flowers. She and her staff have nicknamed their ghost, "Shopping Charlotte."

A candle that lighted itself has been the only sign of the supernatural at the Serendipity Gift Shop at 307 Mill Street. There, the owner opened up one winter morning to find a freshly lighted candle on her front counter. She asked all her workers if they had lit the candle, but no one had been in the shop since the evening before!

Perhaps the most prolific hauntings in town occur at the historic Occoquan Inn, at 301 Mill Street. There have been, for example, numerous sightings of the apparition of a tall Indian "with long black hair and a dignified face." He has been seen in the smoke from a drafty chimney, inside the restaurant, and in the mirror in the upstairs "necessary." Yet when startled viewers turn around, the image disappears.

Chuck Miller and Theresa Owen run "Down Under" at the Inn, a pub-like tavern in the bottom of the building. Chuck says he has not seen the Indian, but when he was first called to comment on psychic phenomena in the building, he offered, "I've got stories you won't believe." Chuck and Theresa say they have a gentleman ghost with a puckish sense of humor.

"He likes to play all kinds of games," Chuck says. "Sometimes we find the door of the ladies' bathroom locked from the inside. We unlock it, and 'he' locks it again and again. Customers coming out of the men's room tell us something keeps turning on the water faucets as they leave. Other times 'he' plays around with things. 'He' will take something, like my hammer, hide it for awhile, and then put it back where he got it in the first place, sometimes a day or two later.

"'He' has a 'thing' about our cash register, too," Chuck continues. "'He' likes to take the quarters and dimes — 'he' never fools with nickels or pennies — and stack them all up in neat rows. I can't explain how it happens, but it does." At other times, Chuck and Theresa have both felt "his" presence. "We'll be sitting in the bar late at night when everyone has gone home, and we'll feel a freezing cold spell. It makes all the hair stand up on your body," Chuck notes. "'He' seems to linger a while and then he moves on and the chill is over."

Chuck thinks it may be the spirit of a gentleman who lived upstairs long ago in a part of the building that is more than 100 years old. "'He's' not mean or anything like that, but every once in a while it seems like 'he' picks on a certain customer. One evening we had a group of gentlemen at the tavern, and one of them was playing a game, Yatsee, or something like that. There was one piece missing from the game and the man was looking around for it. All of a sudden the piece came flying across the room right at him, like somebody had thrown it at him. He wasn't hurt, but it sure unnerved him for a minute."

And so it goes in this picturesque little village. No one knows for sure just when and where one or another of the multiple haunts in Occoquan will flair up, but there does appear to be a whole family of them here, and they seem to thoroughly enjoy themselves.

A Variety of Phantasmal Vignettes

THE MYSTERIOUS WEEPING STATUE
(Lake Ridge)

(Author's note: Some things you just can't explain. In this instance it was a case of rare psychic phenomena that wasn't directly ghost-related, but it was so unusual and fascinating — and virtually impossible to explain rationally — that it is included in this collection.

First, some background. In the year 1913, there was an Abbot named Vachere of Mirebeau, France. At the time he was 59 years old, and was a conscientious member of the church. He had met, and was liked by the Pope, although there was nothing extraordinary about this man, and he had no special talents that anyone knew of.

Vachere had a painting of the figure of Jesus hanging in his private chapel. Inexplicably, Christ's hands and feet in the picture began to bleed, or at least it was reported that "drops of reddish moisture began to ooze from the hands and feet." When word got around, the Bishop asked to see the painting, and it was sent to him, but it failed to bleed. When it was returned to the small chapel, however, it started bleeding again!

Next, a gang of workmen were building Stations of the Cross near the Abbot's home. Vachere pinned up a plain color print of Jesus in their hut. This also began to bleed. Many witnesses attested to this fact. But when the Bishop arrived to see it for himself, nothing happened. He considered Vachere a fake, and had him excommunicated from the church.

Vachere then went to visit some friends at Aix-la-Chapelle. In the house was a statue and a picture of Christ, and both began to bleed when the confused Abbot was in the house. No explanation was ever forthcoming, although experts who investigated the situation were convinced that the phenomena were genuine.

In doing research for my book, "The Ghosts of Charlottesville and Lynchburg," I visited the famous shrine at Swannanoa, on top of a mountain near Waynesboro. It is there that Walter and Lao Russell built a 30 foot statue of Christ of the Blue Ridge. And it is there that I heard an unsubstantiated yet recurring story that a large bird flew into this statue once during a furious storm, and the figure was seen bleeding from the heart! I was never able to confirm this through an eye-witness. All of this leads up to the following, amazing account.)

I n March 1992, newspapers and television newscasts across the United States and around the world carried reports of what some were calling a miracle. A three-foot fiberglass statue of the Blessed Virgin Mary at the St. Elizabeth Ann Seton Church in the small town of Lake Ridge, 30 miles south of Washington, D.C., *was crying!*

It apparently wept only in the presence of the parish priest, the Reverend James Bruse. But witnesses other than Bruse saw it. Parishioner Tom Saunders, for example, has two photos of the statue crying, which he says is proof of the phenomenon. "When you see it," he said, "it's hard to believe at first. But it's there." Another who saw the tears was the Reverend Paul Burns of Our Lady of Angels Catholic Church in nearby Woodbridge. "I saw the water," he said at the time. "It's mind boggling."

As word of the "happening" spread, the church got thousands of phone calls, seeking verification. Hundreds of others came to the church in person, many were afflicted with illnesses and sought a cure. For weeks, after each mass, throngs of people approached the olive-colored statue with their rosaries, their holy cards and their own crosses and statues, hoping to see the tears that appeared "several times" between Christmas 1991 and March 1992.

Even stranger was the fact that Reverend Bruse told a fellow priest, around Christmas, that he had developed welts on his wrists and that his feet had started bleeding, just as Christ's had done 2,000 years ago!

THE HAUNT IN A HOTEL HALLWAY
(Virginia Beach)

n the movie "The Shining," based on Stephen King's classic horror story, actor Jack Nicholson portrays a struggling writer who goes mad while serving as a caretaker at a huge resort hotel in the Rocky Mountains, closed during the harsh, snow-bound winter months. Amidst periodic flashbacks which allude to a horrible multiple murder committed at the hotel 50 years or so earlier, Nicholson kills another hotel employee with an ax and then, for the last third of the movie, tries to slay his wife and young son. They eventually escape, and Nicholson freezes to death while chasing his son through the frozen hedge maze adjacent to the hotel.

The camera then pans to a photograph taken during the resort's heyday in the 1920s, and there, in the front row, is the exact image of Nicholson, leading the viewer to believe he has relived a past life of tragedy.

At the venerable old Cavalier Hotel in Virginia Beach, it is possible that a real life parallel to "The Shining" is in effect. Here, allegedly, sometime in the 1920s or 30s, a debonair young man said to be a member of the Coors family of beer brewery fame, was said to have committed suicide. Several hotel employees believe it is he who has "returned" half a century later to walk the halls of the old section of the resort late at night, and he mysteriously appears in photos of wedding receptions and other events.

"All I can tell you, is that it is one creepy place," says Mac MacAluso, who has worked there as a night bartender. "None of us wanted to work the old, original section of the hotel. You felt eerie there. Sometimes that section would be booked solid with people, yet when you walked down the hallways late at night, it was as if no one was there. It was like walking through a cemetery. You could feel the hair standing up on the back of your neck. I never saw him — the apparition — but others did. They would see him for an instant in the dark passageways, and then he would be gone. Just disappeared.

"But the scariest thing of all," MacAluso says, "was the photographs. People would hold wedding receptions here and when the photos of groups were shown, 'he' would appear, often sitting in the front row. No one knew who he was or where he came from.

And they didn't remember seeing him at the reception!

"He was slender and pale. He had black hair with a touch of gray. It was slicked down. He was very distinguished looking, probably in his late 40s or 50s. And he was dressed in a suit that looked like it was from the 1920s!"

* * * * *

DOES BIGFOOT ROAM VIRGINIA'S BACKWOODS?

Does a ghostly "Bigfoot" monster roam the backwoods of Virginia? Most alleged U.S. sightings of the legendary "Yeti," or "Abominable Snowman" — half man and half beast — have come from the Pacific Northwest,

Bigfoot in Virginia?

although there have been occasional scattered reports from Texas to Pennsylvania. But during a 13-month period in the 1970s, there were two separate accounts of witnesses in different parts of Virginia who said they caught glimpses of the elusive "Sasquatch."

The first of these surfaced in February 1977 at the Quantico Marine base in the northern part of the state. Several sentries there told of "seeing strange sights and hearing strange sounds. "It" was seen in the dark shadows of a tree line outside an ammunition storage area. One marine, who asked that his name not be used, said, "I remember the night I saw it very well. It was about 2 a.m. I was walking my post when I heard something in the woods. I could see a dark figure beyond the fence, so I shined my flashlight at it. I couldn't believe what I saw. It was some type of creature that looked like a cross between an ape and a bear. The first thing I noticed was its large glaring eyes. I then noticed it had arms and was covered with dark brown hair." The young man, understandably shaken, ran for help. But when he and his sergeant of the guard searched the area, they found only a set of mysterious large tracks. The Marine later estimated the "thing" was between six and eight feet tall! Others said they heard loud screaming noises, always between 11 p.m. and 4 a.m., that sounded "as if someone were being mutilated." But they never found the source.

A little over a year later, similar sightings were recorded by utility workers for Virginia Power near Middlebrook, in Augusta County, about 13 miles south of Staunton. "They definitely saw something, and it scared the heck out of them," said Robert Huffman, a company safety supervisor. He added that the workers had been moving through a pasture in a rough-terrain vehicle when they "saw something in their headlights." They told Huffman that the creature "ran upright like a man, but there was no way a man could have run that fast." They said the creature "glided over downed trees without a stumble and turned on them, about 75 yards away at the edge of some woods, and appeared to hold a red light close to its chest."

Skeptics believed the men might have seen a large bear standing up on its hind legs, but the workers were convinced it was something else altogether. Gary Spiers, then district game biologist with the Virginia Commission of Game and Inland Fisheries, said, "As for Bigfoot, I don't know. I'm not going to say it couldn't be. There are a lot of things that go on in the woods that we know nothing about!"

*****

THE MAD SHREW OF FOXCROFT
(Middleburg)

ll has been quiet on the paranormal front the past few years at an exclusive girls' school in the pricey, horsey, upscale town of Middleburg, about 25 miles due west of Washington, DC. And the faculty and administration at Foxcroft School like that just fine. Not that they were unduly frightened by the ghost of a Revolutionary War-era woman, seeking retribution for her murder, but, on the other hand, they consider it just as well that the spirit has found peace and gone on to another "home."

But for most of the 20th century, however, the legend of this apparitional figure hovered about the school like a wispy shroud. Succeeding classes of teenage young ladies passed along the colorful stories — and in some instances, experiences — of the multiple manifestation of a woman named Jane Ball Kyle. Few actually said they saw her, but many heard her scamper about over the years, haunting dormitories and classrooms.

While the school itself began operations in 1914, one of the central buildings, called the Brick House, dates back to the 18th century. It was built for a lawyer named Kyle. According to an unofficial history of Foxcroft, Jane Kyle, in time, became mentally ill and violent. To safeguard her against others, and herself, she was kept chained in the attic of Brick House.

One July, while her husband was in Philadelphia on business, it was alleged that Mrs. Kyle somehow got loose from her bonds, tripped, and fell down the long staircase in the house. According to this version, she broke her neck, died, and was quickly buried in the orchard. But some around the household were not convinced this was the way she expired.

There was a persistent rumor that she had been shot, and this fact was then covered up when she was hastily interred. Exactly who would shoot her, and why, has never been determined, although many exotic theories have been offered, such as Mr. Kyle coming back from his trip unexpectedly and catching her with the gardener, etc.

Whatever happened, Mrs. Kyle's spirit apparently never left the house, as if it were hanging around to correct some misdeed.

187

The recounting of her spectral appearances have been perpetuated, and in all probability considerably embellished, by the generations of young ladies who have come and gone at Foxcroft.

Nevertheless, there is an intriguing footnote here. The school was founded by Charlotte Haxell Noland. She lived with the accounts of the resident ghost for decades, and is said to have favored the thesis that Mrs. Kyle had been shot. The mystery must have absorbed her, because in 1925, just before a new dormitory was to be built on the grounds, Miss Charlotte, as she was known, invited six students to help her dig for the Kyle grave, which was believed to be beneath where the new dorm would stand.

By the second day, using two grave diggers, some human bones were found, but they were a man's bones. Perhaps they were Mr. Kyle's. So they dug to the left of his site, and, on the third day, and before a large crowd of curious students and spectators, the smaller bones of a woman were uncovered. When the skull was lifted out and brushed off it was evident to all that there was a bullet hole right through the middle of her head! The ghostly manifestations subsided once Miss Charlotte had the remains reburied at the end of the orchard and properly marked with a shiny brass plate.

* * * * *

A TIMELY SPECTRAL SIGHTING
(Lynchburg)

ost Lynchburg area ghosts are old ghosts. Most of them have been known at least since the 19th century, and others even before that. The story of "Miss Cornelia," however, only surfaced a few years ago, in fact in the mid-1970s. The house location and the family who experienced her ethereal return are not known, because the people involved requested anonymity, which is not an uncommon occurrence. But this story does include a couple of unusual twists. One concerns a rare apparitional sighting, and the other involves the date on which this phenomenon was observed.

The house is known to be at least a century and a half old, because Miss Cornelia Clopton was born in it sometime around 1850, the daughter of a Baptist minister. The present day family moved in sometime in 1968 and almost immediately began experiencing Cornelia's gentle spirit. There were odd noises for which no source could be found. There was, too, the man of the house said, "some undefinable presence." He said the family joked about it. "We'd say, it's a ghost, because, you know, an old house should have one."

Once, the night of April 4, 1974, it rained very hard. The next morning the man was awakened early, and recalled later, "You know how sometimes you just know someone is in the house." It was precisely 5 a.m. He knew this because the clock had just struck. Quietly, so as not to disturb the others, he got up and went to the top of the stairs. All was deathly still.

Then he was quoted as saying, "I noticed that at the bottom of the stairs, it looked awfully light." He reasoned that it could have been a neighbor's garage light left on overnight, but he could see the garage next door through a window and realized the light wasn't coming from there. As he stared, transfixed, the mysterious light began to concentrate and take a shape. Slowly, it developed into the distinct shape of an old woman. "I was absolutely horrified," he said. "My arms went numb and I was freezing. It didn't give off light, but it had a light of its own. It was a woman, about five feet tall with her hair up and a long skirt and full leg o'mutton sleeves." He said the woman never looked up and never spoke, then moved to another room, out of sight. When he cautiously descended the stairs, the wraith-like form was nowhere to be seen. No doors were opened and shut and no windows were open, but there was nothing.

At this point, the family, which had known Miss Cornelia had lived in the house more than a half century before, decided to do some research. They learned that the woman, then in her 60s, had made a trip to Minnesota in the spring of 1917 to visit her aged parents. Just before she was scheduled to come home, she became ill with the flu and died on March 26. She had left specific instructions that her body was to be returned to Lynchburg, and she was buried in the Spring Hill cemetery on April 8th. Through more checking, the family learned that Miss Cornelia's body probably arrived back in town on April 5th. After more digging, it was discovered that in 1917 an early train arrived in Lynchburg at 5 a.m. on the 5th.

Thus the singular sighting of Miss Cornelia's apparition had been made 57 years later — at precisely the same time and on the same date that she had returned home!

THE CRUEL MISTRESS OF PECATONE

his is a mystery as well as a ghost story. It is true, but it is confusing. The mystery is what was the name of the mansion involved, and where was it located? There also are some conflicting accounts of the details. All that considered, it is still, nevertheless, a compelling tale worthy of inclusion.

According to one published report in a *Reader's Digest* book on American folklore, the manor was known as Peckatone. However, in "Virginia, A Guide to the Old Dominion," compiled by workers of the Writers' Program of the Work Projects Administration in the State of Virginia, first published in 1940 — the same house is called Pecatone. One version says it was "one of the earliest great houses on the Potomac," while the other contends the estate was "between the Yeocomico River and Machodoc Creek."

Just when the large brick structure was built is not specified, although it is said the estate itself dates from 1650. According to the *Digest* book, Peckatone featured a "sweeping facade, porches of marble, and spacious, well-lit rooms." It also had an extensive wine cellar from which "earthenware bottles stamped Peckatone are still being found today."

The legend here centered around the fourth owners of the home, George and Martha Turberville. While no date is given, it is probable that the Turbervilles ruled with tyrannical zeal over their slaves, sometimes yielding to "sadistic urges." For example, George was known to chain his coachman to the coach box when he visited neighbors because "the fellow was inclined to run away." But it was the mistress of the house the servants feared most.

While on the surface Martha appeared to be the belle of Virginia society, throwing lavish parties for the landed gentry, underneath she apparently was a vengeful woman whose wrath knew no bounds of decency. The word was that she secretly used the wine cellar as a dungeon in which she tortured, and at times whipped slaves to death, for even the most ill-perceived slights. She added to her aura of terror and mystique by taking nocturnal rides of undetermined purpose in her coach armed to the teeth with pistols, other guns and an ax!

It was, in fact, on one of these nefarious missions that fate intervened. Here again, there is some uncertainty as to just what happened. One source said she and her coachman "were borne aloft in a terrible hurricane and lost to sight." Another claims, "one night she went out in a storm and was caught in a sudden twister. She, her coach, coachman, and horses were all carried away, lifted into the heart of the whirlwind, never again to be seen."

What happened next is reconcilable. The already-sinister reputation of the house was enhanced by the horrifying screams of a woman thought to be the spirit of Martha, and the frightening groans emanating from the dark cellar, believed to be the painful cries of the slaves brought there for punishment. The haunting sounds were so overpowering that no one would live at Pec(k)atone for years. Yet passersby reported seeing "lights" moving from room to room. The hauntings ceased abruptly when the house burned to the ground in 1888.

* * * * *

THE PHANTOM SKIPPER OF WILMINGTON STAR
(Off the Eastern Shore)

In 1905, two young boys, playing aboard an old, abandoned small brig which had just been bought for scrap, got the scare of their lives. What was odd was this incident occurred in the Harlem River, New York City, whereas the apparition they both witnessed had previously only appeared on the coastal waters off Virginia's east coast.

The ship — *The Wilmington Star* — had not seen service for more than 25 years when it was hauled into drydock to be dismantled. The boys, one the son of the scrapyard owner, were exploring the worn-out vessel before the work started. Below deck, there was an eerie silence to the *Star*, broken only by an inch or two of water sloshing around and the occasional scurrying of rats.

As the boys walked down a particularly dark passageway, they froze in mid-step. Ahead of them, descending a companion ladder, was the shadowy figure of a tall man wearing a sea captain's uniform of a by-gone era. He appeared to be 50 or more years old, with red curly hair and beard, sprinkled with gray, and his skin was an ashen-gray.

The boys stood like stone statues as the man started walking straight towards them. As they huddled against the wall, they noticed that while the captain was looking directly at them, he seemed to be seeing *through* them. He passed within a foot or two of them without any acknowledgement that they were there, and disappeared into one of the empty cabins ahead. It was only after a period of several minutes that the two lads were able to gather their wits and speak. It was only then that they realized that when the captain had walked by them — he had made *no noise*; not a sound, even though he was wading through several inches of water!

Later, when the boys confronted the son of the scrapyard owner's grandfather, he just smiled, shook his head, and then had them sit down so he could tell them why they had seen what they had seen. He had known about the haunting legend of the *Wilmington Star* when he had bought the hulk.

The red-bearded man they had seen — Josiah Marchmont — had been captain of the ship back in July 1861, when it was making regular runs between Charleston, South Carolina, Newport News, Virginia, and New York. Frequently, they anchored off Cape Charles, on the Eastern Shore, or in Chincoteague Bay. One evening while they were in the Bay, Captain Marchmont and his first mate, went ashore. Later that night the men on board were startled to hear a piercing and prolonged scream from the shore.

Some time after that, several crewmen heard a noise on the bridge and looked up to see Captain Marchmont slowly walking down the bridge steps. His red beard was clearly visible in the moonlight. He appeared to be terribly pale. Some of the men spoke to him, but he did not reply or even seem to hear them. He went straight to his cabin.

When the seamen told this to the second mate, he thought they were joking. He told them the captain and the first mate had not yet returned from land. He went to Marchmont's cabin to make sure. No one was there, nor was there any sign that anyone had been there. The next morning the two officers were still not aboard, and the ship had to sail for New York without them.

No one ever found out what happened, but it was strongly speculated that they may have been robbed, beaten and killed in a local bordello, which had an unsavory reputation all along the Virginia and Maryland coastlines. Bodies, it was said, were thrown down an old well.

From that time on, whenever the *Wilmington Star* passed through waters near Cape Charles — and only then — was the wraith of the captain seen. That is, at least until he appeared to the two boys in the drydock on the Harlem River. Perhaps then he was giving his old ship one last once-over before sailing on an other-worldly journey.

The Ghost Coach
of Carter Hall

(Clarke County)

illwood is a small town which lies at the northern end of the Shenandoah Valley somewhat to the east and about halfway between Winchester and Front Royal in Clarke County. Here amidst the rolling rural hill country, stately in its magnificent presence, is Carter Hall, which has been called "the idealized image of a Virginia plantation." It was erected around 1790 for Colonel Nathaniel Burwell who was born at historic Carter's Grove, near Williamsburg. Writing more than 60 years ago, author Margaret DuPont Lee said, "He (Burwell) journeyed from Williamsburg to Clarke County, and there built his splendid mansion, choosing a site commanding superb views of the Blue Ridge Mountains and close to a great spring flowing in the cool shade of immense forest trees… (It) stands today, a massive three-story stone structure some 60 feet in length, and bearing on either end long wings adding grace and symmetry to the whole."

Burwell married Susanna Grymes at Brandon plantation in 1772, and was, it is said, "devotedly attached" to her. They enjoyed years of happiness at Carter Hall, but when she died at the age of 37 in 1788, he was "so crushed and lonely he felt unable to bear his misfortune without a companion in misery who could understand his great loss and render the sympathy he felt he must have."

Just how long he suffered in his "deepest bereavement," is not known. However, it is recorded that sometime later he journeyed across the state to the legendary Page mansion, Rosewell, in Gloucester County in his "immense coach." There, with the help of Rosewell's master, Colonel John Page, he met and subsequently married a beautiful young widow, Lucy, John Page's sister. It is not documented as to just how much consolation Lucy provided to Colonel Burwell in his declining years, but it is thought that he never really got over the untimely death of his first wife. He died in 1814.

In the intervening years a curious phenomenon occurred again and again at Carter Hall. Succeeding generations of owners reported the distinct sounds of a large coach arriving at the front door of the mansion. Yet when they went to see who had come for a visit, no one was ever there. One who experienced this more than once was Townsend Burwell who lived there in the early 1900s.

He was not convinced the mystery coach was of supernatural origins, however. He attributed the occurrence to a limestone cave located beyond the bluff southeast of the house. In a book on the history of Clarke County, he was quoted as saying, "Unlike most ghosts, this one has a scientific reason for being. Often enough, even to this day, a coach may be heard to rumble up to the portico of the house and the old-fashioned folding steps may be heard bumping down as they are unfolded. It is, of course, very probably that the cave extends under the house and on to the west until it passes beneath the highway. Certain it is, that the road sounds queerly hollow at a certain point, and the unbelieving maintain that the sound of the coach is only that of a truck or a wagon passing over the hollow place in the highroad, and that the sound is carried by the cave to the earth under the house a quarter of a mile away."

Seems like a plausible explanation. But is it?

If so, how does one account for the extraordinary vision witnessed by Lucy Burwell Joliffe and her two sons about three quarters of a century ago during a visit to Carter Hall. It was covered both by author Lee and in the book on Clarke County history. Here is what was said: "One night sitting before the fire in the dining room, they heard the sound of a carriage being driven to the front door. Taking a candle, Mrs. Joliffe followed by her sons, opened the door and all three *saw* a big old-fashioned coach with heavy wheels, two large horses, and coachman and footman high upon the box. They could see someone was *in* the carriage. The footman jumped down, opened the door, letting down the steps. *No one descended!*

"Before their astonished gaze he put up the steps, closed the door, and jumping to his seat beside the coachman, the crack of the whip was plainly heard as the great lumbering vehicle disappeared into the night. Mrs. Joliffe's description coincided with what was known of the great coaches belonging to the day of the Master of Carter Hall!"

The limestone cave could possibly explain the origins of the *sounds* of a mystery coach. But how, one may ask, could it possibly account for the coach's *appearance*?

The Vengeful Return
of Hetty Cooley

(Near Middletown)

(Author's note: During the course of a year, I get hundreds of letters and phone calls from people all over Virginia, and, in fact, throughout the country, related to ghostly subjects. Some ask questions, and many relate psychic experiences they have had.

A few years ago, I got a call from a woman, out of the blue, who wanted to tell me what happened to her when she visited a famous plantation a few miles south of Winchester near Middletown, also the site of the Civil War battle of Cedar Creek. This was Belle Grove. The woman said she had never been there before and did not know anything about the history of the house. Yet, she recalled, "As soon as I started down the driveway leading to the mansion, I sensed a ghost. I also sensed a terrible fight between two women on a dark rainy day, and a gruesome murder. I felt all this before I started the tour. And when the tour was over, I had the very strong sensation that a woman ghost followed us down and out of the house."

When the woman told me this, I didn't think too much about it, because I didn't know the tragic history of Belle Grove. When I finally decided to do a book on the ghosts of the entire state, Belle Grove stood high on the list of probable houses "to do," because it is without question one of the most written about haunted houses anywhere. And when I researched the particulars involving what happened here in the days just before the Civil War, and remembered then what the woman had told me over the phone *before* she had taken the tour, I was deeply impressed — because the details of what the woman had envisioned matched precisely the sordid facts. There had been, indeed, a fight between two women, and a murder which could be called far worse than gruesome! The lady who had called me obviously had strong psychic powers.)

␣he magnificent house itself was built from 1794 to 1796 for Major Isaac Hite, Jr., a Revolutionary officer and grandson of Jost Hite, pioneer settler of the Shenandoah Valley. Isaac married James Madison's sister, Nelly, and it is recorded that Madison called upon his friend, Thomas Jefferson, to help in the mansion's elegant design. The interior woodwork is said to be some of the most beautiful and finely crafted in the state. During the Civil War Stonewall Jackson used Belle Grove as his headquarters, as did Union General Philip Sheridan later in the conflict, during the battle of Cedar Grove, after which it served as a hospital.

In 1860, as the war clouds gathered, a bachelor named Benjamin Cooley moved into the mansion, along with a handful of servants. One of these was a young slave girl named Harriette Robinson, who served a dual role as cook and housekeeper. She was feared by the others who worked for Cooley, because she had a fiery temper, a sharp tongue, and a totally intimidating manner. She also was physically strong enough to bully all of the women on the estate, and even some of the men. The other slaves went out of their way not to cross Harriette.

After a few months at Belle Grove, Benjamin met a handsome widow named Hetty, married her, and brought her to the plantation to live. Everyone seemed pleased that the master had finally found a mate, except Harriette Robinson. She was furious. She felt the new mistress would undermine her authority. Sparks seemed to fly from the first time these two domineering women met. In a manner totally uncharacteristic of slave behavior at the time, Harriette openly defied Hetty on virtually every order she was given. Things got so bad that Hetty asked her husband to get rid of the hostile servant, but, for reasons never explained, Benjamin failed to take action.

One day Harriette stormed into the house and brazenly asked Mrs. Cooley if she had found a stocking. Mrs. Cooley said no. Harriette then accused her of purposely hiding the stocking, and of being a liar. This drove Hetty over the edge, and taking out her pent up frustrations, she flailed away at Harriette with a broomstick. This resulted in a wrestling match, and the slave grabbed Hetty by the shoulders and was kicking her senseless when others in the house came to aid and separated the two.

Curiously, Hetty revealed to Mary Moore, a friend living at Belle Grove with the Cooleys, that she didn't think she would be alive to see Abraham Lincoln become President, even though the inauguration was only a short time away. Her words turned out to be frighteningly prophetic. She had somehow experienced a premonition of her own death.

At about 2:30 in the afternoon a few days later, Hetty was sitting in the parlor of the house with Mary Moore. She got up, excused herself, and went outside. When she hadn't returned or been heard from by five o'clock Mary became worried. A little later, James Gordon, a tenant farmer on the Cooley place, walked over to the house. Along the way he said he smelled something strange; it smelled like burning wool. Mary Moore asked Gordon to help her find Hetty. He thought maybe she had gone to the stable, but she was not there. Then an old slave said he had heard something or someone groaning in the smoke house. There was a frantic search for the key to this locked door.

When the men finally opened it and pushed their way inside, they were horrified at the sight; Hetty Cooley lay in a semiconscious state between two hogsheads with her feet sticking in the fire! Her face, head and hair were bloodied and burned almost beyond recognition. The servants carried her, wrapped in a quilt, to the main house and two doctors were sought, one of whom was Hetty's brother.

After a thorough examination, they were appalled at the extent of her injuries. What skin on her face that wasn't burned was badly bruised. Some sort of cord had been tied tightly around her neck. She was bleeding from her nose, there was a "severe wound" on her right cheek, the right cheekbone was shattered, the right eye was "sunken," whilst the left eye was protruded, and there were two flesh wounds on the right side of her forehead running around to the temple. Another wound behind the right ear, an inch and a half long, was laid open to the bone. Her nasal bones were broken and there was an imprint of human knuckles on the left cheek and chin. It also appeared she had been choked as there were fingernail marks between the throat and the collar.

Despite all this, Hetty was conscious enough to recognize the doctors' voices. When asked who had done this to her, she incredibly replied that "there was nothing the matter with her." She, in

Belle Grove

fact, said she had fallen when she had climbed up in the smoke house to get a piece of meat. The doctors later felt she had not been rational when she made these remarks. Dr. Shipley, her brother, said almost immediately that there was nothing he could do for her, and Dr. Guyer more or less agreed. She was found on a Tuesday evening, and died the following Saturday afternoon without uttering anything else of relevance.

But that Tuesday night, both doctors went out to check the smoke house. They found a pool of blood just inside the door. Then they saw Hetty's steel skirt hoops, placed in a neat pile, upon the fire. Both hogsheads, between which the beaten woman was found, had blood on them, and there was "a large splotch of blood" against one of the studdings, and more blood on some boards lying upon a salting trough. Blood also was found in a vacant space on the dirt floor.

Human hair, similar in color and texture to Hetty's was located under the door of the pig room — a room connected to the smoke house that was used for slaughtering animals for food. Dirt on

Hetty's underclothes also was dissimilar to the dirt on the smoke house floor and was believed to have come from the pig room. It was thus obvious to the two doctors that Hetty had not fallen accidentally. She had been attacked viciously and then her battered body had been dragged from the pig room to the spot in the smoke house where she had been discovered.

Harriette Robinson subsequently was charged with the murder of Hetty Cooley. The circumstantial evidence presented by the two doctors was overwhelming. The case was strengthened when several witnesses testified that Harriette had made threats on Hetty's life, and the details of their previous fight were brought out. It was determined that Hetty had died with apoplexy caused by the injuries to her head. The evidence against Harriette, who had remained silent through the trial testimony, mounted when a witness pointed out that the dress Harriette was wearing on the day of the crime was hanging out to dry the next morning after being washed. This was deemed unusual because she had only worn that particular dress for two or three days, and normally she didn't change clothes for two or three weeks at a time. The crowning testimony came from a black woman who said Harriette had asked her if she had any poison, and told her, if she (Harriette) couldn't do anything else, she could poison her (Hetty). When the woman told Harriette that if she did such a thing they would surely hang her, she had replied, "I don't care what they do with me afterwards, I will have my revenge."

Totally without any sign of remorse, Harriette was taken to prison, and although the trial transcript and subsequent official accounts do not specify what her punishment was to be, it is generally believed that she was sentenced to hang. But, ironically, she didn't hang. According to Guy Jones of Annandale, Virginia, who has done research on the history of Middletown for a book he is writing, evidence in the Confederate Congress records states that Harriette died in prison.

In it any wonder then that the ghost of Belle Grove is said to be Hetty Cooley? In the 1870s, only a few years after the tragedy, members of an English family named Rose and one of their intimate friends, a Miss Lucy Jones of Winchester, all reported seeing the same wispy apparition. As recorded by Margaret DuPont Lee in her book, "Virginia Ghosts," written more than 60 years ago, what they saw, frequently, was "a white figure standing by the stone fireplace in the basement gliding along the flag path to the smokehouse..."

Vengeance sometimes is hard to give up.

The Battlefield Ghosts of Cedar Creek

(Near Strasburg)

For Confederate General Jubal Early, it was a time of hard decision. He had about 15,000 tattered and hungry soldiers under his command in October 1864 at a site in the burned out Shenandoah Valley a few miles from the town of Strasburg. Early and his men had been beaten back twice in the past few weeks by the superior-in-strength forces of General Philip Sheridan. In the process, the Union soldiers had torched the Shenandoah to the point where one Reb officer wrote about the "great columns of smoke which almost shut out the sun by day, and in the red glare of bonfires which, all across the Valley, poured out flames and sparks heavenward and crackled mockingly in the night air, and I saw mothers and maidens tearing their hair and shrieking to Heaven in their fright and despair, and little children, voiceless and tearless in their pitiable terror."

Early really had no choice. He could launch an all-out surprise attack on Sheridan's army, encamped comfortably at a site known as Cedar Creek, which flowed from the northwest to join the north fork of the Shenandoah River. Or he could retreat, and cede the Valley to the Yankees. Early, who historian Bruce Catton described as being "as pugnacious a man as ever wore Rebel gray," chose, not surprisingly, to fight.

The historic battle commenced early on the "shivery, misty dawn of October 19, with fog hanging in the low places and the darkness lying thick in the graveyard hour between moonset and dawn." The Confederates rose up out of the gorge and came in yelling and shooting on the "drowsy flank" of Sheridan's army. They caught the Union forces completely off guard.

Amidst the barrage of gunfire and total confusion, one Northern soldier recalled, "We see nothing but that enormous disk (the sun), rising out of the fog, while they could see every man in our line and could take good aim." Another terrified trooper described the attack like this: "Men seemed more like demons than human beings as they struck fiercely at each other with clubbed muskets and bayonets."

The result, for Sheridan's men, was disastrous. There was no orderly retreat. There was a rout. It was, as one witness wrote: "a disorganized, routed, demoralized, terrified mob of fugitives... crowds of officers and men, some shod and some barefoot, many of them coatless and hatless, with and without their rifles, but all rushing wildly to the rear, oaths and blows alike powerless to halt them..."

As the Federals raced as fast as they could scamper north-ward, towards Winchester, a curious thing happened. Many of the Southern troops, instead of chasing and capturing them, stopped instead at the Yankee encampment near Cedar Creek to forage food, clothing, weapons, and anything else left behind in the rush.

And then another remarkable happening occurred. Philip Sheridan, the Northern commander, had been 20 or so miles north in Winchester when Early's attack began. He was on his way to Washington for a conference, but when he heard the artillery shelling, he immediately turned back and rode hard to Cedar Creek. And in so doing, he achieved immortality as a charismatic military leader. Almost singlehandedly, he rallied his forces from chaotic retreat, turned his men around, and led a devastating counter charge against Early's tiring troops. As his-torian Catton phrased it: "The effect was electric." Riding at ͏ men of which legends are made. They followed him with an enthusiasm and a sense of mission almost beyond their physical capabilities.

The result, within hours, was a complete reversal of the morning's rout. The courageous but spent Southerners were driven back almost as fast as they could run, and a resounding Union victory was snatched from the jaws of defeat. For all intents and purposes, the great Valley campaign of 1864 was over. But it was not without an awful cost. As one chronicler wrote, simply, "The victory was dearly bought."

Thousands, on both sides, lay dead or grievously wounded, and the bitter physical and emotional effects would endure long after the last gun fired. In fact, said many of the area's residents, the ghosts of the Blue and the Gray continued to fight shadowy battles along the gentle streams of Cedar Creek and over the blood-soaked ground for years afterward.

Witnesses reported that many of the wounded later died in a nearby Episcopal Church, which had served as a hospital during the battle. Countless bodies were hastily buried in the churchyard. A short time later, many of these men were dug up and placed in pine box coffins, which were then stacked high against the back wall of the church. They stayed there for a month or more. Curiosity seekers pried some of the coffins open. Said one person who was there at the time, "Some of the dead men was very natural and others wasn't fit to look at. One man with a blanket wrapped around him was petrified, and his appearance hadn't changed any since he was buried, only his hair had grown way down and his beard had grown long."

It was while these massed coffins lay stacked against the wall, that ghostly manifestations began to take place. Some of them were recorded in detail during interviews of survivors of the scene by author Clifton Johnson for a book published in 1915 called "Battlefield Adventures." Some said they had seen a strange light come out of the church and dance around the coffins at night, "as if someone was searching around with a candle," although there was no one there. Others saw an unworldly calf-size animal at the site.

Following are selected excerpts from an interview Johnson did with an aged servant who lived near the church in the 1860s: "The boxes was taken away presently, but the ghosts stayed at the church, or came there often at night, and we'd hear them walking, groaning, and carrying on." Several people recalled hearing an army band playing in the church. The servant said everyone around was called out of their houses one night to listen to the mysterious music, and all swore they heard it clearly. It was described this way: "The music sounded way off, but we could hear the lead horn start and the drums tap. The kettle drum would rattle it off and the bass drum would go bum, bum, bum!

"Right after the war we used to hear the soldiers' ghosts shooting here all around the battlefield, and we'd hear horses in the back lane coming klopity, klopity, klopity. The horses would ride right up to you, but you couldn't see a thing. I know one man who lived out on a farm and he come in to the town one night to a prayer meeting. As he was going home, about ten o'clock, he heard the bugle and the rap of the kettle drum. While he was listening, he seen an officer walking ahead of a squad of soldiers. The officer hollered 'halt!' to them and they stopped. But the bugle kept blowing, and pretty soon they marched off."

The interviewee told of another man who came into town often during this time while he was courting. "Some of the nights was tolerable dark. Many a night he'd hear horses coming across the fields, and canteens and swords hitting the sides of saddles, blangity, blangity, blangity!"

He also told of a ghost in a barn near Cedar Creek. "The ghost is supposed to be a soldier that was killed thereabouts. He has Yankee clothes on and wears cavalry boots that come way up to his knees. Some say he has no head, and others say he has a head and wears a plug hat. People see him at night, just about dusk, and he only comes at that time of evening." Apparently, many residents and others saw this apparition, because the old man said the railroad ran excursion trains to the area so people could come and see the ghost. "I went there to see him once, but I was afraid to go in the barn."

One man who had first hand experience with this military apparition was Holt Hottel, who rented the farm. He first saw him one evening as he was in the barn feeding his horses. "It was just after sundown," the old servant remembers, "and (Holt) was going to throw some hay down the hold to the feeding room when he noticed the ghost. But he thought it was a tramp, and he told him to get out of there. The ghost didn't say anything and just stood there. Holt got mad then and tried to gouge the ghost with his pitchfork, and the fork went right through the ghost into the weatherboarding. Holt's horses didn't get no hay that night! There's people who have tried all sorts of ways to see that ghost and never could, and there's plenty of others who have seen it. I know this — that Holt Hottel was a reliable a man as there was in the state. His word was as good as his bond.

"Around here it was only a few years back that we'd see plenty of strange sights and hear plenty of strange noises. We don't see and hear them things so much now because the battlefield has been so stirred up by plowing and raising crops. That's driving nearly all the battlefield ghosts away, but there's some left yet. Yes sir, there's still ghosts. I can take you out with me tonight, and if you'll look across my left shoulder I'll show you something!"

And so it seems, for some poor lost souls, the fighting never ceases; apparitional warriors continue to wield spectral weapons across the hallowed grounds of historic Cedar Creek.

The Searching Spirit
of the Shenandoah

(Shenandoah Valley)

ne was, in his time, a legitimate legend; a wily military genius revered by his men, respected by his enemies and as courageous and unafraid of looking death squarely in the face as a Kamikaze pilot. "Adventures are to the adventurous," he liked to say, and there seemed to be no challenge or dare he would not accept, no matter the odds, in his bold, audacious raids against Union army troops during the Civil War.

In time, he gained a well-earned reputation as a wizard; a guerrilla commander who drove Northern generals to drink or worse with his daring, swift-as-lightning attacks and his equally-quick disappearances, almost before the eyes of his pursuers. Once, as 3,000 Yankees chased his band of but 20 men, after they had captured and burned a Union supply train, he later wrote: "We vanished like the children of the mist." There were even those who considered him a ghost, or myth, so mysteriously were his forays.

His name was John S. Mosby, Colonel, C.S.A. For years, with only a handful of crack-shot calvarymen, he ruled like a military Robin Hood in the northern end of the Shenandoah Valley. But while Mosby and his bands fought as guerrillas, they nevertheless also fought with honor. Other groups at the time, calling themselves guerrillas, were actually no more than a step above being common outlaws, ravaging, pillaging, plundering and terrorizing any local citizens who got in their paths. They also indiscriminately killed any Yankee soldiers straggling away from their units.

Such bushwhacking tactics not only sickened General Robert E. Lee and his officers, who abhorred such maneuvers, but also infuriated the Northern forces. This was one of the reasons the Valley was so devastated during the war, with many farms burned and crops destroyed, until, as historian Bruce Catton phrased it, "Even a crow would not support himself."

It got so bad, that by 1864, whenever a Confederate guerrilla got caught — whether he was a member of Mosby's raiders, or just a common thief-murderer on his own — Union soldiers were determined to punish him on the spot. This generally meant a hasty firing squad or a hanging, whichever was more convenient.

Unfortunately, sometimes the innocent became victims of such wanton revenge. Such was the case of a blameless youth who lived in the Front Royal-Riverton area. He was suspected of being a member of Mosby's raiders, though he wasn't, and he was pummelled by Federal soldiers in "murderous violence." It was said that after the troops were finished with him, his battered body was thrown into a field where cattle stampeded over him.

It was this undefiled youth, many area oldtimers believe, who returned to the Valley in spirit form at varying times for more than 50 years seeking an answer to why he had been so cruelly treated by fate. His nightmarish appearances, spanning a period from the 1870s until at least 1925, stirred stark fear in the few residents who actually saw him; a fear that spread with the telling and retelling of his sightings, throughout entire communities.

It was commonly thought that the apparitional figure reemerged about once every six or seven years, and while there are numerous accounts of his manifestations over the last third of the 19th century, and the early years of the 20th, it was in 1912 that a detailed description of the phenomenon was first preserved through the eyes of a person who can be described as an unimpeachable witness: Judge Sanford Johnson.

The judge was outside feeding his dogs on a freezing wintry day that year on his spacious estate near the village of Riverton, when a sudden movement down near the bank of the creek, which ran across his property, caught his eye. As Johnson looked up he saw the "form" of a young man dressed in a Confederate uniform with a visored cap pulled down low over his eyes, shading his face. Stunned into silence at the unexpected sight, the judge watched open-mouthed as the figure "jerked and stumbled" out of the creek.

The judge's first impulse was to go forward and offer aid to the soaking stranger, but there was something about this whole vision that wasn't right; something that caused Johnson to, instead, race in panic back to his house and bolt the door. He peered out the back window but saw nothing. Then he moved to another window and saw the strange form, again moving rapidly and jerkily, wend its way down the long road past the front of the house. It was at this point that the conservative and practical judge observed something that chilled him to the bone: although there was fresh snow several inches deep on the ground, the form of the soldier *left no tracks*!

In relating his eerie experience to a close friend, the judge's normally logical mind seemed a total blank to explain what he had seen. Where, for example, had this "creature" come from? Had he arisen out of the middle of the half-frozen creek? Secondly, Johnson said not even a bird in direct flight could have moved as rapidly from the river bank to the point down the road where he next appeared in the time it took the judge to go from just outside his back door to the window. And, lastly, how could anything mortal move through the snow without leaving a trace?

The next "major" return of the mystery figure took place at a nearby farmhouse 13 years later, in 1925. The timing of the year and the particular circumstances varied somewhat from those Judge Johnson experienced, including a frightening eruption of psychic activity. But when everything was over, there was no doubt, among four eye witnesses this time, that the young Confederate soldier had reappeared. This visitation took place at the home of the Brad Cook family.

It was late on an autumn afternoon. There was a "friendly stillness" in the air, when, without warning, what has been described as a violent burst of wind shrieked and thrashed through the tall trees down by the river in back of the Cook farmhouse. As two of the Cook women looked on in surprise, the disturbance stopped as abruptly as it had begun, and a deathlike quiet followed.

Next came plodding, heavy footsteps up the path toward the fence gate, and then the gate itself creaked under some burden invisible to Mrs. Cook and one of her daughters who stood in the center of the kitchen looking out, trembling. Gusting winds again whipped up, fearfully shaking the trees. And then, as the shadows seemed to darken along the river banks, the women saw, suspended over the gate, an "odd, ovally massed, silver-greenish light that quavered in a shimmering motion."

In her fine book, "Beyond the Limit of Our Sight," chronicling supernatural stories of the Shenandoah Valley, author Elizabeth Proctor Biggs wrote of what happened next: "Peering uneasily at the strange spectacle, the two women watched in disbelief as the splay of subtly shifting luminescence stirred and began to shape itself. Gradually there appeared the form of a man wearing plain gray trousers and jacket. A visored cap shaded his face. He leaned, arms folded, against the gate and appeared to be intently watching the house...the shimmering countenance commanding the frightened attention of the two women. The form maintained continually the weird wavering motion — never completely stilled."

The two other Cook daughters were called down from upstairs to view the incredible figure. It next moved, in a wink of the eye, from the front to the back gate of the fence, yet maintaining his mesmerizing stare fixed on the women in the house. One daughter then ran back to the front of the house to lock the door, and nearly fainted at the glowing form, which had seemed to follow her back to the front gate. Amidst a whirling wind, the strange apparition stilled itself, its light disintegrated, and it vanished!

Mrs. Cook later was to say there was no humanly way possible for anyone *living* to move that quickly around the yard and up a hill from the front gate to the back and then to the front gate again. Also, an examination of the grounds revealed that although there had been much rain in the area recently, there was not a single footprint or other sign of mortal movement around the house.

Curiously, there have been no reports of the mysterious visitor since 1925. If indeed it was the youth who had been suspected of being a Mosby raider and consequently mauled and stampeded to death in 1864, had he at last somehow found peace? The definitive answer will likely never be known. But it may be fair to surmise that Mosby himself might well have welcomed such a fleeting young man into his guerrilla troop; one who could dart about quick as a whip without even leaving the faintest trace of his surrealistic movements!

CHAPTER 38

Righting a Wrong
from the Grave

(Near Harrisonburg)

o what lengths will a ghost go in returning from his or her grave to right a wrong that he or she may have been responsible for in life? There are on record two accounts of spirits reaching from the beyond to amend circumstances they felt they could not leave unattended. In one instance, a male apparition appeared in a dream, and in the other, a woman "returned" to the scene until her correcting message was received and understood. The first account actually occurred in North Carolina, in the 1920s, but it is so extraordinary, it is well worth the retelling as a prelude to a somewhat similar event which happened near Harrisonburg right after the turn of the 20th century. In both cases, the ghosts came back to see that their wills were changed to more properly reflect their intentions.

The Tar Heel story unfolded in the early 1900s on a farm near the small town of Mocksville, about 25 miles southwest of Winston Salem. It raised the issue of whether or not a person could return from the dead to deliver an important message, and thus right a wrong. It dealt with a time-honored question: are some earthly visitations by spirits caused by nagging guilty consciences, or missions unfulfilled in life?

When James L. Chaffin, a God-fearing, Bible-reading farmer, died in 1921, he left a strange will; one he had written 16 years earlier, in 1905. Although he had a wife and four sons, Chaffin bequeathed his 102-acre farm and everything on it, to one son,

Marshall. No provisions were made for the other members of the family; a situation that caused a great deal of hurt and bitterness.

A year later, Marshall died, and the farm passed on to his wife. Then a very strange thing happened. Pinkney Chaffin, one of Marshall's brothers, had a dream in which his father vividly appeared at his bedside. The same dream occurred several nights in succession. "He just stood there and looked at me with a sorrowful expression," Pinkney recalled. "He seemed to have something on his mind, as if he felt he had done something wrong in his lifetime and wished he could set it right."

When Pinkney told his wife about the sequence, she laughed at him. But several nights later the phenomenon recurred in a different form. This time it wasn't a dream. Pinkney awoke from a deep sleep to see the image of his father standing close to the bed, looking down on him. He was wearing his old black overcoat. As Pinkney sat bolt upright in bed, his father pulled back the coat, pointed to an inside pocket, and said, "You will find something about my last will in my overcoat pocket." Then he vanished before his son's startled eyes.

"I was convinced my father's spirit had come back from the grave and spoken to me," Pinkney said. He found his father's frayed coat at his brother's house and they went through it, but found nothing at first. On closer examination, they discovered a small spot where the lining of the pocket had been stitched to the coat. Inside the lining they found a little roll of paper tied with a string. Written on the paper, in the father's handwriting, was a curious message: "Read the 27th chapter of Genesis in my daddy's old Bible."

After a frantic search, Pinkney finally found the Bible in the bottom of a bureau drawer in the attic. It was falling to pieces. When he turned to the 27th chapter, two leaves had been folded together, forming a pocket. Inside was a handwritten will signed by James Chaffin and dated January 16, 1919 — nearly 14 years after the date of the first will. This one stated that all four sons should share the farm property equally! Coincidentally, the 27th chapter of Genesis is a parable about the two sons of Isaac, Esau and Jacob, in which the younger son, Jacob, by deceit, cheats his older brother out of his birthright.

In June 1925, Pinkney filed suit in Davie County Superior Court claiming this "new" will invalidated the earlier one. Several witnesses testified that the handwriting was that of James Chaffin, and Marshall's widow did not fight the case. The court ruled the second will was legal.

It was a historic ruling which brought widespread interest not only from lawyers, but also from psychic experts. For here was an actual instance in which the apparition of a man who had been dead for nearly four years apparently reappeared to deliver a message from the grave!

* * * * *

(Author's note: I am indebted to attorney Joseph B. Yount III of Waynesboro, who wrote a paper in 1979 about his family and its associated history with Stonewall Cottage in Rockingham County, and was gracious enough to share a copy of it with me. The paper is titled "Ghosts and Frights at Stonewall Cottage," and Mr Yount says, "All of these events happened before I was born. I have done my best to recount them exactly as they were often told me by my late father, Joseph Bryon Yount, Jr. I have tried not to exaggerate... I have tried to be as accurate as possible. Some of my kinsmen may think it ridiculous to record these stories. In doing so I do not intend to dishonor the dead...The various stories about Stonewall Cottage and its haunts...have been a part of my family folklore all my life. Truth is stranger than fiction, they say, and I have no reason to believe that any of this is untrue.")

nder a heading called "Restless Spirits That Wander," Yount writes: "I now come to what I believe to be the 'true' ghost story of Stonewall Cottage. It happened in 1902. For its accuracy I have virtually identical oral accounts from two people, namely (1) my father, who was five and a half years old at the time and present at the occasion, and (2) his first cousin, Addie Yount Wood, who was 15 years old at the time. Addie was a favorite niece of my grandfather, Joseph B. Yount, who also witnessed the events of 1902. She lived on a farm near Waynesboro, Virginia, neighboring his, and she well remembers the excitement caused when he came home from Stonewall Cottage in 1902 and related this story. She says he told it to her many times, and, as she puts it, 'I know that Uncle Joe wouldn't have made up something like that.'

"(I might add that my father's younger sisters have tended to discredit the story. Even while he was living, they tended to discredit it as largely the account of an exaggerated imagination. It seems to embarrass them to think about their grandmother as a ghostly presence. My father always cut them short when they talked that way, insisting that he knew what he had seen. My father was a colorful, educated man, an active practicing attorney for 47 years; he had a keen memory and could imitate voices of long-dead people; he loved to tell stories of old timers. I have no reason whatsoever to believe that he fabricated any part of this story, especially since his account agreed in virtually every detail with what Addie Wood remembers her Uncle Joe telling her in 1902).

"Stonewall Cottage in 1902 was the home of Mary Dovel Stephens, 72, and her two daughters, Laura, 40, and Sallie, 32... Brother Will, who had disappointed the family by his marked lack of responsibility and unwillingness to take over the farm operation, was living in Winchester, Virginia...The Stephens family of Stonewall Cottage was well-to-do, but it was very burdensome work for the three women to operate the big farm with often undependable hired farm labor.

"One late summer day in 1902, Mary Dovel Stephens, while eating a hearty dinner, remarked to her daughters that there was some very important business that she needed to tend to at once. (Some speculated that she intended to write a will that would eliminate her son from sharing in any part of her share of the farm)... Immediately after the dinner at which she had made these remarks, Mary Dovel Stephens lay down to rest on a couch and without warning died instantly of an apparent heart attack. She was buried in the family cemetery south of the house near the orchard. A week of so after the funeral, Sallie and Laura asked their brother-in-law, Joseph B. Yount, to come to Stonewall Cottage for several days to help them with business affairs in connection with the settlement of the estate. Joe brought his five and a half year-old son, Byron, my father, along with him.

"The first night of their visit, Joe and his young son went to bed in the front upstairs bedroom, a room in which an old rocking chair was located. Sallie and Laura were supposedly asleep in the upstairs bedrooms to the rear of the house. Shortly after they went to bed, Joe and his son heard the distinct sound of the front door being opened and the tread of footsteps lightly ascending the main stairs. Suddenly, the door to their bedroom seemed to blow open, and the rocking chair began to rock as if some ghostly figure were sitting in it. Grandfather attributed these strange happenings to the

Stonewall Cottage — 1895. Left to right, Laura Belle Stephens, 1862-1934; Martha Josephine Stephens, 1856-1899; Mary Elizabeth Dovel Stephens, 1829-1902; Sallie Georgiana Stephens, 1870-1938.

wind, arose from bed, and closed the door. He and his son fell asleep. When they awoke, the bedroom door was open again, with no indication that it had been opened by anyone else in the house.

"Grandfather said nothing, not wanting to alarm the recently-bereaved sisters-in-law. The next night, perhaps out of caution, he pulled a side chair against the inside of the bedroom door to insure that the wind would not blow it open. He and his son were nearly asleep when, again, they heard the front door open and close, the sound of footsteps ascending the stairs, and then, to their amazement, the door was pushed open, as if by some invisible force, sliding the side chair back against the wall, and then the rocking chair began to rock.

"This was too much for my grandfather. He abruptly arose, hurriedly dressed, took my father by the hand, and walked down to the rear of the house, where Sallie and Laura were supposed to be sleeping. To his surprise, he found them both awake, each with a frightened look. The expression on his face caused them to say, 'Well, you have heard it, too! It has happened every night since mother was buried. We thought we were losing our minds. If it continues, we will have to move away from here.'

"The next day my grandfather took Sallie and Laura to see their minister and told him of the apparent poltergeist. He was the minister who served the nearby Melrose Church of the Brethren, where the dead woman had also belonged. He contacted one or two fellow pastors...That night at Stonewall Cottage the ministers joined Sallie and Laura, my grandfather and father, for prayers. The ministers read appropriate words from the Bible and led the group in prayer. I have never looked in the Bible for the text, but my father described it as some verse about 'restless spirits who wander' or 'troubled spirits who wander.'

"The prayers and readings were enough to summon the spirit, and the mysterious footsteps were soon heard. They then conducted further prayers, and one of the ministers exhorted the spirit, 'In the name of God, what do you want?' These words were repeated, and when there was no response the ministers then said, 'In the name of God, be at rest.' The prayers and exhortations were effective. Never again during the remaining 36 years of family occupancy did the restless spirit wander the halls of Stonewall Cottage.

"My father always professed to believe that it had been the ghost of Mary Dovel Stephens, who had died before attending to her important business and who could not rest... All I can promise the readers of this account is that I have not exaggerated it one iota. I have written it as it was told to me by one who was there."

A Pair of Heroic Female Phantoms

(Shenandoah Valley)

 alk about spirited women!
Both in life and afterwards!

Their names have been somewhat coated over in the dusty annals of time, yet in their respective days, and for years afterwards, Belle Boyd and Mad Ann Bailey each was the talk of the Commonwealth. Each gained a well-deserved reputation for daring and heroism under fire that earned undying respect from their friends and followers and grudging admiration from their enemies. Boyd's exploits spanned the Civil War years, and Bailey's fame came a century earlier, during almost daily conflicts with then-savage Indians.

There seems to be some controversy among writers and historians as to just how attractive, or unattractive, Belle Boyd really was. Descriptions pretty much run the gamut. Take your pick. She was:

— "Not beautiful, but she was attractive and fascinating to a degree that would charm the heart out of a monk and cause him to break his vows of celibacy."

— "A tall, somewhat long-faced brunette with prominent teeth."

— "Attractive in manner, appearance and personality, she possessed dash, energy, and courage; and she was a skilled rider."

— "Flirtatious and manipulative."

— "Pretty, fair-haired and blue eyed."

Belle Boyd

— "Irrepressible, allegedly pretty, on her record, fascinating."

— "A wildly romantic tomboy."

— "One who thrived upon the stir of war, (and) saw herself as the beautiful female spy of the Confederacy."

Whatever conclusion one may draw, it is a general consensus that Belle fairly well gushed a youthful exuberance and disarming charm which was, to most Yankees she dealt with, somewhat intoxicating, if not downright spellbinding. She had a flair about her that captivated men, old and young, experienced and immature alike. And she used this homespun, backwoods charisma to fullest advantage.

Belle Boyd's legend began in the early months of the War

between the States, at her parents' home in Martinsburg, West Virginia. A troop of northern soldiers appeared at the house one day and insisted that a Union flag be raised on the grounds. Belle's mother said the family would rather die first. At this point, one of the men "spoke insultingly" to Mrs. Boyd, and, impulsively, Belle allegedly drew a pistol from her bosom and shot him dead. Amazingly, when officers heard the story later, they let the young girl go. She was then 16.

Shortly afterwards, Belle moved to Front Royal to live with an aunt, and began gathering information on Federal troop movements and strategies. On May 18, 1862, for instance, she overheard plans for the destruction of munitions and structures in the town, and for the retreat of Union forces as the Confederate army was approaching. She overheard this conversation taking place in her aunt's parlor by General James Shields and his staff through a knothole she had cut in the attic floor.

She then mounted her horse, Fleeter, as darkness fell, and rode 15 miles to the nearest southern camp to relay her intelligence. For the better part of the next two years, she continued her covert actions, by cajoling information out of Yankees, and then braving bullets and swords as she dashed southward to deliver her secret messages. On one occasion she arrived at a Stonewall Jackson camp so breathless she couldn't speak for several minutes. Then she informed the assembled staff officers where the Union soldiers were and what they were up to. This helped lead to a Jacksonian rout. Afterwards, Jackson sent her a note saying, "I thank you, for myself and for the army, for the immense service that you have rendered your country…"

Just how many missions Belle carried out between 1862 and 1864 is not known, but in time her nocturnal journeys between enemy and friendly lines became well known to both sides, and eventually she was arrested and imprisoned. She was tried, found guilty of spying, and sentenced to hard labor in the Fitchburg jail where she nearly died of typhoid fever. Her father somehow managed to free her from prison.

Toward the end of the war, this energetic and totally dedicated young woman set off by sea with important Confederate dispatches for London. The vessel was captured, however, and sent to Boston under guard of a Lieutenant Harding of the United States Navy. Belle worked her magic again, and by the time they docked, she not only had converted the Lieutenant to the southern cause, she also had become engaged to him!

He helped her escape to Canada and then to London and married her! They were divorced in 1868. Belle, in fact, went through several husbands, and wound up writing her memoirs of the war, and then touring the states giving lectures on her many adventures. She billed herself as the "Confederate Heroine Belle Boyd of Stonewall Jackson and Shenandoah Valley fame," and called her dramatic narrative, "North and South — Or the Perils of a Spy." Audiences loved it.

She died peacefully at a ripe old age, but her spirit seems to live on. Her wraith has allegedly been seen many times in the area around Winchester and Front Royal gliding effortlessly across the hills and through the woods, her chestnut curls flying. As one writer put it, "she rushes with messages to a ghostly army commanded by Stonewall Jackson."

Mad Ann Bailey

* * * * *

Mad Ann Bailey preceded Belle Boyd by a century, and although her feats were every bit as daring, if not more so than Belle's, they have been more obscured by the passage of the years.

She did not write her life story and little in written form survived. One can find a monograph or two at the state library in Richmond. One such is called, "Ann Bailey...Thrilling Adventures of the Heroine of the Kanawha Valley...Truth Stranger than Fiction as Related...by Writers Who Knew the Story." It was edited and published by a Mrs. Livia Simpson-Poffenbarger, Point Pleasant, West Virginia, in 1907.

One thing is certain: Mad Ann would not challenge Belle in a contest of captivating looks. In fact, from an old drawing, one might even compare her in appearance to Edgar Allen Poe! She had a broad face, heavy arching eyebrows, and long curly black hair which sprawled down her shoulders. She quite often dressed like, and passed for a man. One historian described her as being "a short, stout woman, very masculine and coarse in her appearance, and seldom or never wore a gown, but usually had on a petticoat, with a man's coat over it, and buckskin breeches...She was profane, often became intoxicated, and could box with the skill of one of the fancy."

Ann Bailey was born in Liverpool, England, in 1742, and after her parents had died, came to America at age 18 and settled near Staunton, then a wild and rugged frontier settlement often besieged by Indians. She married a Richard Trotter in 1765 and they had a son. In 1774, Richard was killed in the bloody Battle of Point Pleasant, and "'Twas at this juncture our heroine donned a semi-male attire made partly of buckskin used in those days and took the gun, determined to protect herself and her little child and also avenge her husband's death." It is written that when she learned that Richard had been killed, "a strange wild dream seemed to possess her and she vowed revenge on the Indian race."

For the next 11 years, she became a terror, leading to the legend of Mad Ann. Here are two brief descriptions, one written more than 50 years ago, the other more than 100 years ago: "She 'halways carried a hax and a hauger and could chop as well as hany man.' Dressed in man's clothes, equipped with rifle, tomahawk and knife, she became a spy, messenger, and scout, killed more than one person's share of Indians (and) saved stockades."

She "abandoned that home life that had once been so dear to her and entered upon that military career which has made her name famous for all time. Clad in the male costume of the Border, with rifle in hand, she attended the militia musters and urged men to go to war against the Indians in defense of helpless women and children; or to enlist in the Continental army and fight the Briton from the sea. Then she became messenger and scout, going from one frontier post to another, thus continuing that career of female heroism which made her name a familiar one to the pioneers."

Still another early account reads, "During the wars with the Indians, she very often acted as a messenger, and conveyed letters from the fort, at Covington, to Point Pleasant (West Virginia). On these occasions she was mounted on a favorite horse of great sagacity, and rode like a man, with a rifle over her shoulder, and a tomahawk and a butcher's knife in her belt. At night she slept in the woods. Her custom was to let her horse go free, and then walk some distance back on his trail, to escape being discovered by the Indians. After the Indian wars, she spent some time in hunting. She pursued and shot deer and bears with the skill of a backwoodsman...The services she rendered in the wars with the Indians endeared her to the people. Mad Ann, and her black pony, Liverpool, were always welcome at every house. Often, she gathered the honest, simple-hearted mountaineers around, and related her adventures and trials while the sympathetic tear would course down their cheeks."

While she has never gotten a fraction of the credit accorded Paul Revere, or even Jack Jouett, Mad Ann Bailey, in 1791, at the age of 48, made one of the most incredible — and dangerous — rides in American history. By this time she had remarried, to John Bailey, a distinguished border leader of Southwest Virginia. She and her husband were at Fort Lee (now the site of Charleston, West Virginia), when they were attacked by a large army of Indians.

Here is how historian Lillian Rozell Messenger described what happened: "The fort was now threatened by a savage horde, hovering not many miles from the beleaguered garrison. Their powder was nearly exhausted, which created the wildest dismay among our men. Col. George Clendenin called the garrison together to know who of the band would volunteer to risk their lives in an effort to save the garrison from slaughter. It meant to ride to, and return from, old Fort Union or Savannah, (now Lewisburg), 100 miles away. Brave men paled and looked at each other in dismay that appalled them. A dead silence fell. Only one voice was heard in a determined tone, and said: 'I will go.' Every inmate of that beleaguered fort recognized the voice of Ann Bailey."

For more than a day and a night she rode hard, dodging Indian spears, tomahawks and bullets. She was warmly received at Fort Savannah, given an extra horse, and laden with powder and ammunition. She declined a guard escort. Mrs. Messenger accorded her return as follows: "Night and day she pressed on; and at last, nearly exhausted, but animated by hope of saving the garrison, she reached Fort Lee amid shouts, the echoes of which died among the wild hills around; she was ushered within the gates, having accomplished the most daring feat recorded in the annals of the West. The savages still hovered near; but the next morning the garrison marched forth, and after a spirited action, forced them to raise the siege, and thus that feeble garrison...was saved from butchery..."

It is said, too, that the Indians called her the "Great White Squaw," and believed that she was protected from their weapons by the "Great Spirit." Perhaps it is under that protection that Mad Ann Bailey apparently still rides through the rugged terrain near Covington. She has been sighted numerous times, always under a full moon, astride her faithful horse, bounding through the foothills.

One who has seen her is B. B. Strum, a teacher at Radford University. "We used to see her during summer camp years ago," Strum says. "She was riding a pale horse, and she was always sighted out towards Lake Moomaw. She seemed to be calling for her son, William." Her apparitional rides became so well known, in fact, that in recent years reenactments of them have been performed during the summer outings at the camp.

But there is no doubt in the minds of B. B. Strum and her companions, a generation ago, that they saw the real, or spirited, Mad Ann Bailey, rifle strapped to her back, gliding effortlessly through the woods on her way to fulfill yet another perilous mission.

C H A P T E R   4 0

Harbingers of Death (and Life)

I n the classic Sherlock Holmes thriller by Sir Arthur Conan Doyle, "The Hound of the Baskervilles," a gigantic hound appeared on the moors before the death of a member of the Baskerville family. Says Daniel Cohen, author of "The Encyclopedia of Ghosts," "though this was entirely fiction, it was based on an ancient and widespread spectral hound tradition in England."

As an example, Cohen documents a case where a Scottish family experienced just such a phenomenon. The father did not believe in the long-standing tradition, but nevertheless did not tell his wife about it for fear of frightening her. Then one of his children fell ill with smallpox. Though it seemed to be a relatively mild attack, smallpox at the time was a dangerous disease, and the family was quite worried.

One evening, as the family sat down to dinner, the mother went upstairs to check on the sick child. A moment later she came running down the stairs in an excited state. She told her husband that the child was asleep but that there was a large black dog lying on the bed. She exhorted him to chase the dog out of the house. The father knew instantly what the appearance of the dog meant. Filled with fear, he rushed upstairs. There was no dog in sight, and the child was dead.

Other stories of spectral hounds abound. It was said that a small white dog appeared at the gates of the notorious Newgate Prison in the United Kingdom before every execution.

In these cases, be they actual recorded instances, legends, or traditions, dogs frequently have served the curiously dubious role of being harbingers of doom. That is, their appearance has been a forewarning of imminent death, usually of a member of the family or person they are associated with.

Other common "harbingers" in the annals of psychic phenomena have included everything from birds to the actual appearance, in apparitional form, of the person who is to die, or who already has died. And sometimes, there are unusual omens announcing the approach of the Grim Reaper, such as an invisible horse and rider, and a group of otherworldly children playing on a lawn. Herewith, are a few examples:

THE DISTURBING VISION OF GENERAL MINOR
(King George County)

General John Minor III was born at Topping Castle in Caroline County in 1761. His second wife was Lucy Landon Carter, of Cleve, an ancestral home of the Carters in King George County. This stately Georgian mansion, one of Virginia's great plantation homes, was destroyed by fire in 1917. The general and his wife are buried in the old Masonic cemetery next to the James Monrow law office and museum in Fredericksburg. A red marble mausoleum marks the site.

John Minor III joined the Revolutionary Army as a "mere boy" and was at the siege and surrender of Yorktown. He later studied law under George Wythe and settled in Fredericksburg, where he gained considerable stature and reputation for his knowledge of law and for his eloquence. He was made a general during the War of 1812.

A few years later, as a member of the Electoral College for the Commonwealth of Virginia, Minor was in Richmond attending a public dinner at the Swan Tavern. That very same evening a number of his wife's relatives had gathered around the parlor fire at Cleve in King George. William McFarland, a brother-in-law, left the group at 11 p.m. and went upstairs to retire. But a moment later he rushed back downstairs in an alarmed state and proclaimed that he had just seen General Minor, wearing his riding clothes, enter the house through the front door, ascend the stairs to the second floor and pass him without so much as a word. He told the gathering at Cleve that he believed it to be the general's ghost.

Everyone laughed at him, and when they followed him up the stairs no one was there.

Early the next morning — as documented in family records — they learned from a messenger that the previous evening, as General Minor had risen at the Swan Tavern to deliver a scheduled speech, he was stricken with apoplexy. He was carried into another room and died a few minutes later — precisely at 11 p.m.!

* * * * *

AN AVIAN SIGN OF DOOM
(Chesterfield County)

lover Hill has been described as one of the most historically significant plantations in Chesterfield County. It is known as the ancestral home of the Cox family, and personal records date the house to the 18th century, although the Virginia Landmarks Register notes that there is no architectural evidence for so early a date. Instead, it states: "Two distinct segments of the house date from the early 19th century, the large two-story section was built shortly after the Civil War, and since then various one-story additions have been put on."

Clover Hill also is known as a house that has suffered through more than its share of sadness and grief. Legends, passed down through the years by slaves and others who have lived there, involve bizarre tragedies, and with them are associated some classic ghost stories. These include tales of a bird swooping through a window at the approach of death; an eerie rapping on a certain side door when an adult member of the family is about to die; phantoms and banshees flitting through the skeletal branches of the once-stately Lombardy poplars; mysterious deaths, including a disembodiment at an old spring; and the often-repeated story of "Cox's snow."

Of all the stories swirling about Clover Hill certainly the most famous concerns the great blizzard of 1857, which has become known in Chesterfield County lore as "Cox's Snow." The date was January 17, and Dr. Joseph Edwin Cox, a cousin of Henry, was called from his home in Petersburg to visit a patient in Chesterfield. According to one account of the incident, published in 1937, "It was snowing furiously, and his horse sloshed through the muck hour after hour. Finally, completely exhausted and chilled to the bone, the doctor and horse reached the gate of Clover Hill in the night. The snow was piled high about the fence posts and the wind whipped around in icy flurries...Ask any oldster in the county, and he will tell you that such a storm has not been seen since.

"Dr. Cox edged his numb body out of the buggy and plodded through the drifts to unlatch the gate. It was icy, frozen, immovable. He called through the black murk of falling snow. He called again and again, until his voice was a faint whisper."

Here, the story is picked up by Mrs. Jennie Patterson, a former slave at Clover Hill born about 1846, who was interviewed when she was 91 years old. She was about 11 years old at the time. "I was up yonder in de big house, settin' knittin' socks fer my master. Dr. Cox...had been drinkin' heavy dat day when he came from Petersburg. When he got most to de house, we heard him callin' but thought t'was some of the t'other folks 'round dar. His daughter (Mrs. Grimes), wouldn't git up to open de do' 'cause we all was gittin' ready to go to bed."

The next morning slaves found Dr. Cox near the gate frozen to death. As Jennie Patterson recalled it: "I seed him dar when dey all went out. Fus' seed his horse an' buggy comin' to de house dout (without) nobody in hit. All got scared an' went a-searchin' an callin' him. An' lo' an' behold, dar was Marse Cox stiff in the snow. Chile, I'se been feard to tell all I know 'bout dis here thing. Dar's bin all kinds of tales de white folks bin all kiverin' hit over. Marse Cox liked his liquors so he was drunk an' couldn' make hit, not bein' of his self. I bet you ain' heard dat. Yes, yes, dar was a big botheration at de big house. Naw, I ain' said nothin' 'tall 'bout dem ghost."

What the ex-slave wouldn't refer to, was what has happened at Clover Hill ever since. "Sperrits," some of the former servants called them. The phenomenon involves a specific upstairs bedroom. Something, or someone — the most commonly offered explanation is that it is the ghost of frozen Dr. Cox — "keeps watch over the bedroom in a most discomfiting (sic) manner." He will not let the sleeper keep any bedcover on himself after midnight, especially if he is the only person in the place.

There apparently is some credibility to this because it is told that once a certain "minister of the gospel (whose word, naturally, goes unquestioned)" spent the night there and was "so harried by this persistent ghost that he grabbed a blanket and spent the night out of doors."

There are a host of other hauntings at Clover Hill, some fanciful, some more difficult to explain away by rational means. For example, cedars now line the old carriage drive, where once tall Lombardy poplars stood. In pre-Civil War days slaves believed "Headless ho'semen" rode at night among them. Looking at the shimmering branches on dark nights, the slaves said they saw "folks made out o'bones wid wings, an' hants flappin' roun'!" They made such a hue and cry that Judge Cox had the trees cut down.

Then there are the gruesome stories of the spring from which fresh water was drawn for the house. Ex-slave Jennie Patterson said: "Dar was a slave amongst us who 'cided to run away an' a 'oman slave heard him doin' his plan. She ups an' tells her mistress, an' mistress sends dis man to de spring to fetch water. Down dat spring dar was dem overseers. De man stayed so long fo' he brought de water up to de house (that) another slave went to look for him an' do you know dat man was found all cut up in de water bucket. Yes, dem buckets was big buckets; no setch buckets like you see now."

In all probability, Jennie's tale has been considerably embellished in the retelling, and the land owners probably did nothing to discourage it because fear was one of the best resources in keeping slaves from running away. Still, there was something mysterious about the spring because there is a much better documented account of what happened there to another slave, Aunt Jensie. She was dispatched one day to the spring for water and when she failed to come back they found her head and upper torso in the water, "dead as a doornail." So profound was the terror among the servants after that, that none would go to the spring again for water, even under threat of a whipping. Subsequently, the spring was bricked up and never used again.

Several members of the Cox family have died suddenly at Clover Hill, and each time, servants say, it was preceded by a harbinger of death. This took the form of a "sharp rapping" on a particular side door of the house. While there is little to substantiate this legend, there is a fairly detailed remembrance of the "swooping bird" who made a sign of death.

It was during the early days of the War between the States. One evening in early October, Judge James H. Cox was "taking his ease in the double parlors." His three sons had recently left to join the Confederate Army, and he was alone in the room. He heard "a fluttering of wings, 'tis said, and instantly a small dark bird circled

228

about his head, then flew out the window."

In a few days the judge and his wife and daughter left for Norfolk, where Edwin, the favorite son, was stationed. The servants said they made the trip, " 'cause de bird had done gib de sign." They found the boy "thin and rosy-cheeked with the flush of ill health." The family brought him back to Clover Hill, where his health became worse. He died the day after Christmas, and was laid out in the parlor where the bird had appeared.

The Coxes called the death, after the appearance of the bird, a coincidence. The servants had another name for it. It was "hants," they said.

* * * * *

ON THE WINGS OF THE SNOW WHITE DOVE
(Danville)

(Editor's note: The following account is paraphrased from an actual interview of a black servant woman named Melviny Brown, who was interviewed in Danville, Virginia, in December 1940. The interviewer was a woman named Bessie Scales, who was working as part of the Virginia Writers' Project, a depression-era program. Melviny Brown talked about what she perceived to be supernatural events which occurred sometime during the early part of the 20th century. The house she refers to and its owners are not identified, but the incident did occur in the Danville area.)

 elviny Brown liked to call it the "big house." She was a servant there nearly 100 years ago. She said that she and all the other servants and field hands loved their "master and mistress." She described her mistress as being pretty and "real smart." Melviny said the lady loved her flower garden and would "set in it, all the time," when the flowers were in bloom. The house's young master, she added, loved his bride "more'n anything," and everyone talked about how happy the two of them were.

And then, suddenly, tragedy struck. One night, when Melviny said the brightest moon she had ever seen was shining, and all the servants were sitting outside in front of their cabins, a huge screech owl, sitting in a big tree over the main house, began making terrible screeching sounds. This apparently went on for some time, and greatly unnerved the more elderly servants, including Melviny's mother. She declared flatly that someone in the big house would soon die. To the blacks in that area at that time, the sign of the great owl screeching in a tree overhanging or near a prominent house was a true harbinger of doom.

According to Melviny, her mistress collapsed in the flower garden a week afterwards as she leaned over to smell a new blossom. She was taken into the house and laid on a bed. There, the young mistress made a startling revelation and a mysterious prophesy. She knew, she said, that she was about to die. Then she said that she would come back to earth in the form of a white dove, and she would perch on the snowball bush in her garden.

Soon after, she, in fact, died. The master, it was said, nearly grieved himself to death, and later closed up the house and went off on a journey that would last for many years. Melviny and others continued their work in the gardens and fields and she looked for the return of the white dove, but it never came. Finally, a letter was received from the master, and he said he was returning to Danville with a new mistress whom he had recently married.

On the day that they arrived, as they stepped onto the front porch, a strange low wail was heard from the garden. Melviny gasped as she saw, on a limb of the snowball bush, then in full bloom, a white dove! From that day on, the dove returned to the bush every evening and moaned. The servants all were scared and certain that this was their original mistress, back as she said she would be. The phenomenon so disturbed the new bride that she wouldn't even enter the garden.

So one evening, Melviny said, the master came out with a shotgun, and stalked down the path to the garden. As he neared the snowball bush, the dove took to flight, directly towards him. Just at twilight, he raised his sights and fired. A woman's scream pierced the air just above the garden, and the dove flew away with a large red stain over its heart.

That night the master died in his bed of unknown causes. The new mistress soon left and the house was abandoned. Melviny told that in time white doves flew in and out of its broken windows.

"It sho' is the old hanted house," she said.

* * * * *

CHILDREN OF ANOTHER WORLD
(Bowling Green)

But of all the harbingers of doom, perhaps none is more scary or sensational than those once experienced at historic "Old Mansion" in Bowling Green, Virginia. It is, without question, the oldest house in Caroline County. Just how old is not precisely known, although historians seem to be certain that it was built "not later than 1675." According to the Virginia Landmarks Register, the property on which "this venerable pre-Georgian manor house" is located originally was called Bowling Green after the long green sward before the entrance. The name was changed to Old Mansion when its owner, a charismatic and colorful fellow named Colonel John Waller Hoomes, donated property for the courthouse and permitted the newly formed county seat to take the name of his estate.

Old Mansion, Bowling Green

Throughout the centuries Old Mansion has maintained a reputation for being haunted. Adding to the aura, a newspaper reporter doing a Halloween feature on the house a few years ago wrote: "from a basement that looks like a tomb — to narrow, winding back stairs ripe for midnight terror — this place has got atmosphere all right." To this, notes Old Mansion owner Peter Lawson, "I definitely think this house has a spirit." He adds that his 10-year-old son won't go upstairs in the house after dark. "He's very frightened of it," Peter says.

As best as can be determined, the plethora of psychic phenomena which seem to swirl around Old Mansion began early in the 18th century during the "reign" of Colonel Hoomes. Again, there are two and possibly three separate accounts, any one of which brought on a premonition of the impending death of a male member of the family.

In his 1924 book on Caroline County history, Maurice Wingfield says that after Colonel Hoomes died, his ghost always appeared to each member of the family before their death, "walking in full view, dressed as when in the flesh and not in grave clothes." Such an appearance is said to have signalled "unfailing warning" of the approach of death to some member of the family. This gets a little confusing, because Wingfield also states that, "another hair-raising ghost story connected with this old place is that a headless horseman, riding furiously around the old race track, always heralded the approaching death of an eldest son."

Now which is it? The third vision has been ascribed to other long-time county residents and has been recorded by several writers, including Margaret DuPont Lee in her book, "Virginia Ghosts." According to Lee and others, the tradition began one night when Colonel Hoomes (apparently then still quite alive) and several guests were seated around the dining hall table, which the host, whimsically or otherwise, always had set for 13 people. During the dinner everyone present heard "distinctly" the sound of horses' hooves galloping rapidly around the track in front of the house.

Since all of the Colonel's horses should by then have been safely locked in their stables, Hoomes and his guests got up from the table and went to the front door. Peering into the twilight, they could see no one around the track (not even the alleged headless rider), but, mysteriously, at the far end of the track near the road gate, they all reported seeing a group of children playing on the grass. No one thought to ask who they were, where they had come from, or why they were there.

"On the morrow," the eldest Hoomes son was suddenly taken ill and died!

Was it coincidence or was it supernatural phenomena that created the exact same circumstances a year later at Old Mansion? Again the horse's hooves were heard, and again the children were seen playing on the grass. And the following day the next son in line of descendance died! This time all the neighbors were called upon and asked if their children had been out at the hour of the apparitional appearance. None had.

The next year the house was filled with fear and apprehension. Yet there appeared to be no escape from the ghostly rider who heralded the approach of death. Sure enough, one night the dreaded hooves were heard once more racing up the gravel track, then dying in the distance, and the same band of spectral children were seen at the far end of the yard. The next day the third son was stricken and died!

Then, for some unexplained reason, there was a welcomed break in the terrifying sequence. Nevertheless, several years later the phenomenon was repeated and another son died. It has been said and written that this eerie experience was repeated until all of Colonel Hoomes' sons — it has never been specified how many there were — had passed on and were buried beyond the box hedge on the left side of the house. Lee penned; "Never was that rider seen; nor were those appearing gaily dancing on the lawn, children of earth."

* * * * *

THE APPROACH OF AN APPARITIONAL ANGEL
(Shenandoah Valley)

ne of the most written about and most oft-told legends of harbingers or premonitions of death occurred in late summer 1806 near Winchester. It has been passed down from generation to generation as the absolute truth, largely because it involved one of the town's most respected citizens, a man of unquestioned veracity. He was Dr. Daniel Conrad, a skilled physician whose reputation extended beyond the bounds of the northern Shenandoah Valley.

That summer a fever epidemic had engulfed the area; many had died and more lay deathly ill. Dr. Conrad was called upon night and day to tend the minions to the point of his own physical exhaustion. Late one evening in September, after a full day and evening of calls, he rode his horse 15 miles into the countryside to see a young woman named Charlotte Norris who had been suffering from what he called a "lingering consumption." She lived on a plantation near Berryville on the banks of the Shenandoah River.

As he came to a fork in the road near an isolated point known as Ash Hollow, the doctor reined his horse up to check what time it was. In the bright light of a near-full moon, he saw that it was precisely 1:30 in the morning, later than he thought. It was at this exact moment that *he saw her*! Coming up the road towards him, on horseback, was none other than Charlotte Norris. She appeared almost apparitional, but there was no mistaking who she was. She appeared to have on a long flowing night dress. As she neared him, she smiled, turned back toward her house, and beckoned him to follow her with a wave of her hand.

Dr. Conrad believed Miss Norris must have eluded her family members and charged into the night in a state of delirium. He spurred his horse onward, but the wraith-like figure had spooked his horse, and it whipped around and raced off in the opposite direction. It took the doctor several minutes to bring the animal under control and redirect it. He rode the rest of the way to the plantation at full gallop, ran up the portico steps, and pounded loudly on the door. An aged butler named John answered and Dr. Conrad asked him where his mistress was. The old man lowered his eyes, and said, almost in a whisper, "she's dead."

"Dead?" exclaimed Conrad. "What time did she die." John pointed to the tall grandfather clock in the hallway. As was the custom in those times, he had stopped the hands of the clock when his mistress had "entered another sphere of existence." The doctor seemed stunned. The hands were set exactly at 1:30 a.m.!

* * * * *

A WINGED MESSENGER OF LIFE
(Lee County)

 ife was hard for the settlers of the Virginia frontier. It was difficult enough just scratching out a living from the harsh land itself. But many pioneering families also lived in constant danger of being attacked by Indians.

Such was the case in June 1785 in Lee County, at the very southwestern tip of Virginia's "toe," near the Cumberland Gap. It was from this remote and dangerous setting that arose the legend of an extraordinary woman, who through uncommon courage and willfulness, assisted by a propitious event of psychic phenomena, managed to survive a horrifying experience in the wilderness.

It began one June night that year when a band of renegade Shawnees, led by the notorious Chief Benge, swept down onto the isolated farmhouse of Archibald Scott and his family. In minutes the war-painted Indians killed Scott and his five children and plundered and burned the house. Mrs. Scott was taken prisoner and forced to march back to a settlement north of the Ohio River. It is written that whenever she faltered on the trail, nearly collapsing from exhaustion, the Shawnees slapped her in the face with her husband's scalp and forced her to continue.

It is estimated they traveled for about 200 miles before finally stopping at a favorite hunting ground. While the braves were out after fresh game, and when her lone guard fell asleep, Mrs. Scott escaped from her captors. Hearing the Indians all around her, she fled through the woods and then waded for some distance up a brook to conceal her tracks. She wandered for days, her clothes torn and tattered, surviving on roots, plants and berries.

Several times, she heard Indians nearby. Applying resourcefulness beyond her years, she successfully hid in a hole in a tree one time, and later in a hollow log as her pursuers came frighteningly close. When they left, she continued her arduous journey. Eventually, she came upon a major fork in the path. She didn't know which way to go. She chose the left-hand path, but had gone only a short distance, when a bird flew right in front of her — and crossed over to the other path.

Mrs. Scott stopped. She believe the bird to be the spirit of one of her dead children, one who had loved birds. She felt it was a divine sign from heaven to guide her. She switched paths. Several days later she came upon the head of Elkhown Creek, then onto Pound Gap, and finally to Castlewood where many of her relatives lived. She was saved! She remarried, raised a large family and died at an advanced age.

The Insolent Hostess of Castle Hill

(Charlottesville)

"If there is any place by man's creation which approaches the great secret of nature, like the untouched woods or the ocean's floor, which calls forth our solemn admiration — that place is Castle Hill. Let us have the shimmering fields 'neath an atmosphere which has created poets and philosophers."

— Quote from *Historic Virginia Magazine.*

 funny thing happened to British Colonel Banastre Tarleton at Historic Castle Hill in Charlottesville during the early morning hours of June 4, 1781. He and his troops got waylaid, in a friendly sort of way, by genial host Dr. Thomas Walker. And had not the good doctor detained the colonel and his men for as long as he did, the course of U.S. history may have been inexorably altered, and some have even surmised that America might have remained under English rule for years, perhaps decades or generations longer than it did!

More than 200 years after this curious yet crucial episode occurred, it almost mystically remains little more than an obscure historical footnote. Equally perplexing is the fact that the hero of this underplayed drama — Jack Jouett — likely would stump the panel on Jeopardy. Yet in terms of the importance of his contributions to the liberation of his nation, Jouett, experts will tell you, should rank as high on the scale, if not higher, than Paul Revere!

All Jouett did, through nearly superhuman effort, plus a welcome and necessary helping hand from Dr. Walker, was save the fledgling country's key legislators, including Thomas Jefferson himself, from virtually certain capture by Tarleton's forces. The ramifications of such an act are staggering to imagine. It would have been like the Union Army ensnaring generals Robert E. Lee and Stonewall Jackson together in the first months of the Civil War.

Here's how the story unfolded: On the evening of June 3, 1781, Jouett, a happy-go-lucky giant of a man at six foot four, and a captain in the Virginia militia, happened to be supping at the Cuckoo Tavern in Louisa County. He saw a large group of British cavalrymen outside, moving through the area. In fact, it was Colonial Tarleton, admiringly called by his contemporaries, "The Hunting Leopard." He had a force of 180 dragoons and 70 mounted infantrymen.

The fast-thinking Jouett quickly analyzed the seriousness of the moment. General Cornwallis had launched a spirited attack across Virginia, and as a precautionary measure, Jefferson, then Governor of Virginia, and about 40 key members of the legislature had "strategically retreated" from the colonial capitol in Richmond to the more remote Monticello. Jouett correctly surmised that Tarleton was sweeping stealthily toward Charlottesville in a surprise move to capture the Virginians. In addition to Jefferson, Patrick Henry, Richard Henry Lee, Thomas Nelson, Benjamin Harrison, and many other noteworthy leaders were among the intended prey.

At about 10 p.m., after the troops had passed by, Jouett slipped onto his steed and headed due west to warn his fellow countrymen. As Tarleton took the main road, the redoubtable captain, aided by a full moon, struck out along an old Indian trail which had not been used for years. It was a rough and dangerous ride through forests, thick patches of thistles and hanging wild grapevines. Jouett was to carry facial scars caused by the boughs of trees for the rest of his life. Nevertheless, he rode so hard for about 40 miles, that his horse gave out near Castle Hill. He told Dr. Walker of the situation and was given a fresh mount in the predawn blackness. He continued on without rest.

A short time later, near daybreak, Tarleton and his men arrived at Castle Hill, stopped to rest, and demanded food. Dr. Walker and his wife obliged them. First, allegedly, they plied the officers with rounds of well spiked mint juleps, all the while telling the kitchen help to delay breakfast preparations as long as possible. The ploy worked. In fact, in a *Historic Virginia Magazine* article some years ago the writer reported that Tarleton "became quite irate at the delay in serving the meal, and stalked into the kitchen demanding the cause, whereupon the worthy functionary, the colored cook, said 'De soldiers dun eat up two breafuses as fast as I kin cook 'em.' " Tarleton then "ordered the men to be flogged, being first tied to a cherry tree, the site of which is still shown. They were most unmercifully whipped, their loud cries resounding over the place." By the time the colonel was able to remount his troops, Jouett had reached Monticello, and Jefferson and most of the legislators were able to escape.

It was a brilliant and heroic maneuver that helped shorten the war and secure the independence of the colonies. Yet, interestingly, it was, in the estimation of many historians, an event that has never been given due credit. For example, says eminent author Virginius Dabney, "It was a ride that overshadows Paul Revere's much more famous but far less difficult feat." Adds noted biographer Ellie Marcus Marx, in her book, "Virginia and the Virginians," published in 1930: "Had it not been for Jack Jouett's brave and timely ride, there would have been no Jefferson to help bring peace, happiness, and success to the American people."

Thus, stately Castle Hill not only figured prominently in a fascinating vignette of our heritage, but it also, through the centuries, had been host to a series of psychic manifestations. Strangely, they involve neither Jouett, Tarleton, nor Dr. Walker. Rather they center around the fussy and selective spirit of a woman who probably was an early resident in the mansion, and has "stayed around" to see that no further unwelcome intruders overindulge in the house's long-time reputation for outstanding hospitality.

The earliest portion of this two-part house was built by Dr. Walker in 1764 in the colonial Virginia frame tradition. It should be said here that Walker himself is a much under-publicized contributor to the growth and success of the colony. John Hammond Moore, in his impressive history of the area, "Albemarle ...Jefferson's County," published in 1976, wrote: "Although 18th century Albemarle was the home of many distinguished citizens, one man, more than any other, left an indelible imprint upon the county's early history. For over half a century, whether tending to the sick, exploring the far slopes of the Appalachians and beyond, establishing the town of Charlottesville, speaking up for the welfare of the Piedmont in the House of Burgesses, supplying the

Castle Hill

Virginians fighting with Braddock, negotiating with Indian chiefs, or pursuing his special interests in scientific agriculture, religion, and commerce, Thomas Walker was a force to be reckoned with."

Thus it should be no surprise to learn that some of the intellectual giants of that era were close friends of Walker, and often were guests at Castle Hill. It is recorded, for example, that Jefferson played his fiddle there on occasion, and that the youthful James Madison danced to the lively music. The original house was reportedly destroyed by Indians. The old porch in the rear was laid with large square stones that once were used for the walls of the structure.

The brick addition was erected in 1823-24 for then-owner William Cabell Rives, himself a U.S. Senator and Confederate congressman. It was, says the Virginia Landmarks Register, "an example of Jeffersonian classicism by the master builder John M. Perry." The brick was imported from England, with Tuscan Doric columns of white stucco running all across the front. The small panes of glass and brass door locks came from London.

In time, Castle Hill descended to Rives' granddaughter, Amelie, a distinguished novelist of her time. A remarkable woman in her own right, she began writing fiction and poetry as a pre and early teen, but was discouraged by a grandmother who took away her papers and pencils. Undaunted, she began writing her verses on the wide hems of her white starched petticoats. When her novel, "The Quick and the Dead," was published, in the late 1880s, she was but 25 years old and became instantly famous.

Photographs and sketches of Amelie lend physical proof to the general acknowledgement that she was one of the great beauties of the day, and that she carried this beauty throughout her life into old age. Born to the "social graces," she first married John Armstrong Chaloner, a man described as being the most eccentric in Albemarle County's history. While the marriage lasted only a short while, Chaloner was such a fanciful character, with a deep abiding interest in the occult, that it is worthwhile to briefly mention a few highlights of his life. On a trip to New York, he was somehow committed to an insane asylum. Several years later he escaped and returned to the Charlottesville area, where he was declared legally sane.

In March 1909, Chaloner shot and killed a drunken neighbor named John Gillard. Incredibly, when the police arrived, they found Chaloner, in his leather pajamas, eating his customary breakfast of duck and vanilla ice cream. He told the officers he had spent the night with Gillard's body "to test his nerve." Apparently, it was ruled self-defense, and later Chaloner went on the lecture circuit to talk about this bizarre affair. He also lectured on hell, lunacy reform laws, and on buzzards which, he feared, were facing extinction.

Irascible and unpredictable, Chaloner, according to historian/author John Hammond Moore, used his cane to smash windows of autos that came too close to him as he strolled city streets. He also reportedly once held a University of Virginia professor prisoner in his mansion, Merrie Mills, while he impersonated great figures of history. For all his eccentricities, however, he was, too, a generous man who gave a considerable portion of his sizeable fortune to the needy.

Divorced early from Chaloner, Amelie Rives next married Prince Pierre Troubetzkoy, a Russian painter of international repute. During their long tenure at Castle Hill it became a showcase for the Charlottesville gentry, complete with a magnificent garden shaped like an hour glass, and a fairway-sized lawn lined by immense boxwoods.

It was also during these years, including the early decades of the 20th century, that the hauntings first surfaced.

The manifestations took many forms. Guests reported to the Troubetzkoys that they heard footsteps ascending and descending the stairs late at night. Or they heard heavy pieces of furniture being moved around during the post-midnight hours. Some said they heard voices, but in leaving their bedrooms to check on the nocturnal conversationalists, found nothing. A number of visitors, plus the prince himself, told of smelling the distinct scent of roses, particularly on the stairways. Mrs. Troubetzkoy did not wear such perfume. Shaken servants came to the princess on several different occasions to tell her they had seen an apparition of her grandfather.

A former housekeeper at Castle Hill, identified in a 1982 article in *Holiday Magazine* as a "Mrs. Brown," said she was standing at the entrance to the study one day when "something grabbed my keys." She turned around, but no one was there. She lived in a cottage on the estate and said also there were times when "something would grab her ankle if she slept on the bed without covers. She was asked if she thought these incidents were caused by a ghost. "I don't know how else you'd explain them," she replied. In more recent years, according to a 1985 article in the *Charlottesville Daily Progress*, overnight visitors have heard the "sounds of a lively party going on downstairs. They heard doors opening and shutting, chairs being pushed back against the drawing room walls, glasses clinking and music playing." No source for the apparent merry making was ever discovered.

While such phenomena was spread throughout the house, there was one particularly persistent spirit who seemed to confine her lively appearances to a certain room in the back of the house on the ground floor. It was known as the pink bedroom. Her exact identification has never been fully determined, although Mrs. Troubetzkoy, taking into account the descriptions given her by quite a few of her overnight guests, once said she believed the ghost to be her aunt, Amelie Sigourney, who drowned with her husband and three children when their ship sank on their way to France in 1870. Those who caught glimpses of her said she was "not very old, rather pretty, and at times playful." Other contended she was downright frightful.

One who encountered her was writer Julian Green, who didn't believe in such things as spirits. However, after spending a night in the pink bedroom, he abruptly left Castle Hill early the next morning with scarcely a word of explanation to his hosts. Another who experienced a meeting with a strange lady was a gentleman from the University of Virginia who was to spend a Saturday and Sunday night in the house. When he appeared Sunday morning, though, he was pale and obviously uncomfortable. Without saying why, he, too, left in a rush.

It wasn't until a month later that the Troubetzkoys found out the reason for his hasty departure. A friend told the princess that the gentleman said he had been awakened in the middle of the night by a "charming looking woman dressed in the fashion of long ago, and carrying a tiny fan." He was, understandably, unnerved at the sight. The woman then told him, over and over, "You must please go. You must go away. You must not stay here."

The warning was more than enough. The gentleman said he would never again stay in that house. Later, when asked about specifics of the incident, he would mumble incoherently, wave his arms anxiously, and refuse steadfastly to discuss it further. Nor were these two the only ones to share the inhospitality of the apparitional hostess. At least three other people, including one woman, declared they not only were asked to leave the premises, they were, in their words, literally "pushed out of the house" by a sensation "not wanting them."

Yet, apparently, this ghost was selective in who she chose to drive out. Many visitors slept peacefully in the pink bedroom without a disturbance. The legend is that this room once belonged to the lady ghost and she, and only she, determines who may occupy it in peace. All others are given explicit psychic messages which they unfailingly obeyed.

One must admit, it is a novel way to get rid of guests who have overstayed their welcome.

The Insolent Hostess of Castle Hill

Evil in the English Basement

(Charlottesville)

here have been cases, although admittedly rare, in the annals of recorded psychic history where ghosts have literally followed families from house to house, sometimes great distances apart. In terms of spectral phenomena, this is extremely unusual because most spirits are associated with a residence in which they were born and raised, or lived in for a number of years, or suffered some tragic and traumatic experience. In most instances, if the dwelling occupants move, either to get away from the hauntings or for other reasons, they generally leave the ethereal beings behind, some happier at getting rid of the "intruders"; some sadder at losing the company of mortal friends or relatives.

In the few documented occasions where ghosts followed people from one house to another and continued to make their presences known, it usually involved poltergeist-type activity. The spirit had an axe to grind, so to speak, and its "business" was not finished.

Jim and Sue Anne Elmore of Charlottesville must have thought something like this happened to them when they moved from one house to another in the city a few years ago, because extraordinary things happened to them in two separate homes. Yet, as it turned out, this was, in fact, even a rarer event, because there were two *different* sets of ghosts involved, and they were totally unrelated!

It all began in 1978, when the Elmores moved to Albemarle

County from Athens, West Virginia, a small town near Bluefield. They bought a house on East Market Street. The original portion of it had been built in the 1820s. "It was one of the largest houses in the neighborhood," says Jim Elmore. "We were about a mile from city hall. It has three floors and an old English basement. There were beautiful flower gardens, and it was in a kind of historic area. Charlottesville's old woolen mills were nearby, as was the river, a graveyard, and railroad tracks. Two major additions had been made to the house; one in the 1880s and one in the 1920s. It was owned for a long time by the Graves family. The elder Mr. Graves had been one of the stockholders in the town's hardware store decades ago.

"We heard stories of Nora Graves, who lived there for a long time. The whole family was sort of eccentric, and one of Nora's brothers went out back one day, laid across the tracks, and was killed by a train," Elmore continues. "In her later years, Nora became sort of reclusive. She spent her last years living in an apartment in the English basement, and she rarely went out. Neighbors told us she was withdrawn and kept mostly to herself. And apparently, she had enough money to live independently. After she died, I think in the early 1970s, the Albemarle Baptist Church bought the house and used it for a while for Sunday School services. We bought it in the spring of 1978 and lived there four years, till the summer of 1982. It was during that time that my wife and I and several of our friends experienced a number of unusual things, and almost all of them happened in the basement."

What were some of the "unusual things?"

"Sue Anne can probably tell you a lot more than I can," Jim says. "She was in the house more. One thing that I will always remember, however, was the cold, icy blast of air you would feel in the basement, and it didn't matter what time of year it was, winter or summer. Now, I'm not talking about a little draft of air coming through a crack in a window or anything like that. These were blasts of air. They would make you stop and take notice. A lot of our friends encountered this as well as us. The other thing I can't forget was the odor. It was indescribable. I don't know how to describe it. It was the foulest, nastiest, most rank smell I ever experienced. It was beyond rotting, organic matter. It would stop you in your tracks, and you would ask yourself, what the hell is that? It was startling. It would only last for a few seconds at a time, but I assure you that was enough."

Jim Elmore also recalls one particular, and frightening manifestation which happened to him one day in the English cellar. "I was walking through the little kitchen down there, on my way outside, when I felt this strong force pushing me. It was like the palm of someone's hand pressed into my back shoving me as hard as it could. I jerked around, but there was no one there. It was very unnerving."

"What I remember specifically about the 'Nora Graves' house, is that we didn't experience any problems until our son, Seth, was born," adds Sue Anne. "That's when I began noticing that awful stench in the basement. It was like rotting, putrid flesh. It was awful, almost like it was a kind of evil spirit oozing up from the center of the earth. I would scrub and scrub and it had no effect. Then it would just disappear. There were a number of times when I had the distinct feeling that I was being ushered out of the basement, and there were a couple of times when I was actually pushed, like Jim. Once, it caused me to trip on my feet. I didn't fall down, but it was a definite push. It felt like bony fingers shoving me in the back. Often I had the feeling that there was a presence there. I could feel a current go past me. At first, I was really scared, and then I got indignant."

It was at this point that Sue Anne started reading up on the subject of how to deal with disquieted spirits. "I put lavender, rosemary and distilled extracts around in the basement," she says. "Then we had a conversation with 'Nora.' I told her that we knew she had lived in the house for a long time and that the English basement was her place. But I said that we lived in the house now, and we would have to learn to co-exist. Jim laughed about this. Here we were, grownups, talking to a ghost. But it must have worked, because there was a noticeable quiet after that."

In the summer of 1982, the Elmores moved to a house called Tufton, which was on property that had been part of Thomas Jefferson's Monticello estate. When Jefferson's daughter had to sell off the land to help pay her father's debts, a family named Mason purchased this particular tract and the house is said to have been built in the 1820s or 1830s. The Rivanna River runs through nearby, and Jim calls the area "a lush piece of land." It didn't take long, after moving in, for the Elmores to think that Nora may have moved with them, because spirit-like manifestations began to occur right away. But there seemed to be a difference, and, in time, Jim and Sue Anne realized that there was a whole new set of ghosts at Tufton.

The house is very large, with about 5,000 square feet of living space. The rooms are huge on the first two floors, and there is an attic on the third floor. The "activities" began soon after the Elmores moved in. "It was really curious," says Sue Anne. "I would be in the house and it would be very, very quiet, and I had this sense that I could hear people laboring, like picking up heavy things and moving them. Yet there was no one else in the house. It was not uncommon to hear someone walking in the attic, and then you would hear a door slam. There was a sense of somebody coming through the backside of the house," Jim concurs. "We heard these type noises many times. Doors would open and shut. One night I was upstairs and I thought I heard someone in the kitchen, cooking. I was sure of it, and I assumed it was Sue Anne. I called down from the top of the stairs, and when there was no answer I went down to look. There was no one there."

One of the most unusual occurrences was witnessed by both Jim and Sue Anne. Says Jim: "It was about dusk, and I still can't tell you exactly what it was we saw. It was standing in the main hall when we first saw it. It was an amber colored figure moving in the back of the house. It literally shimmered. I had the strangest feeling. And as it moved, there were intense, laboring footsteps, like it was carrying something very heavy. It appeared to be human-like, and yet it wasn't human. I don't quite know how to describe it. It walked through the hallway and did not seem to be in any hurry or anything. It was just like a friend of yours would walk by you. At first, I didn't believe that I saw it, then I realized that I did see it."

"I believe it was a male," says Sue Anne. "It apparently had come up from the basement. It was in full color. It was amber and it was in a shape that was not well defined, but it seemed to be the shape of a person. It was awesome, but for some reason I was not at all frightened by it. We were mind blown. Neither Jim or I said a word. We were speechless. It took your breath away. We just stared. It moved by us and appeared to be going outside, paying no attention to us. The hair raised on my arms and I had goosebumps all over."

Sue Anne also had another extraordinary experience at Tufton. She had done some research on the house and believed that it had been occupied at one time, perhaps while Thomas Jefferson was still alive, by indentured servants. Sue Anne thinks they were white servants, and possible house servants at Monticello. She isn't sure. "A lot of people lived in that place and they left a lot of spiritual activity behind," she says.

"I was alone in the house one day. I remember it was very hot, and I was carrying a load of clothes up the stairs. There was no air conditioning. About half way up the stairs I stopped, leaned against the wall, and shut my eyes for a moment. I felt a very strong presence. I mean very strong! I don't know how to put it in words. This may sound crazy, but it was as if I had slipped into a time warp, and I became that presence; I became another person. It was the presence of a young girl, a servant or a slave. I think she was either white or mulatto. She, or I, was wearing an old muslin type dress. It was gray and had no buttons. It wasn't fancy at all, maybe like a uniform, with a fitted bodice and long sleeves.

"It was like a feeling of regression, like I had gone back in time and assumed this person's body. Although she was young, I felt that she was worn out. She had too many children, and she had been worked too hard. There was an overwhelming sense of weariness of her body. I felt the total sadness and tiredness of that young woman. I felt her smallness and her utter fatigue, so much so, in fact, that I didn't have the strength to carry the clothes upstairs. I don't know how long I stood there on the stairs. It might have been four or five minutes. And then the feeling lifted, and I was back in present time again. I had a feeling of astonishment. It was so real."

CHAPTER 4 3

The Mystery Hummer of Monticello

(Charlottesville)

hat can be said about the grandeur, the magnificence of Monticello that has not already been said thousands of times over by the most gifted of writers during the past two centuries? One of the brochures on the racks at the Thomas Jefferson Visitor Center three miles southeast of Charlottesville just off Route 20 puts it well: "often described as one of our country's foremost architectural masterpieces... Monticello remains today as a testimony to its creator's ingenuity and breadth of interests. Located on a mountaintop in Albemarle County, the house commands a view of the rolling Virginia Countryside that Jefferson so dearly loved. It was here that he retreated from the pressures of public office..."

Jefferson began his complex dwelling on the "Little Mountain" in 1770 and worked on it for over 40 years, altering and enlarging it as his taste developed...when an extensive revision was finished in 1809, it had become an amalgam of Roman, Palladian, and French architectural ideals, all rendered in native materials and scale to form a unique statement by one of history's great individuals.

But of all the literary efforts of 200 years, who could paint the scene with more heart-felt exquisiteness than the Man himself. In 1786, he penned: "And our own dear Monticello, where has nature spread so rich a mantle under the eye? Mountains, forests, rocks, rivers. With what majesty do we there ride above the storms! How sublime to look down into the workhouse of nature, to see her clouds, hail, snow, rain, thunder, all fabricated at our feet! And the glorious sun, when rising as if out of a distant water, just gilding the tops of the mountains, and giving life to all nature!"

One young hostess did say that back in the 1920s when Monticello was first opened to public tours the guides were "older black men" whose only pay was tips from the tourists. "They figured the better the stories they told, the better their tips would be, and they came up with some good ones," she said. "They told of soldiers during the Civil War riding their horses in the house, and there were tales of beds rising up to the ceiling, but there never was any substantiation."

Surely, it would be this author's capstone if there were an epic ghost story to relate about Monticello; if Jefferson's imposing figure would occasionally reappear on the grounds or in the house, inspecting, tinkering, observing, enjoying again the splendors of his beloved estate. But such is not the case. Most of the historical interpreters politely say that they know of no Jeffersonian spirit, full of pluck and curiosity, roaming about. What a shame!

And yet, privately, there are a few references, here and there, to mysterious footsteps and other sounds; to certain "things" that

Monticello

admittedly are difficult to explain in television-age rationality. And there are even some who, through inexplicable personal experiences, have been persuaded that, indeed, perhaps there is an otherworldly presense here.

Certainly, one could make a case for the justification of a Jefferson reappearance at Monticello, aside from his unquestioned love for the place. He could have been unhappy that his survivors, weighted in heavy debts, had to sell the plantation in 1831, five years after he died, to a druggist who tried, unsuccessfully, to grow silkworms on the farm. (Although it could be said, too, that Jefferson might have been pleased with such an experiment, since he was interested in just about everything!) Or he could have been upset when a subsequent owner, Uriah Phillips Levy of New York, tried to will the house to the Commonwealth of Virginia, only to have a nephew overturn the will. (The Thomas Jefferson Memorial Foundation eventually bought the property in 1923.)

The Man could have been displeased at all the unfavorable publicity that had swirled about him in recent years. Although generally unfounded and totally refuted by most historians, such gossip persists, contending that Jefferson had illicit liaisons with a slave or slaves at Monticello. It is alleged that he had a long standing tryst with Sally Hemings, and that they met often in a small dependent building on the grounds, and that Sally bore his children.

One well known writer on psychic phenomena said that there apparently had always been "a problem between Jefferson and his wife concerning other women. All of this did not contribute to Mrs. Jefferson's happiness." The author went on to ask, "Could it be that part of Thomas Jefferson still clings to this little cottage where he found much happiness?" Would such besmirching of his long-unassailable reputation not be sound reason for him to come back and clear the air, so to speak?

And then there is the long unpleasantness that clouded his final resting place, down the mountainside a ways, west of the house. Jefferson himself had carefully designed his own tombstone, and left instructions that he was to be buried beside his brother-in-law and closest friend, Dabney Carr. The family cemetery was laid out over a choice acre of ground about half way up on the north side of the mountain. No one, not even the Sage of Monticello himself, could have imagined the terrible desecrations that were to follow his interment.

In 1879, his great-grandson, Dr. Wilson Cary Nicholas

Gravesite of Thomas Jefferson

Randolph, wrote in the *Jeffersonian Gazette*: " ...Where it was certain that no creditor would lose aught by Jefferson, his grandson erected a monument over his grave as was designed before his death by Jefferson...Twice has the marble slab over his wife and daughter been renewed, and once the granite obelisk over Jefferson's own grave. Now there is not a vestige of the slabs left, and the last obelisk chipped and battered by so called relic seekers, is a standing monument to American Vandalism ..."

It was bad enough that armies of tourists were boldly stalking off with chunks of tombstones, but then, from nowhere, came a movement to have Jefferson's body uplifted and taken north, to the

Washington area. The northern press picked up on the idea and favored it strongly. Family descendants had to literally mount an attack to keep the body at rest at home. Finally, one newspaper, *The New York Mercury*, brought some sensibility to the bizarre situation. The paper said that, "Jefferson's bones had no business in such a place as Washington in 1882,...to which the angels must pay few visits indeed. At Monticello, lifted near the sky, and situated amid sylvan glories, there is peace and purity. Mountain ozone is there, instead of the malaria of the Potomac flats, and the effusoria of political corruption. Let Jefferson's bones alone. They are in honest earth, in an honest atmosphere, and among honest citizens..."

With that, the ill-conceived movement subsided. But the vandals continued defacing the small cemetery for years afterward. Ordinary people with ghoulish bents squeezed through the iron bars surrounding the small cemetery and chipped with their hammers at anything they could find. Those who couldn't wriggle through the bars hired young boys to do their damage.

It really wasn't until well into the 20th century, when the Thomas Jefferson Memorial Foundation began restoring the buildings and grounds, and Monticello became a national shrine, that the vandalism ceased. Only then, as his great-granddaughter, Sara Randolph, wrote, could "he sleep amid scenes of surpassing beauty and grandeur, on that lovely mountainside, surrounded by the graves of his children and grandchildren to the fifth generation... The modesty of the spot is in striking contrast with the celebrity of its dead, and there are few in America of greater historical interest or more deserving of the nation's care."

Again, would not such actions stir the dead? Would it not be fitting for Jefferson to return to answer his caustic critics and to scold those who would disturb his gravesite?

Or he might just return for the simple reason that, in life, he enjoyed so much happiness here.

Perhaps he does!

Some staff members at Monticello say that on occasion, after the mansion is closed for the day, they have heard the sound of a man humming a cheerful tune when there is no living mortal around.

Jefferson's overseer, Edmund Bacon, once wrote that Jefferson " ...was nearly always humming some tune or singing in a low tone to himself."

The Legendary Moon Ghost of Scottsville

or 74 years, 'Echoes of the Moon Ghost' have resounded from our low-lying hills to the beautiful Blue Ridge Mountains of Virginia, and on to places far beyond. These echoes have persisted, not alone because, as a manifestation of the social unrest and insecurity of a crucial period, the story of the so-called 'Moon Ghost' belongs to the history and folklore of Albemarle county, and therefore to the ages and to all of the people."

This is how Frances Moon Butts began her reading of a paper before the Albemarle County Historical Society on July 24, 1940. The paper covered her recollections — as recounted to her by her father, by other members of the Moon family, and by servants and other "live" witnesses — of one of the most extraordinary, and most widely publicized ghost stories in the annals of Virginia.

Surprisingly, very little is known about the legendary "Moon Ghost" of Scottsville today. In fact, in 1930, when Margaret DuPont Lee published her classic book, "Virginia Ghosts," no mention was made of this bizarre episode. Yet, 125 years ago when the *Scottsville Register* ran a detailed account of the strange happenings which occurred at John Schuyler Moon's house over a sustained two year period, the news caused a sensation. The newspaper, said Frances Moon Butts, Moon's niece, "sold like 'War Specials' in Richmond, and the Packet Boat came for more! Reprints were made and still Lynchburg and other places clamored for papers." One writer, in summing up the sequence of events noted that "Scottsville's peaceful image was badly blemished...bringing national fame to that once sleepy town."

Not only were people all over the Commonwealth clamoring for more information about the on-going escapades of the alleged spirit, but thousands of them streamed into the small town from all directions in hopes of personally witnessing a slice of psychic phenomena. At one point, for example, about 25 University of Virginia students decided to venture over to Scottsville and keep a midnight vigil at the Moon residence. During the night they were not disappointed. It is said that when they saw, or thought they saw, a "mysterious shape" on the roof of the house, "15 guns fired in vain." Detectives and psychic experts from as far away as Washington, D.C. came to the area and literally camped out "many long nights" waiting to observe the specter.

It got so out of hand, wrote Frances Butts, that "my uncle, a man of dignity and reserve, seems to have been more resentful of the exaggerated publicity the ghost brought than of its almost nightly depredations. He finally refused to let anything be published that he did not write."

Though the incredible running series of manifestations occurred from August 1866 to 1868, the mystery of the Moon Ghost has never been satisfactorily solved. In fact, even today, there remains a large, overriding question: was it a ghost at all? Or was it a vengeful human being, or more than one person? As Moon's niece put it in her talk in 1940, "The details of nearly everything the ghost is said to have done are equally controversial, and contradictory."

There is no question that the events happened. They were described and documented in detail, and in most instances, they were witnessed by more than one member of the family, and in many instances they were witnessed by large numbers of people. The question is were these events staged by an ethereal presence or by a living man or men?

A reasonable argument can be made for the latter possibility. It was during the reconstruction period when the nation was still recovering from the great wounds of the Civil War. Conditions were unsettled. One President of the United States had been assassinated and another one nearly impeached. Frances Butts said "the newly-freed slaves, untrained to habits of self-support, were mostly unemployed, often unrestrained...Even justice was irrational and often severe."

She adds that her uncle was a lawyer and that he once defended a neighbor who had been attacked by an armed intruder. Apparently, he was successful, because Mrs. Butts said, "when driven away, this Negro left vowing vengeance on my uncle." John Moon also was successful in the conviction of Lucian Beard, a notorious leader of a horse-thief gang. After the ghostly episodes finally ended, Beard wrote Moon from the penitentiary in Richmond and offered to explain the ghost if Moon would secure his pardon. Moon never answered him.

Could the ghost, in reality, have been either the vengeful intruder or perhaps one of Beard's gang of rowdies? That would make sense. But then again, could that person, or persons, have sustained a series of events over a two year period, which included penetration of the Moon house on a continuous basis, sometimes every night for weeks at a time? Could such a person have eluded scores of gunmen who kept watch at night during this period? Many times the house and grounds were ringed solid with family members, neighbors, law officers and the just plain curious. Could such a person have escaped the gunfire aimed at them on numerous occasions? It is reported that more than once bullets found their marks on the mystery trespasser, but each time he bounded up immediately and eluded posses of men chasing him. How would one explain this?

Perhaps it is best, at this point, to examine some of the specific occurrences, so readers may judge for themselves. Preceding the beginning of the ghostly manifestations, one Sunday morning in the summer of 1866, someone banged on the front door of John Moon's estate, known as Church Hill, five miles north of Scottsville. Two "rough men" demanded to see the head of the house. A grandson explained that Moon had gone to church. The strangers then "whirled away on their mounts." Some neighbors saw them ride in the direction of a nearby graveyard. When Moon returned, he and some friends rode off around the neighborhood in search of the two men, but never found them. Shortly after that, the Moon Ghost began appearing.

The specifics of the intrusions were covered in graphic detail in a long article in the *Scottsville Register* issue of November 11, 1867, more than a year after the phenomena started. The article was written by J. L. Brandy, editor of the *Register*, and it was headlined, "The Mysterious Affair at the Residence of Mr. J. S. Moon." The article was reprinted five days later in the *Charlottesville Chronicle*, and a copy of this is on file at the Alderman Library of the University of Virginia.

The following excerpts were taken from this edition. The article began with a preamble:

"Our readers are aware that we have heretofore studiously avoided publishing anything in connection with what has occurred at the residence of Mr. John S. Moon, (five miles from our town,) during the past few months. Mr. Moon is a lawyer by profession, and has quite an extensive practice; but while he is well known to the public in this respect, it is exceedingly unpleasant to him to have a notoriety forced upon him by the remarkable circumstances related below.

"If the mysteries are kept up, we will make a weekly report; and the reader may rest assured that we will state nothing but what is strictly true. A matter so serious should, and shall be, by us, handled seriously and truthfully."

And then editor Brady began his article under a Scottsville dateline: "About ten months ago, a candle box, filled with rags saturated with whiskey was placed against a side of Mr. J. S. Moon's house, five miles from this place, and ignited. About 1 o'clock at night the fire was discovered and extinguished; and the unburnt rags discovered to be fragments of garments missing from Mr. Moon's house, in the then past several months. Whether this effort to burn the house had any connection with what has followed, is not known…

"During Mr. Moon's absence, attending court about that time, his parlor door which had been carefully shut and locked (the key being left in the lock at night) was found open in the morning.

"In a night or so afterwards, a parlor window which had been fixed with a straw stuck in a crack of it, was found to have been hoisted; the store room door was found open, (unaccountably), several mornings about that time.

"After this, Mr. M. fixed his inside and outside doors and windows in such a way as to know if they were disturbed, and found they were repeatedly opened. He watched on the inside of his house for a good many nights or only all night, but failed to detect any one attempting to enter. No one disturbed the house the nights he watched.

"One night, about six weeks ago, Mr. M. fastened all doors and windows carefully. He was the first one to get up the next morning, and found his inside dining room door had been opened — a store room door opening into the dining room had been unlocked and opened — a door opening into the kitchen from the dining room had also been unlocked and opened, and the sliding kitchen door had been moved back. A light had been seen to flash about the house that night after the family had all retired. From the store room about four or five pounds of sugar, gotten and weighed that evening, had been taken, and the whiskey out of a demijohn known to have been full the night before, was missing.

"The next night Mr. Moon's son, about 14 years old, was sleeping in his father's office, which is about 100 yards from the house. On this night an effort was made to hoist the window, which awakened his son. He jumped up, saw a man run off, got his gun and made ineffectual pursuit.

"The next night some one was heard to stumble on an open shed over the back passage door — a loud crash immediately followed. Upon going out, Mr. Moon found on the ground, not far from the shed several ladies' and children's garments, taken from the upper part of the house and the remains of two plates taken from the dining room, wrapped up in them — also a Bible taken from the dining room mantle piece a few feet off.

"The next night was windy and dark, and the rain fell in torrents. Every door and window was carefully closed by Mr. Moon except the back passage door, and he placed all of his family in his chamber — in a room opening next to him. He sat in this open door with his gun in his hand about two hours, when suddenly the window around the corner from his was busted in with a loud crash. He rushed to the spot, but could not have seen or heard a man moving in three feet of him on account of the darkness, wind and rain, and the outcry of his family.

"The next day was clear, and Mr. Moon made arrangements for eight of his neighbors to surround the house about half an hour after the moon went down, which it did that night about 11 o'clock. If anyone entered the house, it was understood that Mrs. Moon, at one of the windows upstairs, and one of his sisters at the other, were to raise signal lights. Mr. Moon retired to his chamber in his usual way, so as to deceive the burglar, and locking the door, extinguishing the light, and rustling the bed clothes, sat with his gun in his hand. His son crept down, and peeping into the dining room, saw that a window had been hoisted. Upon going back and reporting, the ladies doubted the report. He went down a second time, satisfied himself fully, and coming back, it was determined he should shoot the rogue as he went out of the open window.

"In a few minutes he saw a man about 20 steps from the house and fired on him. The signal lights went up — the man fell flat and crept off. At the same instant that young Moon fired, a man ran between two of the guards, about 200 yards off, on the other side of the yard, and was fired at by one of them with a pistol. The other guard could not fire for fear of shooting one of his companions. The next morning tracks made by a coarse boot, or shoe, were found coursing down the hill from that point. That night the store room door was found locked, but upon going in they found a bag, with two compartments to it, left on the flour barrel, and about a double handful of coffee spilt in with the flour. A shawl, missing from the dining room, was dropped at the spot Mr. Moon's son shot at the man. It seemed to have been perforated with three shots. The entrance and exit of the thief had evidently been made through the back passage door by means of a false key, although the door was found locked.

"The next night, by moonlight, a man was observed from an upstairs window, crawling cautiously by a flower border from the front gate. It seemed to take him nearly half an hour to reach the house. He had in his hand a long rod, which was supposed to be a ramrod. Approaching near to the house he seemed to prefer exposing the front part of his person and crawled with his back to the ground. Upon reaching the foundation of the house, he reached around with his rod and smashed a side light in the face of Mr. Moon's brother who immediately fired through the door, under the mistaken impression that he was about to enter the house. He was observed to move off rapidly, but with his body kept very near to the ground.

"The next night there were 14 men around the house — two of them, however, made a gap by leaving their posts early in the night. Mr. Moon's brother was on duty about 60 yards directly in front. At a late hour he heard someone step boldly on the platform before the front door and unlock the door and go in. He supposed it was some member of the family. One of the ladies upstairs heard a noise below and awoke Mr. Moon's son. She afterwards saw a man go out of the front door and crouch by the side of the platform. Mr. Moon's son went to the window and fired down at the spot she indicated. The guards rushed to the house and found, as they supposed that night, a large blood stain on the steps, over which they exulted very much.

"The next night there were three men on guard about the house. One of them stationed at the yard fence, reports that he saw a man rise up from among a clump of bushes and walk off a short distance and take a position as if to watch the house. He fired at him with a shotgun. The man, he says, fell immediately. He fired again at the spot where he fell. There was no result from this shooting. Mr. Moon's impression is that the object shot at, fell just before the first shot, or it may have been a man with defensive armor on.

"The next night there were 10 or 12 men around the house. Two of them reported that they saw a man creeping on all fours along the garden fence — one of them shot at him with a pistol without result. At a later hour they saw the same object, and made chase, but he escaped among the grape vines and high weeds nearby...

"The next week Mr. Moon was compelled to attend court again. After an interval of several nights, which two of Mr. Moon's neighbors were inside watching the front door, someone came to it and struck forcibly on the door or sill, from appearances, seen through the side and top lights, most probably with the butt end of a musket. The first strike aroused the whole family. One of the men fired through the door at him. Mr. Moon's sister-in-law saw him, from an upper window, run around the corner of the house and pause to peep back to see if he was pursued. She fired at him twice from the window, which was open, with a little pocket pistol. He fell to the ground (at) the first fire, and moved off after some hesitation. The men rushed out in wrong directions to hunt for him.

"The next night Mr. Moon's sister-in-law saw from the closet window a tall man coming from the direction of the ice house door, which is about 25 yards from the house. She immediately reported to the three men then on guard in the house. The lady went back to the closet window — the man on the shed had been alarmed and had disappeared. In a few minutes, however, he appeared again, and Mr. Moon's sister-in-law again reported his presence to the guard at the back passage window. She went back immediately to the closet window to look out, she saw a man crouched close to the wall between the two windows — a scraping of matches was heard — a light flashed in at both windows, and the man on the shed rushing by the closet window on the roof of Mr. Moon's chamber, fired a pistol at her, barely missing her head, and singeing her eyebrows, and hair. The powder blackened the side of the house next to the window, and the ball struck and glanced off. The man ran over Mr. Moon's chamber, and jumping down on the other side, escaped.

"Since this last described night, several weeks have elapsed, but no night has passed in which the burglars did not demonstrate their presence, unmistakably in some way or other. Lights have been thrown in at Mr. Moon's windows every night, and frequently over the heads of from 10 to 40 armed men. Sometimes a small light, no larger than a quarter of a dollar is played upon the walls of his house — sometimes a much larger spot — than a broad or narrow streak — sometimes a flash, and sometimes a broad glare. A bright, radiating light has been seen on the shed at the chamber window, and at the office window.

"Nearly every night knocking or scraping sounds have been heard on the sides of the house. Stones have been thrown on top or against the house. Footsteps have been heard on the shed and chamber roofs — windows have been opened, or attempts made to open them, or something of the sort has occurred.

"One morning, a roll of cloth about six inches long, and an inch in diameter, saturated with kerosene oil, and burnt at one end, evidently a wick for a large light, was found on top of Mr. Moon's shed.

"We should add that in the last several weeks, the burglars have been seen five or six times and shot at twice. The demonstrations last night were violent and daring."

And so it went, night after night, the absurdities and terrors continuing with increasing variety and tenacity. One night some bricks and rocks that children had piled up, were lugged by the phantom to the roof of the house. On another occasion, a "figure" sailed china plates off the roof. A brick hurled at a nurse rocking an infant grazed the baby's hand.

Four weary neighbors, armed with muskets, sat up most of the night one evening, when toward dawn, with all quiet around the house, they laid down on the parlor carpet and went to sleep. As they did, someone, or something, tiptoed his (or her) way across them to a table in the far corner, removed a heavy music box and family Bible, took off a linen table cover, replaced the objects and dumped the cover by the door, which was slammed. Jerking awake at the sudden noise, the four men saw "lights playing on the door," but no sign of the prowling prankster.

Mrs. Butts, Moon's niece, adds more manifestations to the account, which occurred after the *Scottsville Register* article appeared. She told of the experiences of their uncle's butler at the house. "He said the bed of my uncle's beautiful young daughter used to rise up to the ceiling when the ghost came near. The butler said the ghost left the silver and other valuables untouched, but would always drink up the whiskey and brandy from my uncle's decanters; and that once he actually consumed a demijohn known to have been full at bedtime."

Mrs. Butts continued: "One night the butler returned late and left his groceries on the dining room table. The ghost emptied everything together, coffee, sugar, flour, meal, salt and soda, and then poured New Orleans molasses over the mixture. Gathering up the four corners of the cloth, he deposited his 'witches brew' and a family Bible on the roof, a favorite spot with him.

"It was from the shed roof that he fired a shot which singed the hair and eyebrow of my uncle's sister-in-law, Miss Kate Tompkins, and at other times hurled rocks and dinner plates through the air. Able to aim close without inflicting injury, the ghost was equally adept at escaping bullets.

"Although the ghost made many peculiar noises, the only complete sentence ever heard from him was: 'Surround the house, boys!' spoken when he and a number of his confederates rushed madly toward the house, masked and clad in overcoats and Confederate capes. They were off again before the watchers had time to shoot. The ghost apparently wore armor, for chains were heard to rattle at times, especially when he raced around the cottage, shaking windows and doors as he went. One night toward the last when he appeared on the front porch, and was shot at, the clank of chains was heard when he fell, but he was up and off before the watchers could reach the porch. They found a puddle of blood where he fell. Some claim this 'blood' was pokeberry juice; others say an examination at the University of Virginia showed it to be either ox blood or human blood.

"The butler said that late that night four men were ferried across the river at Scottsville, carrying something which looked like a litter with a covered body on it. He also said that thereafter one of his old colored friends had been 'so pestered by the ghost of the ghost' that he was forced to move back and forth across James River every six weeks to keep the ghost away, because 'it takes a ghost six weeks to cross water.'"

Finally in the summer of 1868, the ghost or person ceased his nocturnal activities at the Moon House. He left his "visiting card" in the form of a note tied to a long reed. Mrs. Butts said, "when my uncle opened the front door, pistol in hand, in response to some pebbles thrown against the door, the reed fell into the hall...It was written in pencil on cheap paper with a zig-zag scroll drawn around these words: 'Master Jack...I will not pester you any more...Jack Ghost.' "

There were no more manifestations at Moon House.

Was the Moon ghost a ghost? Or was he a persistent prankster seeking revenge for some real or perceived past slight? A case could be made either way. Whoever heard of a ghost writing a note...or even more implausibly, firing a gun? Still, if it wasn't a ghost, how would one explain the Houdini-like escapes which continued, sometimes nightly, for two years? Surely, in all that time, with all the hundreds of guards and witnesses who kept watch at the Moon house from 1866 to 1868 — somewhere, somehow, someone would have seen or run into someone mortal. And so it remains — to this day — one of the great unsolved mysteries of the Commonwealth of Virginia.

There is even a surreal footnote to this absorbing saga. In her talk to the Albemarle Historical Society, Frances Moon Butts said that she had received many letters from people all over the world regarding her uncle's famous ghost. One came from a woman in Pennsylvania who said that there was a spirit which appeared every 50 years at the "old Moon stronghold" in England.

Her curiosity piqued, Mrs. Butts did some extensive research, and traced the Virginia Moons back to Dunster Castle in the "Lorna Doone" country of England. "In 1933," she said, "I visited Dunster Castle. Built on a 'tor' or small mountain, as at Monticello, it overlooks the southern shores of the Bristol Channel and dates back to an original grant from William the Conqueror.

"A young man guided me through the old entrance gate, around a wall ten-feet thick at places, until finally we left the winding road to continue our ascent up a long flight of foot-worn stone steps through a darkly wooded section. I was wondering about the ghost but dared not ask, for fear of hearing a story 'built to please,' but when suddenly the guide turned and said: 'They call this Jacob's Ladder, because the ghost walks here.' I replied as innocently as possible: 'Do you have a ghost at Dunster Castle?' He answered: 'Yes, every 50 years. His last visit was in 1916, and the people who were living down in Dunster Town at the time say they used to hear him moan and scream up and down this path.'

"Nineteen sixteen was exactly 50 years from 1866!"

Stone Showers from Hell

(Augusta County)

(Author's note: Forget all the far-out fiction you may have seen in movies about poltergeists, leading to a vast array of Hollywood's most imaginative (and ugly) monsters, black pits of seemingly endless depths, extra-terrestrial type flights to another world and all that. Such fanciful nonsense has no semblance of relationship to the very real world of psychic phenomena. So cleanse your minds of any past remembrances of hideous, blood-covered creations snatching curly-haired little girls into the bottomless chasms of the beyond. It doesn't happen.

The German word poltergeist (from poltern — to knock) means "a noisy, usually mischievous ghost held to be responsible for unexplained noise (as rappings)." Poltergeists also long have been credited with the supernatural ability to move objects and throw things around on occasion. Some believe this is an angry type of ghost, and there have been cases where the manifestations have been abusive in nature. The notorious Bell Witch of Tennessee quickly comes to mind. In this well-documented case which occurred near Nashville in 1817, members of the Bell family were physically harassed by the spirit of a dead woman who believed she had been cheated by them. They were slapped, pinched, choked and haunted nearly out of their wits.

In "The Ghosts of Richmond and Nearby Environs," I wrote about an agitated poltergeist at the famous Dodson Tavern in Petersburg who "threw things around the house in fits of rage" which eventually attracted large crowds of witnesses. In this instance, books flew off shelves and across rooms, one hitting a workman in the chest. In "The Ghosts of Tidewater," I reported on the "return" of a mother from her watery grave to continually scold two teenage daughters who had disobeyed her. She allegedly even braided their pigtails together as they slept.

I also told of a house in Portsmouth where so many objects — from glass vases to tobacco cans — sailed from room to room, flung by unseen hands. It became so dangerous the occupants had to move out. And there was another occurrence in Virginia Beach where a teenage girl, upset because her parents had grounded her, walked by her mother who was preparing soup in the kitchen. Eye witnesses swore the soup came out of the pot and soaked the mother.

Were all these incredible instances the work of poltergeists? Some experts believe not. They contend the flying objects and unexplained loud noises were, in reality, caused by human beings rather than ghosts, generally adolescent youths. They cite a phenomena known as Recurrent Spontaneous Psycho-kinesis, or RSPK. Dr. William G. Roll is a nationally known and respected scientist who has studied RSPK for decades. He says, "our focus on such eruptions has been on the individual who is at the center of the disturbances," which he concludes are sparked by tension or certain neurological features.

Another expert, Dr. Helmut Schmidt, former director of the Institute for Parapsychology in Durham, North Carolina, has written extensively on the subject. He sees a consistent pattern in the agents Dr. Roll has examined. "Poltergeist agents usually have a low ability at verbal expression," he has written. "This is coupled with built-up hostility that is being repressed from consciousness. These agents seem to be persons who have a deep feeling of hostility." Dr. Schmidt believes that often the person involved, such as the daughter in the soup incident, tries to repress such feelings in the hidden regions of their unconscious, therefore they may be unaware they are actually causing an action. To this, Dr. Roll adds that the thrown objects seem to indicate that some "moving force field or vortex" is responsible.

It is an intriguing dilemma. Can the human mind affect the outside world by pure thought? Dr. Schmidt says this question has captured our imagination throughout the ages, and he summarizes that during the last half century, careful laboratory work "has shown that man can, to a certain degree, influence the outside world by pure thought." But he also points out that the "psychologically induced RSPK explanation cannot fully explain *all* the manifestations of the poltergeist. He warns, too, that while significant breakthroughs have been made in the psychological study of the poltergeist, the poltergeist has not yet been explained nor has its actual mechanisms been explored. He admits the door to the eventual understanding of such phenomena may have been opened, but there is still much to learn before the full mysteries of poltergeists can be understood.

And so the question remains today. Are the actions of poltergeists triggered by ghosts from the past or by those who were living at the time? Was the mother's pot of soup spilled by her angry teenage daughter or by the unseen hands of a spirit who was sympathetic to the daughter?

All of this is a prelude to the following account of one of the most bizarre and celebrated cases of poltergeist activity on record. In fact, one of the nation's leading experts of extra-sensory perception and supernatural manifestations has called the *McChesney Ghost* "one of the five authentic poltergeists in the U.S.," to which no natural explanation can be given. One of the first major accounts of this extraordinary phenomenon was given in the "Annals of Augusta County, Virginia from 1726 to 1871" by Joseph Waddell, a member of the Virginia Historical Society. While this activity occurred over a two year period beginning in 1825, it is still talked about in the area and has been passed down from generation to generation by the descendants of Dr. John McChesney and Thomas Steel, many of whom still live in the Staunton area west of Charlottesville.

Even the conservative Virginia Historic Landmarks Commission, in its usually stilted architectural survey form outlining the McChesney house noted, "This is the house known locally as the Haunted House. Before the War Between the States, it was the scene of tongs dancing on the hearth, fire and brimstone raining down, etc."

The following account was taken from many sources, including the recollections of William Steele, son of Thomas, who in 1889 was one of the last surviving witnesses of what had happened. It was at that time, at age 70, that he told of what he had witnessed in the 1820s when he was a child of six. In the 1950s, Margaret McChesney was the last living link between the time of the occurrences and the present. She then was in her nineties, and had heard the story first-hand both from her aunt, Amanda, and from Dr. McChesney himself, her grandfather. Despite her advanced age, she maintained an exceptionally keen and alert mind, and she had said that someday the "last of the McChesneys" would tell the entire story that had never been known outside the family. For it was said that only the family knew the whole story, and it was a subject upon which they maintained an unbroken silence for well over a century. This is so, because even Waddell's well researched report did not include some of the strangest — and saddest — details.

When her sister died, Margaret became the last of the McChesneys to know the complete story, and in 1954, when she was 92, she dictated it to her niece, Evelyn Jones Yarbrough. As one newspaper reporter later wrote, "Why would a woman on her death bed record such a tale? She had nothing to gain, surely, and neither did the distinguished family. There is no other explanation except it is the truth."

This is the story.)

r. McChesney has been described as an "intelligent physician" who lived on his farm in a house called Greenwood about a mile north of the village of Newport in Augusta County just off the main road leading from Staunton to Lexington. He was, "a respected physician, a stern but just man, and a staunch Presbyterian." He lived a busy, well-ordered life, and was accustomed to having his word and his wishes obeyed without question. His wife was a sister of Thomas Steele (William's father) who lived about a mile away. Mrs. Mary Steele, widow of Captain William Steele and mother of Thomas and Mrs. McChesney, lived in Rockbridge, two miles west of Midway.

Then, Dr. McChesney's family consisted of his wife and four young children. A prosperous man, he owned a number of slaves. Among them was a girl named Maria who was, at the time, around 12 years old. And it began with Maria — the first episode that was to lead to total disruption of the peaceful, orderly life at Greenwood.

It was, as Margaret McChesney recounted, "a warm spring afternoon. In the kitchen the servants were busy with preparations for the evening meal. Mrs. McChesney was seated in a chair in the parlor rocking her infant son, James, when the quiet was pierced by loud screams from the yard. Almost immediately, Maria burst into the room obviously terrified and screaming that an old woman with her 'head tied up' had beaten and chased her. Mrs. McChesney, trying to soothe both Maria and James, could see that there were welts and bruises on the girl, but could make no sense out of what Maria was saying about the old woman. Finally she lost patience and ordered Maria out of the room.

"Soon Mrs. McChesney succeeded in quieting James and rocking him to sleep. Then she heard the tinkle of glasses in the nearby dining room. A decanter of wine and some wine glasses stayed on the tray on the sideboard and the house slaves were known to get into the wine whenever an opportunity presented itself. So, thinking to catch the culprit, Mrs. McChesney, still holding the baby, crept softly to the dining room door. The room was empty, but the tray with the decanter and bottles intact had been pushed so far to the edge of the sideboard that only the rim rested against the board. Yet it was perfectly level...simply hanging there in mid-air defying every natural law.

"Dumbfounded, Mrs. McChesney returned the tray to its proper place and returned to the parlor. Promptly, the tinkle of wine glasses could be heard in the dining room, and when she went back, the tray again was suspended in the air with its rim barely touching the sideboard.

"The months of misery had begun.

"Now began a steady barrage of clods of mud and rocks hurled through the house and in the yard. Sometimes they came from *inside the house*, sometimes from the outside, yet no one could determine where they came from and they followed no directional pattern. Often, the rocks were hot and actually singed the spots where they fell, and they left great dents in the furniture.

"Maria was the special target for abuse. Frequently, the girl would go into convulsive screaming fits crying that she was being beaten. The sounds of heavy slaps and blows could be heard distinctly above her cries, and, before the eyes of the members of the family, great welts would appear on her body."

While the children found some of these "peculiarities" amusing and exciting, and Mrs. McChesney was "extremely perturbed," Dr. McChesney pronounced the whole affair "utter nonsense" and refused to discuss it or allow anyone to mention it to him.

Margaret McChesney continued with her remembrances: "Before events got really serious, the children and some cousins decided it would be a great idea to have a table seance and try to contact whatever it was that kept throwing things around the house. Into this gleeful gathering came the doctor, and he was outraged to find members of his family solemnly trying to establish contact with a spook. In terms so stern that his daughter Amanda never forgot them, he berated them for their sinful ways and ordered that there never again be any talk of ghosts in his home. For his decisive stand, he was promptly showered with clods and mud pelted him from every direction. Incredibly, he chose to ignore this!"

In succeeding weeks, the volleys of stones continued, thundering down on the roof of the house in broad daylight as well as at night. One writer said, "sometimes they came thickly, like a barrage of gunfire, sometimes only one at a time, and hours apart. It is said the stones averaged "the size of a man's fist," and some of them were "too large to be thrown by a person of ordinary strength." Not once, during any of the incidents, was anyone seen hurling stones at the house.

Word of the strange and ominous events at Greenwood started to seep through the countryside, and curiosity seekers began arriving. This, said Margaret McChesney, "was a bitter blow to Dr. McChesney and soon he abandoned all attempts to be courteous and drove strangers away the minute he set eyes on them. One day a man arrived at the front door which, by chance, was opened by the doctor. The stranger announced that he had heard from someone in Richmond of the occurrences at Greenwood so he had come to stay awhile and make an investigation of the phenomena. Dr. McChesney wrathfully retorted that he would be glad to have him stay provided the man would tell him the name of the damn fool in Richmond who had the idea Greenwood was a hotel." (The family thought this incident was particularly humorous, because the doctor never swore in their presence.)

And still they came! Even in that day of sluggish travel and poor communications, the word continued to spread throughout an ever-expanding area. Literally hundreds of people from miles around travelled to the farm to see the "devil's handiwork" for themselves. Some were rewarded, some were not, because the stones did not fall every day. Along with the curious came the crackpots offering all kinds of unsought and unheeded advice. Even the doctor's vigilance and righteous indignation failed to keep them away.

There is one report that a group of church elders from one of the nearby towns ventured to the McChesney farm. They were cordially received, but when the subject of the stones was brought up "a shadow crossed the doctor's face." The men were invited to dinner, and according to the legend, as one of them reached for a biscuit, a sharp black stone flew from a corner of the ceiling across the room and sliced the biscuit in half!

McChesney Farm

It was during this period that a frightened Mrs. McChesney pleaded with her husband to move, but he adamantly refused, contending that "no intelligent person could believe for a minute that his home had been invaded by ghosts." Stubbornly, he stuck to the firm assumption that as long as he refused to admit anything was wrong, everything was bound to be all right.

Margaret McChesney continued: "Mrs. McChesney was increasingly aware that the bulk of the disturbances seemed to center around Maria, the young slave girl. The beatings were more frequent, more severe. During one of them, Maria screamed that 'the old woman with her head tied up' was demanding that Maria give her a white lacy shawl belonging to Mrs. McChesney. Despite her anxiety, Mrs. McChesney firmly refused to give the shawl to a malicious unseen character who was making their lives so miserable.

"On another occasion, Maria, in a whining petulant mood, was hanging around the kitchen getting in everybody's way and complaining that she was hungry. Finally, she became such a nuisance that the cook shoved her out the door. While the girl stood crying on the back porch, she was fiercely pelted with large floppy objects that appeared to be soggy oversized pancakes. Members of the family, hastily summoned by the servants, saw and handled these objects.

"During one of the flying rock episodes, a large rock was thrown into a pitcher. The pitcher had a broad rounded base and a long narrow neck — the neck impossibly small for a rock of that size to pass through without shattering it. But the rock was there — almost covering the bottom of the pitcher — and there it stayed for many, many years."

Now the harassment took a sinister turn. The baby James began to have strange and frightening seizures. Lying in his crib one day, he suddenly went into a screaming fit, and what appeared to be tiny bloody pinpricks spread rapidly across his body." Mrs. McChesney demanded that something be done, and the doctor reluctantly agreed to send Maria away — to the home of his brother-in-law.

"Brother-in-law and his family, in total ignorance of the proposed visit from Maria, were seated on the lawn entertaining guests when from inside the house, came the clatter of horses hooves — indeed, it sounded like a stampede. Rushing into the house, they found that every stick of furniture and all the knick-knacks in the parlor had been piled in the middle of the floor. While they stared in disbelief, clods and rocks began to sail through the room and crash into the furniture. Panic-stricken, they rushed outside and saw Maria approaching the house. She was immediately sent back to Greenwood!

"Following this, the beatings of Maria were intensified...night and day the rocks and clods of mud sailed through the house and yard...and James' seizures grew more frequent and more terrifying. One day Mrs. McChesney, rocking her son, was badly shaken when a chair, which was placed sedately against the wall, 'walked' across the room and came to rest beside her. Hastily, she moved to the other side of the room, and when the chair followed her, she became hysterical and ran screaming from the house, still clutching her child.

"It seems incredible that Dr. McChesney still could not bring himself to acknowledge that he and his family were up against something that defied reason or explanation. To him the very question of a ghost was both a sin and a disgrace, and he had no intention of giving in. Convinced that he, a physician, could cure the baby of whatever was afflicting him, he refused to leave Greenwood or seek outside help.

"While the doctor tried with all his medical skill and knowledge to cure his son, the seizures increased and with each one James grew weaker. And finally he died in the convulsive throes of a screaming fit while his tiny body flamed with the bloody pinpricks.

"Only then did the stunned, grieving doctor face the harsh fact that he had so long tried to ignore: that some terrible and evil force had been unleashed in their lives.

"The day of the baby's funeral, after the family had returned from the cemetery, Amanda and some cousins were standing on the front porch near the open door. From inside the house came the by now all-too-familiar thuds of rocks and clods being hurled against the furniture. In a reckless frenzy of rage and grief, Amanda stepped through the doorway and screamed, 'Consarn ye! Why don't you pick on somebody old enough to fight back?' Immediately, from inside the house, came a large rock which struck her in the forehead cutting a long deep gash. The injury was so severe that she carried the scar for the rest of her life. Although many people were hit by mud and rocks, Amanda was the only person injured by one of the flying rocks."

Indignant, Thomas Steele cursed the "invisible agent" for taking its spite on a woman and not him. He then sat defiantly in the front door, and instantly was "pelted with clods of sod and earth, coming from the inside of the house." He sat until he was almost covered with "missiles piled around him, moving only after his mother screamed that "the thing" would kill him.

Fearing for the safety of his family, Dr. McChesney moved his children to their grandmother's house near Midway. Maria went, too. Soon, the disturbances began in this house, with some new variations. Stones flew about and furniture in the kitchen "moved of its own accord." One day a large kitchen bench "pranced over the floor like a horse." The children thought this was funny, and one of them said he was going to ride the bucking bronco, but he became so alarmed that he fainted. Nor were the manifestations limited to the house itself. Farm hands said that food and tools that were taken by them to the fields, "disappeared." They turned up in the house.

Aunt Lucy Anderson, an old slave who lived and worked at the farm during this time was quoted as saying she had gone into the wine closet under the stairway in the hall one day and saw the bottles "turn upside down and start dancing with nobody near them." She also told of benches that "walked by themselves" on the porch.

At Mrs. Steele's house, Maria complained of being beaten by unseen hands. Mrs. Steele took the girl between her knees, drew her skirts up and struck all around Maria with a stick "as if to beat off an invisible foe." Maria then cried out that she was being pricked with pins and slapped. William Steele said the slaps could be distinctly heard, but "no one could see the vindictive enemy." Finally, Maria fell in exhaustion to the floor, "apparently dead." She was soon revived, but she continued to be punished by her ghostly tormenter.

All of this — the death of her infant son, the stoning of Amanda, and the continuing blitz of clods and rocks and other inexplicable occurrences — was too much for Mrs. McChesney. She told the doctor if he wouldn't move she would leave without him. As a last resort, Dr. McChesney sold Maria and her parents, sending them away forever. From that day on, the disturbances stopped and never reoccurred. The doctor and his family subsequently moved to Staunton, and he refused, for the rest of his life, to discuss the poltergeist activities.

The whole affair is considered psychically important for a couple of reasons. One, the family was known as one of respectability and prominence, and the McChesneys were much embarrassed by the occurrences and were reluctant to talk about them. Secondly, the incidents were eye witnessed by scores of credible people over an extended period of time.

Was the phenomenon caused by the young girl herself? Was she unhappy in her surroundings, and venting her wrath by means of psycho-kinesis? Or were she and the McChesney and Steele families being taunted by a vicious spirit who used Maria as the medium for the malicious actions, avenging some past offense? Or could there be yet a third explanation? William Steele said that there was an "old Negro woman who lived in the neighborhood and 'walked with a stick and chewed tobacco.' " William apparently feared the woman because he said that in his boyhood he always was careful "to give her the road when they met." Maria, who had a reputation for having "an evil tongue," was said to have sassed the woman and in return was threatened with punishment. William added that the old woman was reputed to be a witch. Had she cast a spell on Maria?

And, finally, there is this footnote. More than half a century ago Margaret F. Wade wrote a prize-winning story about the McChesney ghost. She claimed the phenomena actually started at the near-simultaneous births of Maria and Aunt Liza in the slave quarters and Ellen McChesney in the "big house." She wrote: "A gust of wind shattered a window and swept out the lights in the farmhouse near Brownsburgh, and large rocks fell at Dr. John McChesney's feet, while in the slaves' quarters, the wind was so strong it turned Aunt Liza's bed completely around."

The deep questions involved here likely will never be satisfactorily answered. But from witnesses who said they saw the stones fall, and from the first-hand testimony of William Steele, there is little doubt that something very strange occurred in Augusta County, Virginia, in 1825. They still talk about it today.

When Elizabeth Sterrett wrote about the phenomena, telling what she had been told by the 92-year-old Margaret McChesney, she said to a newspaper interviewer, "Perhaps this article and the work of the Augusta County Historical Society might not only free the McChesney name from ridicule, but once and for all the truth can conquer the legend of the McChesney ghost.

"It was real and it was evil and no one will ever know exactly what it was."

Maria at the McChesney Farm

CHAPTER 46

The Extraordinary
Rocking Cradle

(Lynchburg)

(Author's note: From the beginnings of my research for this book, every time I had talked about the Lynchburg area, people would mention the "Rocking Cradle House." They would say that I had to include a story on this, because it was the most famous haunted house in the city. Everyone, it seemed, had heard about the house, but seemingly no one could provide any details on where it was, or when the phenomena occurred.

Finally, in a book called "The Oldest Living Resident of Lynchburg - 1858," by Mrs. Margaret Cabell, there was a specific reference to the rocking cradle, but even here the facts were obscure. The incident was said to have happened in 1839, but Mrs. Cabell was so sure that everyone had heard about it by then that she failed to discuss the particulars.

Eventually, the trail led to the Lynchburg Public Library, where there were a couple of 40-year-old newspaper clippings that mentioned the cradle that rocked by itself. Then, there was a chapter in Margaret DuPont Lee's 1930 book, "Virginia Ghosts," entitled "Telekinesis in Lynchburg." It covered a plethora of psychic manifestations which took place at a house "at the corner of Jackson and Eleventh Streets in Lynchburg." Could this be the house? One of the newspaper articles, published in 1951, said the house was located at 1104 Jackson Street.

Next, I went upstairs over the Lynchburg Library to the Jones Memorial Library, one of the best sources of genealogical material in Virginia. After checking on a number of stories in Amherst

County, I casually mentioned to the librarian if he had heard of the rocking cradle house and did he have any information on it. He smiled and said as a matter of fact, he did. And then he brought me a copy of Works Progress Administration (WPA) of Virginia Historical Inventory Research Report. It was part of a depression-era project sponsored by the Virginia Conservation Commission under the direction of its Division of History.

The report was titled, simply, "The Poston Home." It had been written June 2, 1937, by Susan R. Beardsworth. As I turned the pages of the report, I had to restrain myself from getting up and shouting "Eureka!" There it was! On page two, under the heading, "Historical Significance," were the magic words I had been searching for: "This house," wrote Susan Beardsworth, "is of interest chiefly because of the legends and ghost stories connected with it, the best known of which occurred in the spring of 1839. The house is generally known as 'the house where the cradle rocked.' ")

Lynchburg's "Rocking Cradle" House

he Poston House is named for W. C. Poston who bought the property in 1902. It is not known exactly when the house was built. Says Ms. Beardsworth: "The property passed through so many hands in the early days that it is impossible to determine who built it, but a careful study of all records on this and surrounding property and a comparison of dates and amounts involved in the sales, would strongly indicate it having been built about 1819, by Edmund B. Norvell, or by Thomas Wyatt, before 1813.

"This story and a half brick house originally faced on the Salem Turnpike, which is now 12th Street, and was built in three sections," the report read. "The main one consisted of two rooms with a closed center stairway on the first floor, and two rooms and hall on the second floor. On either corner of the back yard were the other two sections, one a two room office, the other a two room kitchen, all built of brick. The house has been remodelled or rebuilt twice; in 1875, the office was torn down and incorporated in the main structure, and in 1904, the kitchen was also built into the house, forming a wing, so now there are eight rooms and two halls.

"It is all very plain, simple and quaint looking, the only one of its kind left standing in the city."

Ms. Lee, in her book, says the house at the corner of Jackson and Eleventh Streets was built about 1840 by a Colonel James Maurice Langhorne, which is in dispute with Ms. Beardsworth's account. Yet a cradle that rocked on its own is also mentioned as one of the supernatural events that took place at the house. Is it the same house, or were there two different houses involved?

The residence Ms. Lee discusses was "dreadfully haunted," according to William Nelson Wellford, Colonel Langhorne's grandson. "The ghosts were at work as far back as I can remember," he wrote Ms. Lee. Wellford's sister, Mrs. John Wallace added: "The remarkable phenomena were so numerous and of such frequency she could by no means recollect them all. She did remember her mother telling her that she had seen servants in the house drop on their knees and exclaim: "Oh God! A ghost brushed by me."

Mrs. Wallace's mother also said that on "numerous occasions" after the servants finished their chores in the kitchen, late in the afternoon, and everything was cleaned up and secured, she would hear all sorts of noises coming from the area. She said it sounded like a group of servants preparing for a great banquet. There were hurried footsteps back and forth across the floor; the opening and shutting of doors, and the rattling of china and silver among other things. Subsequent investigations would reveal pots and pans strewn all about, pantry and kitchen range doors open, flour and sugar spilled, and in general, "everything in confusion." Never, did Mrs. Wallace's mother, or anyone else in the house, ever find a rational explanation for such activities.

At other times, the Wallaces found beds unsheeted, linen and bedclothes piled in a bundle in the center of the floor, and the rooms in a "state of utter confusion." Mrs. Wallace's mother also had seen keys in an old leather basket kept on the side of the table, jump up and down "as if someone was shaking the basket violently." Mrs. Wallace herself saw "the walls shake up and down, and felt it, too." When two young nephews came to witness the strange goings on, they became so frightened by the manifestations, including "unseen hands touching them," that they abruptly left. Welford added that the phenomena became so frequent and so frightening, that no one would buy or rent the house for a long time.

The major account of the rocking cradle house, however, came from testimony given by Trueheart Poston to Ms. Beardsworth. He was the son of the man who bought the house in 1902, and he was an architect. Here is what Poston had to say: "The following are

The Rocking Cradle

some legends and stories connected with the house at 1104 Jackson Street...Mr. Asbury Christian in his book, 'Lynchburg and Its People,' gives the account of the rocking cradle...The house at that time (1839) was occupied by a Rev. Smith, who was a cousin of Bishop Early. I do not know whether this cradle belonged to the Smiths or was loaned them by the Earlys, but the tale has it that the Rev. Smith, upon returning home from his duties, found the Negro nanny in a state of hysteria and was told that the cradle had been rocking with the baby in it for some hours and would not stop.

"Upon hearing this, Rev. Smith went into the room and found that the cradle was indeed rocking. Being a very religious man, he commanded the cradle to stop rocking in the name of Beelzebub, whereupon the cradle immediately stopped. Rev. Smith then suggested that Beelzebub start rocking the cradle again, whereupon he apparently did so. This constant rocking under orders continued for a period of some days, during which, as the rumors spread, most of the town folk dropped by and witnessed this sight for themselves. (One "contemporary account" of the event states that "hundreds closed their places of business" and went to see the rocking cradle.) Apparently, after just so long, the cradle ceased rocking and would rock only by human efforts from then on.

"The cradle itself is a very beautiful Sheraton mahogany high poster affair with turned spindle sides and a field bed canopy. It gives the effect of being a miniature Sheraton field bed on rockers.

"There is another tale," Poston continued, "which apparently had its origin with Mr. Walter Additon, who was, up to the time of his death, about 10 years ago, editor of the *Lynchburg News*. The house was in our possession at the time, and Mr. and Mrs. Additon were staying with us. They occupied a downstairs bedroom at the foot of the steps. Mr. Additon would generally return home at two or three o'clock in the morning after checking over his editorial for the morning paper. Upon one of these occasions, he opened the door and saw, on the landing, an old lady, apparently about 80 years old, dressed in a rather old fashioned costume and it being very late and he imagining she was probably deaf, merely nodded and went into his room, naturally assuming that she was some relative of ours.

"The next morning at breakfast when no such lady appeared, Mr. Additon asked my mother if aunt was not well. Of course, there was no such person visiting us at the time and the rumor has gotten around that the old lady is a constant and cheerful ghost occupant of the house. I cannot recall any person having seen her since that date, although many visitors report that they are sure they have heard her moving her feet and heard the cushions in chairs sink as though she were sitting and noticed such other sounds as might be made by such a lady.

"There is also the story connected with a major in the Confederate Army who at one time lived here...What with material losses caused by the war and the general tendency which some men have towards alcohol, the major eventually got to the delirium tremens stage in his drinking and upon such occasions was locked in the dining room by his family.

"During his periods of intoxication, it was his habit to beat his way out with a poker or any handy object. The woodwork in this room shows the results of his attempts at freedom in a very obvious manner. All woodwork around various windows and doors shows evidence of where the major had inserted his poker to pry loose the locks and also evidence of where, apparently at the height of his rages, he took great pleasure in merely pounding the woodwork with his poker.

"Various rumors have arisen in connection with this episode, chiefly concerning the fact that at midnight the doors from this room would all open whether locked or not. When we bought the place in 1902, the original batten doors were still in place, though sadly chewed by the major's poker. Not believing the tale of the opening doors, my parents spent their first night in the first floor bedroom, only to be awakened promptly at 12 o'clock by the creaking of two doors, which they had securely latched before retiring. It appears that at slightly irregular intervals, these same two doors would invariably unlatch themselves and open in a very slow and creaking fashion, as though the major had finally won his freedom.

"I cannot recall any other tales concerning the house," Poston concluded, "except a very vague rumor of a body which drops out of an upstairs dormer. I have not been able to find out whether there is a qualified event for this tale, but do know that for a long time during my boyhood, I was constantly terrified by a sound such as a body dropping out of the windows."

A Devilish Force in Botetourt County

When is a poltergeist not a poltergeist? When an adolescent child is around. Or so say many psychic experts. Poltergeists have been described as "noisy ghosts"; ones responsible for moving or throwing objects about including even heavy furniture. But Dr. William Roll, a psycho-kinetic specialist, claims most if not all of what is often believed to be poltergeist activity is, in fact, caused by the release of emotional energy. Generally, at the center of this is a person, usually, but not always an adolescent, whose pent-up frustrations explode in a burst of some form of supernatural energy that can move inanimate objects. This mysterious force is so powerful it can cause objects to move or fly about a room.

"It's very unlikely that these occurrences involved any kind of ghosts or spirits," Roll once said in a national newspaper interview. "It's a release of psychological or neurological tension in the personality of the brain." He added his beliefs stem from more than 100 cases of alleged poltergeist activity that he has investigated, dating back to the 1600s. Another expert, George Owen, professor of bio-statistics at the University of Toronto, says, "Poltergeist activity is an expression of emotional disturbance in a human being. It seems to be a release of (such) energy that causes objects to move about."

(Author's note: I would tend to agree, at least to the extent that a number of cases I have researched, including "Stone Showers from Hell," included in this book, have strongly indicated that a teen or pre-teen might well be involved. Yet the final answer on the origins of such phenomena is still to be found. No one really knows for sure. If a child is responsible for moving objects about, how would one explain the confounding circumstances surrounding an innocent Baptist minister in the tiny town of Buchanan in Botetourt County (about 20 miles from Lexington) in the 1870s? In this instance there were children around, but they were purposely isolated from the scenes of activity. Here is what happened:)

The disturbances began innocently enough in November 1870 in the home of Mr. G. C. Thrasher. The first indication was the finding of a sack of corn, which had been removed from a padlocked bin and poured on the floor about 20 yards away. It appeared to be only a childish prank and nothing more was thought of it.

But soon after, the manifestations began to pick up in intensity. Windows barred on the inside were opened unaccountably; knockings were heard; doors were locked and unlocked; and furniture was moved around. More scary, utensils were hurled across the kitchen, from counter to counter and wall to wall, some slamming with considerable force.

At first, suspicions were cast upon Thrasher's three boys, all under the age of 12, and upon a young girl servant. But these were lifted in time, because some of the now-frightening phenomena occurred when they were out of the room or out of the house altogether. Also, it became clear that some of the acts were beyond their physical strength.

As in the case of the famous Scottsville Ghost, Thrasher brought in friends and others (the activities were causing considerable curiosity) to stand guard during the night in an effort to determine the cause. One evening when several young men were present, a knocking at the door became "very violent and frequent." It was written that "they resorted to every effort to detect the cause, but in vain." Another person in the house said he "saw chips fly about the house in a way that was utterly inexplicable."

Describing the seriousness of the incidents, Thrasher wrote the following letter which was published in the Lexington Gazette: "For five days during the past week the manifestations were frequent, varied and violent. Brickbats, old bones, billets of wood, ears of corn, stones, etc., were thrown about the house in the most unaccountable manner and again and again everything would be turned topsy-turvy in the parlour and the chambers without their being able to detect the agent.

"One day, two young ladies being at the house, were determined to use every effort to ferret out the mystery. Accordingly, they arranged the parlour, locked all the doors, sent Anna Pring (the servant girl) to the kitchen with my little boy to watch, and carried all the keys to my room. They waited by a few minutes, and returned to find that the doors had been opened, the books from the center table scattered over the floor, the lamps from the mantlepiece put on the ground, and things disarranged generally; and, to increase the mystery, they found a strange key that would neither unlock nor lock any door in the house, sticking in the keyhole of the parlour door.

"One day I left the dining room, carefully locked the door, and went upstairs to my wife's chamber. Just as I was about to enter, I heard a noise downstairs and returned immediately, not having been absent from the room more than three minutes. I found the door open, the furniture disarranged, and all the dishes from the cabinet distributed over the ground."

The Gazette also reported that a visitor to the house was dreadfully shaken when the coverlet of his bed was pulled violently in the middle of the night, waking him instantly. There was no one else in the room.

Unable to cope with whatever devilish force was at work, Thrasher abruptly moved his family to Tennessee. Upon leaving, he noted: "The manifestations continued at my house in Virginia for four months, and only ceased about one week before I moved. I have not been able to make any discovery as to the cause; it is still wrapped in profound mystery!" Nor was any motive for the unusual behavior, which created hysteria in the town of Buchanan, ever brought to light.

But those who served as witnesses during this time were convinced the children in this case had nothing to do with the outbreaks. How would the experts explain this one?

A Dreadful Dream
of Doom

(Buckingham County)

 here is an incredibly vivid psychic vision which occurred in dream form to a farmer in rural Buckingham County, Virginia, early this century. It resulted in a bizarre, precedent-setting episode that ranks among the classic experiences of inexplicable phenomena. As has often been said, truth is stranger than fiction.

In the year 1909, two elderly bachelor brothers — T. C. and W. J. Stuart — lived in a simple log cabin in the woods in Buckingham County. They were a reclusive pair and were rarely seen. They only walked into town occasionally to replenish their supplies. Little was known of them. Under such circumstances, a rumor about the Stuart brothers was fostered and embellished over the years. It was said that they were filthy rich and that there was a hidden treasure somewhere in their cabin or buried in the nearby grounds. In fact, just the opposite was true. They were dirt poor, but with no one to refute the spreading stories, they continued to grow.

Against such a backdrop, on the night of April 17, 1909, the Stuarts' nearest neighbor, a farmer, had an extraordinary dream. It was totally unlike any other dream he had ever had. What he dreamed was not only crystal clear, but he also remembered every minute detail of it.

In his dream, the farmer saw three men sneaking up the road towards the cabin — two black men and one white man. They appeared as plain as day. It seemed obvious that they were headed towards the brothers' log cabin, and there also was no doubt that they were up to no good. The farmer followed them from a distance in his dream, but lost sight of them at a turn in the road. He did not see them enter the cabin.

The time sequence of the dream now skipped ahead, and the farmer's next vision was inside the cabin. There, to his horror, he saw the two brothers lying dead on the floor. One lay near the fireplace. One of his hands pointed towards a hole in the floor, and in the hole was a tin box. Papers were scattered about the crude room. The other Stuart was slumped in a corner with his head crushed.

At this point, the farmer awakened. The dream had been so real he was badly shaken. He told his wife about it and asked if she had seen the brothers pass by their house recently. She said she hadn't seen them for several days. Unable to return to sleep, he got up at daybreak and called the sheriff, describing his dream in explicit detail. Knowing the farmer to be a serious man not taken to fancy, the sheriff and others came out, and with the farmer proceeded to check on the Stuarts.

As they got to the turn in the road where the farmer lost sight of the three men in his dream, they found an empty tin box with papers strewn about. They went on to the cabin and were shocked to see that it had been set afire and was still burning. In the court records on the case, in the Virginia Review, the following gruesome account was published: "When the neighbors appeared on the scene they found in the still burning building the partially consumed trunks of two human bodies which were identified with reasonable certainty as the remains of the Stuart brothers.

"The smaller of the two skeletons, answering in size to that of W. J. Stuart, was lying near the fireplace; and a physician who examined fragments of the skull discovered a number of lead pellets embedded in the inside of the parietal bone taken from the left side of the skull, which he identified as shot. The witness also testified that the passage of those shot from one side of a human skull to the other would cause instant death. The remains of the other brother were found in a corner of the room with the head missing and the neck smooth as though the head had been severed from the body."

The court report added that, "The Stuarts were reputed to have had money, and it was generally believed throughout the county that they were murdered and robbed and their home burned to conceal the crime."

The farmer's description of the alleged assailants he had seen in his dream was so precise that it led, according to Margaret DuPont Lee, who wrote about the case in her 1930 book, "Virginia Ghosts" — to the subsequent arrest of three men. That the farmer had seen the actual perpetrators of the crime in his vision seemed to be substantiated when a 17-year-old black boy came forward and declared he had witnessed the murders.

Ms. Lee wrote, "To date this was the only record of a dream being admitted as evidence in a trial for murder."

* * * * *

There were, however, still other ironic turns to the ending of this remarkable story. In the summer of 1909, a grand jury of the Circuit Court of Buckingham County returned a joint indictment against the three parties, charging them with the murder of the Stuarts. Each of the defendants elected to be tried separately. The jury failed to agree in the white man's case, but they found one of the black men guilty of murder in the first degree. The judge, however, set aside the verdict as contrary to the law and evidence. After a searching review of the testimony of the alleged eye-witnesses (a second man had come forth after the 17-year-old boy), the judge characterized their statements as being "so incredible as to challenge human belief."

At this juncture, emotions in the county arose to a fever pitch. One local publication summed up the feeling of many: "We trust that the people of Buckingham will demand the punishment of red-handed fire-brands and bloody criminals and refuse to let money, spent in hiring tricksters, unlock all our jail doors and turn loose all our dangerous men." Lawyers for the accused men pleaded for a change of venue, but were denied.

Meanwhile, the second charged black man was picked up at his house one night by a deputy sheriff and his son, even though they showed no warrant. As they headed toward town, according to a court review of the case, "He was set upon by a mob of armed men, who took him from the custody of the deputy sheriff, and, putting a rope around his neck, repeatedly drew him up and over a limb of a tree for the purpose of extorting a confession. Facing what must have appeared to him immediate death at the hands of these lawless people, he stoutly proclaimed his innocence." The mob then released him and the deputy sheriff, who allegedly had been in on this cruel action, let him go.

A short time after this, deputy sheriff Eddie Carter — it is not documented whether he was the same deputy who had been in on the harassment of one of the accused men — was murdered one night while on his way home near Sper's Mountain. His body was left lying in the road. From then on, for decades afterwards, those who passed this spot in the road at night reported seeing a strange light about the size of a grave. They said it shined until one got close to it, and then it would go out, only to reappear when one moved away from it. This peculiar phenomenon lasted for at least 40 years of more and was said to have been witnessed by many.

Eventually, the Court of Appeals ruled that the three men had not been given a fair trial, and they were freed. Or were they? Two of the accused murderers died "soon" afterwards, allegedly of tuberculosis. The third man went to work in a West Virginia coal mine, and was "burned alive" in an underground fire.

Was it fate or coincidence? Possibly. But many Buckingham County oldtimers are convinced the Stuart brothers somehow reached out from beyond their graves to avenge their cruel deaths.

CHAPTER 49

Roanoke's Woman in Black

She appeared out of nowhere. One witness "victim" described the unnerving experience like this: "It was as if she had arisen out of the earth." Her voice sounded real. Her touch felt real. She appeared to be real, although quite a few of the gentlemen involved had great difficulty looking her in the eye. A peripheral glance was the best some of them could manage in their fright. She never caused any physical harm, or at least none was reported. It seemed obvious at the time that for every man who summoned up enough courage to report her presence, there were probably three or four others who, for a variety of reasons, kept the mysterious meetings quiet.

Those who did look at her, and did talk, were unanimous in at least one phase of her description: she was beautiful. Breathtakingly beautiful! One man said she was tall and handsome, with "dancing eyes." Another said she was about five feet nine or ten, dressed entirely in black, "with something like a black turban on her head." It was, he added, fixed in such a manner so that it was drawn around her face just below her eyes, forming a perfect mask. She also wore a long black Ragian cloak. "Her eyes," the man said, "were large and her brows and lashes heavy, and if her forehead and eyes are proper index of that portion of her face concealed, she was very beautiful."

And then, in a flash, she would be gone. She would disappear, vanish, evaporate, leaving the men she escorted stunned and speechless.

This was the legendary "Woman in Black," who, for a brief

The Woman in Black

period in March 1902, struck terror into the hearts of the citizenry of Roanoke. Said the *Roanoke Times*: "Her name was on every lip; strong men trembled when her name was spoke; children cried and clung to their mothers' dresses; terror reigned supreme!"

Who was this woman of dark intrigue? And what was her mission? Why was she so feared? As the newspaper pointed out, "Just why the 'Woman in Black' should be so terrible, has never been known. She made no attack on anyone. It was probably due to the unexpected appearance in places unthought of, and at hours when the last person of the city is expected about should be a woman."

She apparently had gone north from the city of Bristol, which, the *Times* reported: "is just recovering from the effects of the scare produced amongst the citizens of the town by what was known as the 'Woman in Black.' Hardly a day passed for weeks that the press of the town failed to have a long account of the antics and performance of the 'Woman in Black' on the night before." On March 18, 1902, the *Times* said, "for the last 10 days she has been unheard of; has completely disappeared from the city of Bristol... and expectation has been rife as to where she would make her next manifestation.

"More or less anxiety has been felt by a few people of Roanoke, who through necessity or otherwise are kept up until a late hour at night, lest she make her appearance before them; and true to the presentiment, to Roanoke she has come and in a quiet way is beginning to stir up some uneasiness and not a little excitement. Just what her mission here can be, what her object is in waylaying certain parties, has not exactly been figured out; but of one thing there seems to be a unanimity of opinion, and that is, she has a proclivity for attacking the married men, if 'attack' is the proper word."

The *Times* said there had been several recent encounters with the mystery woman. Here was one: "The most recent instance is that of a prominent merchant of the city, who on the night after payday, having been detained at his store until after midnight, was making his way home, buried in mental abstractions, when at his side the woman in black suddenly appeared, calling him by his name. The woman was only a couple of feet behind him, and he naturally increased his pace; faster and faster he walked, but in spite of his efforts, the woman gained on him until, with the greatest of ease and without any apparent effort she kept along side of him. 'Where do you turn off?' she asked of him. He replied in a hoarse voice, 'Twelfth Avenue.' Ere he was aware, she had her hand upon his shoulder. He tried to shake it off, but without success. 'You are not the first married man I have seen to his home this night,' she spoke in a low and musical voice.

"Reaching the front gate. He made certain she would then leave him; but into the yard she went. This was a little more than he bargained for. It was bad enough to be brought home by a tall and handsome woman with dancing eyes; but to march up to the front door with her — well, he knew his wife was accustomed to wait for him when he was detained, and he did not dare to go to the trouble of making an explanation to her; besides, such explanations are not always satisfactory. The merchant admits that he was a nervy man, but that in spite of his efforts, he could not help being at least a little frightened. 'Twas the suddenness of the thing,' is the way he expressed it." But as he reached the door, he looked around. She was gone. Where she had gone, and how, he didn't know. But he didn't tarry on the doorstep either.

Two others who experienced these strange visitations were a black porter and a young telegraph operator. Both were married, and in both cases she appeared to them late at night on deserted streets. Each said she moved over the sidewalk with an "almost noiseless tread." The porter was terrified by the apparition. He ran "two squares as fast as his legs could carry him," and "fell into the door almost in a fit." The telegraph operator said she called out to him to "wait a minute," but, like the porter, he ran hard all the way home. Both men later said the woman had called them by name.

Whoever she was, she stayed in Roanoke only a short time. Within a few days the reports of her appearances ceased altogether. But soon there were accounts of her nightly sojourns in the town of Bluefield. And, curiously, in that same month of March 1902, the *Roanoke Times* carried a short article from Alma, Nebraska. It was headlined, "Prominent Men See Ghost." The story said, "The spirit form of a young woman is walking the streets of Alma...She exudes from the depths of some dark alley and rushes past lone pedestrians." One man said he saw it vanish in the moonlight, and another was chased by "it" after he scoffed at it. The dispatch added: "The Alma ghost is remarkable in that instead of being garbed in proverbial white, it walks about clothed in *deep black*."

Who was she? Why did she appear only to prominent married men, always late at night while they were on their way home? It has been speculated that perhaps she was a wife herself once who had found her husband unfaithful. And thereafter she returned to make sure potentially wayward mates did not succumb to temptations of the night.

The Man Who Was Buried Standing Up

(Elliston)

f you happen to be driving south from Roanoke on highway 11, a short distance past the town of Elliston, and if the sun is just right, you might catch the shiny glint of a crumbling, marbleized tomb which has stood as a solemn sentinel on the side of a sloping hill back-dropped by mountains for 175 years or so.

Therein lies one of the most colorful legends of Southwest Virginia.

Obscured today by dense underbrush, wild rose bushes, and the roots, trunks and heavy limbs of centuries old trees, the 10-foot-high tomb itself, and the wall which once surrounded it, lie in scattered ruins; the steep path to the craggy site high above Fotheringay Mansion has been long lost in jungle-like growth.

Nevertheless, the stories persist, undiminished by the memory erosions of time. It is at this particular spot, on the hill-site, that many area oldtimers will tell you, a man was buried standing up!

His name was Colonel George Hancock, a spirited, debonair, and slightly eccentric gentleman who served as a Virginia Congressman during George Washington's administration. He fought through the Revolutionary War, and, it is said, his commander, General Pulaski, died in his arms at the siege of Savannah.

After the war, he settled in Elliston, and in 1796, bought Fotheringay and about 600 acres of land. According to the Virginia Landmarks Register, the great house was built soon afterwards. It is, says the Register, "sited dramatically against the Blue Ridge Mountains overlooking the bottomlands of the South Fork of the Roanoke River," and "is an elegant provincial interpretation of the Federal style." It also features unusually ornate interior woodwork, highlighted by delicately carved chimneypieces and doorways, exhibiting the "high quality of the area's post-Revolutionary craftsmanship." Hancock completed the central section and one wing. A second wing was added 150 years later.

Oddly, Fotheringay was named for the English castle in which Mary, Queen of Scotts, was beheaded.

This much is fact. But from here, the authenticity of the legend skates on thinner ice. It is known that Hancock's daughter, Julia, in 1807 married William Clark, brother of George Rogers Clark of Lewis and Clark exploration fame. It is also widely held that Hancock had a strong distrust of the loyalty and willingness-to-work of his slaves. It is said that when he was running the estate himself, he kept it in pristine shape, but that when military and political tenures kept him away from Fotheringay, he would return to find it run down and in disarray. This perhaps contributed to one of the Colonel's characteristics, described by one writer thusly: "He was a gentleman of no uncertain temperament."

Julia died unexpectedly in 1820, and Colonel Hancock, grieving over her death, also died that year. One historian said that a double funeral service was held at the estate for father and daughter.

The accounts of Hancock's burial vary considerably, depending upon whom you read, or ask. Many Montgomery County residents swear that the Colonel was buried, at his specific request, standing up. One writer noted, "to the rear of the old home and several hundred yards higher...is the tomb of Colonel Hancock, who...was placed in it in an upright position so that he could always keep an eye on the slaves at work in the fields below...and keep them from loafing on the job."

Robert and Sarah Nutt, who inherited Fotheringay in the late 1950s, disagree with such a theory. Mr. Nutt reported that the bones in the vault were "mostly in niches" the last time he looked. An earlier owner of the home, Eskridge Edmundson, recalled entering the vault as a boy with several older men and "seeing remains of skeletons on the sides on shelf-like niches" with Hancock's bones in the middle, supposedly recognizable by the size of the skull. The other remains are those of Julia, son John, and the Colonel's mother-in-law.

It is, however, believed that the tall vault has been opened, or "invaded," a number of times over the past century and three quarters. Mrs. Nutt, for example, says curious Civil War soldiers "poked a hole in the roof and rummaged around a bit." One person who steadfastly believed Hancock was buried in a standing position was C. G. Gasham. He was the Nutt's gardener and had lived near the area all his life. As a youngster, he used to play at the tomb site. In 1979, at age 67, he told a reporter, "Folks have been in that vault and could have changed things."

Others who deeply believed that the Colonel was still standing and watching over them were Hancock's slaves. It is said they toiled harder in the fields after his death than before he died. This is supported by a passage in a book written years ago by Sophie Radford De Mussner. It states: "High on the hillside overlooking Happy Valley where flow the headwaters of the Roanoke River, in a white mausoleum, he had himself caused to be excavated from solid rock, the earthly remains of Colonel George Hancock and his daughter Julia, were laid, and to this day the darkies of the region say with trembling, 'De Cunnel he set up dah in a stone chair so's he cud look down de valley and see his slaves at work.' "

And so, the legend carries on. The Colonel would have loved it.

CHAPTER 5 1

The Guest Ghost
in Room 403

(Abingdon)

t the southern end of western Virginia's chain of valleys, bordering the Tennessee line, Washington County was formed in 1776, and it is the first locality in the United States known to have been named for George Washington. The county seat is Abingdon, a few miles northeast of Bristol. The town's rich historic district extends along Main Street, and, says the Virginia Landmarks Register, Abingdon "is unusual for its large quantity of federal and antebellum buildings of brick, which serve to give the district an air of permanence and prosperity lacking in similar settlements containing mostly wooden buildings." Confederate General Joseph E. Johnston, and no less than three Virginia governors lived in Abingdon.

General Francis Preston built one of the largest houses in the Commonwealth here in the 1830s. This was later converted to Martha Washington College for girls, and is now the famous Martha Washington Inn. It is a four-star, four-diamond hotel adorned with antiques and period furniture that serves, in addition to champagne brunches, complimentary tea and crumpets on the scenic veranda. The dining room features such traditional dishes as Virginia country ham and hot spoonbread.

This venerable old inn, steeped in southern custom and old fashioned, pamper-the-guest service, also is host to a variety of spectral activity. In fact, it may well be one of Virginia's most haunted edifices. If not, it certainly is one of the most discussed

295

and written about. Most of the active psychic phenomena here swirls around incidents which occurred during the Civil War.

There is, for example, an alleged apparitional horse which sometimes roams the grounds on moonless nights, seeking its rider, a Union officer who was shot down in front of the college in 1864. There, too, is the touching saga of a young Confederate soldier who raced into the Martha Washington Inn one day to warn of approaching Federal troops. He ran up the spiral stairway just as his pursuers broke down the front door. From the top of the stairs, it is said that he felled seven men before he was mortally wounded and bled to death in the arms of one of the student nurses outside the door of the governor's suite.

The legend is his blood stains could never be washed away, and still can be seen under the carpeting. "It's a strange thing about that spot in the carpet," says Pete Sheffey, a bellhop who has worked at the hotel for more than 30 years. Every time new carpet

Martha Washington Inn

was put down, it seemed like a hole would somehow appear where the young Confederate soldier had fallen. "I can remember my grandfather talking about it back in the 1930s," Pete says. "He saw the blood stains then, and he said every time they covered it up, a hole would show through at that spot. I think they have replaced the carpet there six or seven times since 1937. No one could ever explain why that happened."

Pete says many hotel workers have experienced various forms of otherworldly manifestations over the years. "There were old slave quarters here on the grounds, and I've been told that some of the slaves were buried under the hotel and even in the walls of the old quarters. I don't know if that means anything, but I can tell you a lot of peculiar things have happened here." Steffey's grandfather said he once encountered the spirit of a Confederate soldier while walking down a long, darkened corridor one night more than 50 years ago. "He said the man had on a gray uniform and that part of one leg had been shot off."

A number of employees have reported seeing wispy figures "floating around." Maids have entered certain rooms and walked into inexplicable icy cold spots, even in the middle of summer. Others have seen door knobs turning when no one was outside the door. A housekeeper said she once encountered a "smoky-like object" at 6:30 in the morning as she sat in the lounge. Stunned into silence, she watched as it drifted across the room and then headed toward the door and vanished. Desk clerks have seen a similar figure appear and then disappear in the lobby during the pre-dawn hours. Others have seen apparitions ascending and descending the stairs, and one woman screamed one night when she said she woke up and "something" was hovering over her in bed.

It is an old building, Pete Sheffey points out. "There are a lot of long hallways and high ceilings and creaking stairs and the such. But too many things have happened here to dismiss them all as being the settling sounds of an old hotel," he says. "I've seen what I could call 'floaters' myself, like something or something was passing by you and you just caught a sidelong glimpse of it. But when you turned around, there was nothing there."

Of all the episodes at the Martha Washington Inn, however, perhaps none is more intriguing, or more romantic for that matter, than the periodic return of a lovely young lady named Beth, who infrequently comes back to room 403 to care for the handsome young man who died there more than 130 years ago! She was a student at the college in early 1863 — a time when part of the school had been turned into a hospital to tend grievously wounded soldiers.

One of these was John Stoves. He had been brought in one day, half shot full of musket balls, and placed in what is now room 403. Beth changed his bandages and comforted him as best she could. When Stoves learned that she could play the violin, he asked her to do so. She happily obliged, and although he was suffering from severe pain, her playing seemed to put him at ease. He would fall asleep listening to her. As the young officer slipped ever closer to the "other side," Beth, it is said, fell in love with him.

One day she was summoned to come to the room quickly. Lying near death, he smiled and asked her to play her violin for him. As she did, he closed his eyes and passed on. She grabbed his hand and cried. She never got over the shock, and within a few weeks she, too, was dead. Some said of complications from typhoid fever. Other said of a broken heart.

Ever since that time there has been a haunting presence that has kind of enveloped room 403. A security guard at the inn recalls one night when making his rounds, he passed a milky-like figure with long flowing hair on the stairway. He asked if he could help her. She did not reply. She instead seemed to glide up the stairs and then she went *through* the door to that room! Maids have told of seeing the wraith of a slim young girl sitting in a chair by the bed. Others say that in the late hours of the night they have some-times heard the soft wafting refrains of a violin being played.

The "Red Fox" of the Cumberlands

(Wise County)

t is said that before the turn of the 20th century, when railroads first began winding their way through the narrow valleys, that the "mountain folk" of Wise County were governed largely by a "code of the hills." As one writer put it more than 50 years ago: "Rugged individualists, they settled their difficulties without recourse to the law, made and sold their 'mountain dew,' and viewed all 'furriners' with suspicion."

Perhaps that is why it took a native son — John Fox of nearby Big Stone Gap — to capture the colorful life styles of these hardy backwoods people who battled bears, Indians and the harsh elements to carve a living from this "toe" of land in the extreme southwestern portion of the state in the Cumberland Mountains area. Fox immortalized some of these legendary characters in his classic book, "On the Trail of the Lonesome Pine." (There actually was a huge evergreen tree which stood on the side of a mountain for years and was known as the Lonesome Pine.)

And what wonderful characters! One, for example, was called "Devil" John Wright, who was married three times and fathered 37 children. Another was a wizened old moon shiner named Ira Mullins. But perhaps the most notorious of all was the fabled "Red Fox of the Cumberlands" — Dr. Marshall B. Taylor, commonly known as Doc Taylor. He was a medical doctor, a preacher and a sanctioned law officer all rolled into one. But he was much more, too. He was charismatic, enigmatic, eccentric to the border line of madness, and widely feared. He was once described as "having a dual character, showing in his face kindness and benevolence on one side; a wolfish snarl on the other; and both plain to any eye that looked."

How much time has embellished the mystique that surrounds Taylor is not certain. It is said that he was born in Scott County and that his parents and brother and three sisters were all "honorable and respected." He, too, reared "a respectable family." As a young man, Taylor went to Lee County to study medicine, and later moved to Wise (then called Gladeville) to practice. It was during this period of time that his extraordinary feats, mostly taking place in the surrounding mountains, began to take root.

He was, for example, noted for having a "ghostly presence" in the woods. One tale involved a man called Riley Mullins. He was walking down an old trail near Pound Gap one day when all was quiet and he felt no one was within a mile or two. Suddenly, out of nowhere, Doc Taylor appeared, and began walking beside Riley, never saying a word. Riley, who himself had a local reputation as being "mean as the Devil," got so spooked when Taylor just as mysteriously disappeared, that he could barely speak. Then, down the road a ways, he found a little piece of "candy poke," and written on the wrapper were the words, "Watch out Uncle Riley or the Devil will get you when you mess with the Fox." At this admonition, Riley ran as hard as he could till he got to a house at the foot of the mountain. He was so sure that he had left Taylor far behind, that when the doctor stepped out in front of him, Riley, as his nephew later described it, "like to a-tore the whole woods down getting away from there." Taylor then took his ever-present Winchester rifle and "cut down the bushes all around him as he run." Riley, who often bragged he was afraid of no man, never made that claim in Doc's presence again.

Taylor sometimes also practiced medicine in strange ways. Whether or not he was psychic is not known, but he would occasionally hold seances to help heal his patients. One oft-told story is that he was treating a man for some undisclosed ailment, and then he went outside the house, lifted his hands skyward in a supplicating position, and stood for an hour. He went back in to his patient, laid his hands on him, and pronounced him better. Again he went outside and resumed his stance, looking to the heavens for another solid hour. This time when he went back in, he pronounced the man cured, and the afflicted patient "arose and went his way."

The Red Fox of the Cumberlands

Taylor showed as much zeal in his part-time job as a law officer as he did as a doctor, and he gained many enemies among the
mountain folks by bringing in a number of moon shiners. There
were so many threats on his life that he began taking the evasive
measures in the woods that eventually earned him the name "Red
Fox." In a 1941 interview, Jeff Mullins told a writer about some of
these exploits. "They was always trying to get a pot-shot at him,

but they'd follow him for days some times and then find out he'd been in the other end of the county all the time. He fooled them by his tracks being made backwards." One of his pursuers claimed he was so sly and smart that he "was as slick as a red fox." Mullins said he would wear his moccasins backwards, so that those tracking him would always be going in the opposite direction. Mullins said that after awhile outlaws quit trying to ambush Taylor, "as it was too dangerous to try. A fellow wasn't apt to get back from such a trip!"

By 1892, Taylor, now in his 60s, had been involved in a running feud with a moon shiner named Ira Mullins for years. Ira, allegedly, had offered $300 to anyone who would kill the doctor. It was because of this, it is believed, that on the morning of May 14th of that year, Taylor and two brothers, Calvin and Henon Fleming, hid behind covering rocks at a point in a mountain pass near Pound Gap since called the "Killing Rock." They had learned that Ira Mullins and his family were headed that way. Sometime between nine and ten a.m., Taylor and the Flemings opened fire on the unsuspecting Mullins, and within minutes had killed Ira, his wife, and three others, plus two horses. Said one historian, "the trail was soon running red with mixed human and animal blood."

Two members of the party, a woman and Ira's 14-year-old son, John, somehow escaped the blazing fusillade, although John's suspenders were shot in two. Although they wore masks, Doc Taylor and the Fleming brothers were identified by the survivors, and went into hiding. Taylor had himself crated in a box and shipped on a freight train to Bluefield, West Virginia. But word of his innovative escape attempt had leaked out and he was apprehended and brought to trial in Wise County.

Even his trial was bizarre. Taylor said he had a witness who would speak for him, and when the judge asked who it was, the defendant answered, "Jesus Christ. Will you hear Him?" When the judge said he would, Taylor pulled a small bible from his coat pocket and began reading passages dealing with false witnesses and oppression. Nevertheless, he was found guilty and sentenced to hang.

In his 1938 book, "A Narrative History of Wise County," author Charles A. Johnson vividly described the scene: "The little courthouse town of Gladeville (Wise) was packed full of people in spite of the drizzling rain that fell all the afternoon. The farmer, the business man, the cross-road merchant, the water-wheel miller, the 'seng digger,' the fur gatherer, the herb doctor, the spiritualists, the witch and the witch doctor, the backtown sightseer, the old and the young, men, women and children, the halt and the blind, the fool and the 'smart-alec,' had all come to see and hear, and if not to see and hear, to be told by others of the scene and the agonies of another dying man, at the end of a hangman's rope. House-tops were groaning with the weight of the curious, tree-tops were swaying with the bodies of the curious, fence-tops were lined in black with the curious, and hill-slopes were crowded with the excited curious — all striving to get one glimpse of the condemned man, over the open top of the enclosed scaffold...Such is human nature."

At his specific, incredible request, Taylor was attired, from neck to foot, in snow white linen, topped with a brown derby hat. After reading from the Bible, his hands were tied with a white handkerchief, and a white cape, instead of a black one, was pulled over his face. As the props were being removed under the trap door, jostling Taylor, he fell in a heap on the platform, and had to be helped up. Author Johnson then said, "the trap door swung from under him, and the body of 'Doc' Taylor, the 'Red Fox,' hung between heaven and earth, and his spirit went to another world than ours."

But did it?

Even in apparent death, the strange nature of this unusual man asserted itself. He had asked that his body be kept unburied for three days. At the end of that time, he had told all who would listen to him, that he would "arise from the dead and go about preaching the gospel."

After the three days he was buried in the town cemetery on a hill overlooking his home in an unmarked grave. The mound was, Johnson wrote, covered by green briar in summer and by blankets of snow in winter.

And while there were no eye-witness accounts of the Red Fox's resurrection, there were some old timers who contend Doc Taylor's spirit does appear on occasion in the darkened woods of the Cumberland Mountains he so loved to roam in life. Only these times, they said, he leaves no tracks at all!

CHAPTER 53

A Galaxy of
Ghostly Humor

ho said ghosts can't be fun? Most people think spirits of the dead are at the least scary and frightening, and at the most, downright harmful. I have sometimes found just the opposite. Ninety nine percent of the ghosts people have told me that they experienced were either quiet and shy, or just plain friendly ghosts. And every once in a while you run across an incident that turns out to be, I think, hilarious. Herewith, are a few such anecdotes I have collected over the years.

A HELPFUL REFERENCE SOURCE

n doing research for my regional book, "The Ghosts of Tidewater," I talked to one young lady in Gloucester who, in trying to be helpful, told me that her mother had a "marvelous" book all about ghosts and that if I could locate a copy in a library she was sure I would find everything I was looking for. She would ask her mother what the title was and get back to me. The next day she called and said the book was "The Ghosts of Richmond." The author was L. B. Taylor, Jr. We both had a hearty laugh over that when she realized who I was.

* * * * *

"MISS LIZZIE" AND THE NON-BELIEVER
(Charles City County)

 t the Victorian mansion Edgewood, located on Route 5 in Charles City County halfway between Williamsburg and Richmond, owner Dot Boulware was entertaining a dinner table full of women guests one evening. She was telling them about her resident ghost, a "Miss Lizzie," who since losing her lover in the Civil War, has allegedly appeared occasionally at an upstairs window, candle in hand. Many people have claimed to have seen her, and others have heard or felt her presence in the house. One of the guests was having none of it, however. She said she didn't believe in such things and anyone who did was crazy. Whether by pure coincidence, or by psychic manifestation, at that precise instant, a brass plate that had been atop a cabinet suddenly fell off and bonked the skeptical woman on the head. Mrs. Boulware says everyone sat in stunned silence for a few seconds as the startling event soaked in. And then everyone got up and rushed out of the room in such a hurry several chairs were toppled.

* * * * *

NEVER INSULT A GHOST
(Charles City County)

 strikingly similar event took place a few miles east of Edgewood on Route 5 at Sherwood Forest, the home of President John Tyler. The ghost here is called the "Gray Lady," and is believed to be a 19th century nanny. Apparently a child in her care died at the house, and she returns to rock the baby in a rocking chair. Payne Tyler, mistress of the house, said she witnessed a number of unexplained manifestations and once sat down and had a talk with her ghost, telling her they had to learn to co-exist in the house. Sometime later, Payne was telling her cousin about the chat, and the cousin laughed and chided her, saying she thought Payne had more intelligence than that. "Then," said Payne, "the most amazing thing happened. The room we were in, the Gray Room, began vibrating wildly. A harsh downdraft of icy cold air seemed to pervade the room, and there were loud bangs, like shutters slamming against the house, although there was no wind to speak of. It was an eerie feeling." Payne said her cousin hurriedly departed, and didn't return to Sherwood Forest for several years!

* * * * *

HOODED VISIONS RISE FROM THE MIST
(New Kent)

once appeared on a radio show about psychic phenomena with the Reverend Richard (Dick) Hughes Carter of Williamsburg, a walking encyclopedia on local lore. Rev. Carter told the following true anecdote: Seems one day in the winter, five Colonial Williamsburg historical interpreters, all women, were driven out to St. Peters Episcopal Church in New Kent County one afternoon for a tour of the facilities and a briefing on the history of the church. The ladies were all dressed in the traditional colonial costumes, covered with hooded capes, since the weather was a bit nasty.

As they left the church late in the afternoon, a mist was rising in the darkening gloom. The ladies pulled their hoods up over their heads and sat down on a bench to await their ride back to Williamsburg. The bench was next to the church cemetery. Soon they heard a vehicle approaching, and assuming this was their driver, the ladies arose from the bench. However, it was not their driver. It was a tourist from New Jersey who apparently was lost. From the road, in the rising mist, he saw five hooded figures in colonial costume suddenly appear out of nowhere, among the towering tombstones. The ladies said the man let out an audible gasp, slammed his foot on the accelerator, and promptly drove into a tree! He then backed up and sped off, spinning his tires, without even bothering to stop and see what damage he had done to his car.

* * * * *

306

A SCARY SCENE AT STONEWALL COTTAGE
(Near Harrisonburg)

ome downright scary things have happened over the years at Stonewall Cottage on the valley turnpike just north of Harrisonburg. Some of the occurrences remain inexplicable and are linked with the supernatural, while others have been caused by quite natural and rational, if unusual, means. Yet the effect has been much the same — spine-tingling chills!

Take the case of the reburial of Uncle Joseph Dovel, for example. This, "ghostly excitement at Stonewall Cottage is not really extra-terrestrial, but must have been equally hair-raising," writes J. B. Yount, an attorney in Waynesboro, and family member. It seems that in 1938, several family graves were to be moved from the land at Stonewall Cottage to lots in Woodbine Cemetery at Harrisonburg. Among those to be moved was Captain Joseph M. Dovel, "the young lawyer who had joined the Confederate Army and became a captain of the celebrated Valley Rangers of the Stonewall Brigade, only to become injured and ill with camp fever and return home to die in 1863 at age 23." The undertaker hired a crew of black laborers to exhume the bodies. They found Captain Dovel buried in a cast iron, bullet-shaped coffin with a glass window over his face. The hinged coffin was held shut by two large bolts.

"Aunt Bettie Post and my father were present when the iron casket was raised. The men dusted off the window, and there was Captain Dovel, looking as if he were merely asleep," says Yount. "He was buried in his Confederate uniform, with a crimson sash for decoration. Aunt Bettie asked the undertaker if he would open the casket for a moment, to enable her to see her uncle 'in full regalia.' The men unscrewed the screws and lifted the top." As soon as the air hit inside, there was a mild, soundless explosion. The body disintegrated instantly into dust before their eyes. Yount adds that it is doubtful if an Olympic sprinter could have outraced the laborers in getting away from the grave site that day!

* * * * *

Yount's father was the sole witness to another of the "colorful after effects" of the haunted stories that circulated about the cottage. This occurred in 1934, when Aunt Laura died sitting up in her chair one night. She had apparently suffered a fatal attack during the evening, before coming upstairs to bed, and her body was not discovered until the next morning. Aunt Laura had left instructions that she wanted to be buried in a shroud, and this request proved to be somewhat difficult to fulfill. Yount's father went from store to store in Harrisonburg "trying to locate the old-fashioned, long out-of-date garment. He could not find one, and one of the neighbors commissioned a nearby Mennonite lady to make one.

"The undertaker had prepared the body in the coffin and placed it, as was the custom, in the front parlor," Yount writes. "The house was dark, the shutters still closed in the front, seldom-used rooms. My father went around to the rear where the family and friends were gathered. After a while, Aunt Sallie asked my father to go over the parlor to get her something from behind the organ. He had to pass through several rooms and the hall to get to the parlor. It had been the aunts' custom to carry keys and lock the doors behind them as they went from room to room at Stonewall Cottage.

"My father always said he wasn't afraid of anyone living, but didn't like to fool with the dead. Nervously, he entered the parlor ...(he) glanced at Aunt Laura, her eyes closed, her form lying stiffly in the coffin. He walked past to the end of the room and reached behind the organ. Suddenly, he heard a loud snap, which he always described as sounding like a 'rat' trap going off. He looked around and saw Aunt Laura in the coffin, her eyes opened and apparently staring at him, her head turned in his direction, her false teeth half out of her opened mouth.

"My father claimed he was so much in shock that it took what seemed an hour for him to walk past the coffin and leave the parlor. He called out the front door to the undertaker, who came immediately. What had happened? Because of the delay in discovering the body, staying as it was in a sitting position all night long, rigor mortis had set in. The undertaker had braced her mouth shut with a brace under her chin, obscured by the high collar of the shroud. My father apparently jarred it loose as he walked across the creaky floor. The brace slipped, throwing the head ajar...My mother remembered well how white and pale he looked when he returned to the Stonewall Cottage kitchen."

* * * * *

ARISEN FROM THE DEAD
(Henry County)

nd finally, Carl DeHart, a Martinsville historian associated with the Blue Ridge
Regional Library, tells of a scary-funny event which occurred
sometime in 1938 on a dairy farm adjoining the famous Hairston
plantation in Henry County. This estate, says DeHart, was called
Beaver Creek, and at one time stretched for several thousand acres,
all the way to Rockingham County, North Carolina.

A black man named "Doc" Smith and his aged grandmother
lived on a dairy farm. She was described as wraith-like, with long
white hair strung down her back. Youngsters in the area referred
to her as "the ghost woman."

One day in the winter of '38, when there was five inches of
snow on the ground, "Doc" found his grandmother apparently
dead. He could discern no pulse or heartbeat. As was the custom in
those days, a "sitting up with the dead" session was held. The
grandmother was laid out on a table in the main room of a two
room log cabin with a sheet over her. Close friends and relatives
gathered to pay their respects.

As it was freezing cold outside, a fire was going full blast in
the fireplace and everyone was gathered around it, with their
backs to the table. Suddenly, the sheet moved. Grandmother supposedly had lapsed into some sort of catatonic, coma-like condition
which included no detectable heartbeat or pulse. Something, perhaps the fire, or the group of people, had aroused her from this
deep sleep state. The elderly woman then sat up for a second,
unnoticed by the others, slid off the end of the table, walked over
to the group, tapped a couple of them on the shoulder, and said
something like, "sure is cold out tonight, ain't it?"

As one might well imagine, there was an immediate stampede
for the exit. The terrified relatives and friends banged into each other
heading for the door in a crazed dash. Hysteric screams filled the tiny
cabin and there was a frantic pile up at the door as the men and
women clawed at each other in panic trying to get through the narrow opening. It was said that one gentleman was so rattled by the old
woman's sudden resurrection, that he tried desperately to squeeze
his body up the chimney, even though the fire was still going!

It must have been quite a scene.

The Ghost of
Governor's Mansion

(Richmond)

"I was awakened from a slumber, like the slumber of death, by the pressing of spiritual lips upon my own."

— *Eleonora*

he Governor's Mansion in Richmond, the construction of which commenced in 1813, has seemed to mellow and improve with age, as has its acceptance among Virginians. Today, for example, a Virginia Historic Landmarks Commission report calls it, "one of the state's outstanding examples of Federal style architecture." And a booklet prepared at the direction of Mrs. Mills E. Godwin, Jr., wife of the former governor, describes the mansion thusly: "The solid old house still seems relatively unaffected by the passage of its many gubernatorial generations. Despite renovations, restorations, and re-arrangements, it remains the very essence of Virginia."

Such was not always the case. Certainly, it was, when built, an improvement over the "unpretentious" four room wooden house that stood at the same site housing earlier chief executives. It had fallen into "bad repair" and was torn down to make room for the new building.

Boston architect Alexander Parris was commissioned to draw preliminary plans for the mansion, but the Commissioners of Public Buildings were not satisfied that these properly reflected the "honor and dignity of the state," so they added some embellishments of their own. Whatever it was they did, it apparently didn't please many people.

Not long after it was finished, for instance, a Richmond newspaper stated the building was furnished in a style of inferiority "almost discreditable to Virginia." It further called the mansion's exterior "one of the homeliest dwellings in the city." One later governor's wife was even more sarcastic in her criticism. When she moved in, she said there were only three antiques in the house — "a tin roof, ugly floors, and copper bathtubs." She also noted that the carpets hadn't been taken up for 40 years.

The furniture at one time was in such a rickety state that a visiting chairman of the General Assembly's finance committee — admittedly, he was a rather large man — demolished a gilt chair when he sat down. It splintered beneath his bulk into kindling and so embarrassed him, he tried to hide the remains of the chair in a potted palm.

In time, however, a number of improvements were made to the house.

The attitude of the public about the mansion also has evolved through the decades, from one described once in a report as "indifference and sometimes caustic criticism," to respect and affection. This feeling has been presumably shared by some of the notable guests of the house, including five U.S. Presidents, Winston Churchill, King Edward VII, Queen Mother Elizabeth of England, Charles Lindbergh, and Admiral Richard E. Byrd.

Add to this prestigious list the fact that four future U.S. Presidents — Thomas Jefferson, James Monroe, William Henry Harrison, and John Tyler, plus Patrick Henry have all lived at the site, and General Stonewall Jackson's body lay in state in the house in 1863.

It is against all this colorful background that we learn that an intruder, too, has tenanted the Governor's Mansion, in the form of the apparition of a beautiful young lady. She reputedly was first encountered in the early 1890s by none other than Governor Philip W. McKinney himself, surely a credible witness.

He came in one hot August afternoon from the Capitol, took his coat off and washed up in a bathroom, and then entered a bedroom, only to be startled by "a young lady sitting in the window." He quietly and quickly retreated to his wife's room and asked her who her guest was. She replied, "I haven't any guest," whereupon he reentered the bedroom and the lady had vanished. A search of the mansion turned up no clues as to her identity or mission.

There was one other occasion where the mystery woman was actually seen. According to officer Robert Toms of the Capitol police, one of his fellow patrolmen saw a woman standing at the curtains of an upstairs bedroom in an area where no unauthorized guests were allowed. When he walked over to tell her she shouldn't be in that area, she disappeared before his eyes, leaving only a scary fluttering of the curtains.

While these are the only recorded sightings of the wispy visitor, she has more frequently been heard, and, at least once, felt. "I've heard footsteps more than once and there wasn't anyone in the house but me," says one mansion security officer. A number of servants have sworn they also have heard her walking about in a "rustling taffeta gown." Once, a butler chased her down a flight of stairs into the basement, where she allegedly "escaped."

She has frequently been heard by security men as they sat at a table in the kitchen hallway in the basement. Says one officer, "Many a night I've been sitting there when the Governor and his wife are away, and I've heard doors slam and someone walking upstairs. I've gone upstairs to look, and all the doors were locked tight and no one was around."

A curious incident occurred during the tenure of Linwood Holton in 1972 that added to the ghost's credibility. When

The Governor's Mansion in Richmond

Hurricane Agnes whipped through Richmond that year, it caused a blackout downtown, including the Capitol and the Governor's Mansion. All was dark, that is except for a single lightbulb in the ladies' stairwell of the mansion. It continued shining like a beacon in the storm.

One who remembers this well is Ann Compton, ABC-TV's White House correspondent who then was on assignment at the state Capitol. She was called to the house to witness the phenomenon by one of Holton's staff secretaries. Recalls Ms. Compton: "Every light switch we tried didn't affect it. Jinx Holton (the governor's wife) always told me she thought there was a ghost. Rationally, I suppose I'd like to think it was a fluke in the wiring. Irrationally, I'd like to think I'm as romantic as most Virginians about their history and that she (the ghost) was the spirit that brought the light to the Governor's Mansion when the rest of the city was dark and wet."

As an eerie sidelight to this episode, Governor Holton later told the Richmond *Times-Dispatch* that during the blackout someone or something moved several of the paintings in his bedroom.

Whoever, or whatever, the presence is which inhabits the Governor's mansion, it apparently was real enough to scare one Capitol policeman clean out of his job. Officer Toms says this particular officer, who prefers to remain nameless, was in the basement one night when he distinctly felt something touch his face. He was so terrified, he ran out of the house, throwing down his badge along the way and quit the force. He came back only to collect his paycheck.

Once, during Governor Dalton's time in office, yet another officer had a hair-raising experience in the basement. He became curious when the Governor's dog, the hair on its back raised, barked furiously at a window. As he stepped over to investigate, he felt a frigid chill in the room. He noticed that although it was in the middle of a summer heat wave, the window had frosted over! And the curtains were swirling about madly. In a few seconds the curtains stilled and the frosting on the window disappeared.

During the time of Governor Andrew Montague, just after the turn of the 20th century, Robert Lynch and Dr. Horace Hoskins were living in the mansion. One night they both were awakened by the unmistakable sound of footsteps in their room, accompanied by the "swish of a silk skirt." They got up and followed the sound along the corridor and down the hallway below the stairs where they lost it. And according to the official "Mansion Tour Script," the brother of Governor Montague once chased the ghostly lady down a staircase and into the street.

Who is she, and why has she chosen the Governor's Mansion, of all places, to make her periodic presence known? No one has ever come up with even a hint of an answer.

CHAPTER 55

The Catastrophe
at the Capitol

(Richmond)

"The very air from the South seemed to be redolent with death."
— *The Sphinx*

hey are heard only late at night, the sounds. Some say they are but the normal creaks, groans and wind whistles of an old building. But there are others, including members of the security force, who swear there are voices; soft muted voices sobbing and moaning in the darkened stillness of the State Capitol building.

Certainly, if the sounds are voices there is good reason for their anguished cries.

Thomas Jefferson conceived the plan for the Capitol, patterning it after the Maison Carrée, a Roman temple built in Nimes, France, in the first century after Christ. It was the first public building in the New World constructed in the Classical Revival style of architecture, and is the second oldest working Capitol in the United States. It has been in continuous use since October 1788.

According to the official Capitol brochure, the structure drew high praise from its earliest days. "Even in its present unfinished state," wrote a visitor in 1796, "the building, is, beyond comparison, the finest, the most noble, and the greatest in all America." The brochure calls it, "a magnificent monument to Virginia's past." Here, in the grand rotunda, is the state's most treasured work of art, a life-sized statue of George Washington carved in Carrara marble by the brilliant French artist Jean Antoine Houdon in 1788. There also are busts of the seven other Virginia-born U.S. Presidents as well as a bronze statue of Robert E. Lee by Rudolph Evans.

Ironically, although the building served as the Capitol of the Confederacy from 1861 to 1865, it escaped damage during the Civil War, only to suffer a tragedy of enormous proportions five years later. The date was April 27, 1870. It was Richmond's second major catastrophe in less than 60 years, the other being the ruinous theatre fire of 1811.

The circumstances leading up to it were these: Although military rule had ended, there was still confusion and turmoil in the governing of the city and state. The general assembly authorized the governor to appoint a new city council, which he did. The council elected Henry Ellyson, publisher of the Richmond Dispatch, as the new mayor.

However, George Chahoon, who had been serving as mayor, refused to relinquish his office. This led to what has been described as "a chaotic state of affairs," as the two rival forces struggled to gain control. The dispute got nasty and eventually wound up in the Virginia Supreme Court of Appeals, which convened to hear the case on April 27, 1870.

Everybody who was anybody in the city, jammed into the Capitol that day to hear the proceedings in what was to be a landmark decision. Hundreds of participants and spectators shoehorned into the courtroom, on an upper floor, and overflowed the gallery.

Minutes before the court convened there was a "loud cracking noise" and then pandemonium. The gallery floor collapsed under the weight of the overflow crowd, and bricks, iron bars, plaster, planks, furniture and a mass of people fell onto the courtroom floor below. Under the impact of this tremendous amount of debris and humanity, the floor buckled and gave way, careening to the ground floor some 40 feet below.

Scores of people were crushed to death immediately, while others suffocated under the huge cloud of dust from tons of plaster that made it all but impossible to see anything. Many were buried alive under the rubble. The pain and suffering were incalculable, and there were screams, cries and moans everywhere. The lucky ones ran, walked and crawled outside and fell, gasping, to the lawn.

The fire alarm was sounded and firemen, police and other rescuers arrived, but it took hours to disentangle the bodies. Survivors

The Capitol at Richmond

were carried out to the lawn covered with blood and lime dust to the point of being unrecognizable. One eye witness said they looked more like "bloody ghosts" than human beings. Rescuers commandeered passing carriages, hacks and other vehicles to convey the injured to hospitals. Every doctor and nurse in Richmond was summoned, and when word of the disaster spread, wives, relatives and friends rushed to the Capitol, adding to the anguish and chaos. Some did not learn of their loved ones fate for a considerable period of time.

Grown men cried openly at the ghastly scene and one witness was moved to write, "I can't dwell upon these awful scenes, they were so heartrending, so appalling that they unman me when I recall them."

In all, 62 men lost their lives — just 10 less than the number killed in the 1811 fire. More than 250 were injured, some dreadfully, their bodies mangled and their bones crushed. The victims included many prominent citizens, among them Patrick Henry's grandson and several well-known lawyers. Fortunately, the House of Delegates was not in session, otherwise the list would have been even more lengthy.

A curious twist of fate spared the members of the Supreme Court of Appeals. The proceedings were delayed for 15 minutes as the judges conferred over some changes in their written opinion of the case. They were just starting into the court room from an adjoining conference room when the gallery floor gave way, and they stood on the very brink of the "awful abysm."

Once again, Richmond was plunged into municipal mourning, just five years after the city had been sacked and burned. Business houses closed and crepe was displayed widely. Resolutions were introduced in the Senate calling for the demolition of the Capitol, and the erection of a new one, but it finally was decided to strengthen and rebuild the existing building.

Ellyson eventually was declared the rightful mayor, and Chahoon later was sent to prison on forgery charges. He was pardoned by the governor on the condition that he leave the state. In time, the Capitol was rebuilt and the business of running the Commonwealth went on.

But although more than a century has passed, and the tragedy is but a black-bordered footnote in history, some say the eerie cries and mournful voices, muted under tons of debris, can still be heard in the hallowed corridors of the Capitol.

C H A P T E R   5 6

The Skeleton with the Tortoise Shell Comb

(Richmond)

"… I have been sleeping — and now — now — I am dead."
— The Facts in the Case of M. Valdemar

he first account of the 19th century hauntings of Hawes House in Richmond was
published in 1910 by renowned local author, Mrs. Edward
Terhune, who under the pen name of Marion Harland, wrote the
"Lassie" books among others. Subsequently, Margaret DuPont Lee
retold the story in her 1930 book, "Virginia Ghosts," and over the
years other authors also have referred to this bizarre tale.

Mrs. Terhune, whose maiden name was Mary Virginia Hawes,
devoted a chapter of her autobiography, "The Story of My Life," to
the intriguing "heroine" who has been called everything from the
"Little Gray Lady" to the "Tortoise Shell Ghost." Whatever, it is a
richly colorful legend that has not tarnished with time. Here goes.

The Hawes family home stood from the 1840s till 1875 was
located at 506 East Leigh Street in Richmond. It was a good sized
Colonial brick house, built early in the 19th century, that featured
large rooms and long passages. The once extensive and beautiful
grounds and gardens, including many large shade trees, slowly
gave way to the encroaching demands of a growing city.

Nevertheless, it was on a cold winter night in the late 1840s
when the young author-to-be, Virginia Hawes, first experienced
the ghost that was to make itself well known to the family for

nearly 30 years. After entertaining a male guest, Virginia saw him off, locked the front door, stopped by her parents room to say good night, and then, lamp in hand, started across a small passageway that divided the two first floor bedrooms.

The light shone bright in this confined area, and she suddenly gasped as she saw, directly in front of her, what she described as a small woman dressed in gray "glide noiselessly along the wall," and then disappear at the Venetian blinds at the end of the front hall, leading into the reception room beyond. The woman appeared to be small and lithe, with her head bowed in her hands. Peculiarly, she wore a high, carved tortoise shell comb in her hair.

Years later Virginia was to write of the occasion: "I have reviewed the moment and its incident a thousand times to persuade myself that the apparition was an optical illusion or a trick of fancy. The 1,001st attempt results as did the first. I shut my eyes to see — always the one figure, the same motion, the same disappearance. She was dressed in gray; she was small and lithe; her head was bowed upon her hands, and she slipped away, hugging the wall as if in flight, vanishing at the closed door. The door I had heard myself latch itself five minutes ago! It did not open to let her through."

At the time, the sighting terrified Virginia. She immediately went back to her parents' room, entered, and exclaimed, "If there is any such thing as a ghost, I have seen one."

Startled, her father reacted immediately, comforting his daughter. He then walked her to her room and told her to try and sleep. The next morning he called Virginia aside and asked her to keep what she had seen to herself. Odd, Virginia thought.

About a month later she and her father were in the drawing room one evening, talking, when her mother came in excitedly and announced, "I have just seen Virginia's ghost. I saw it in the same place and it went in the same direction. It was all in gray, but something white, like a turban, was wrapped around its head."

Young Virginia could see that the revelation had shocked her father, but he gathered himself and asked them not to speak of the incident again. They abided. But while they remained quiet, the ghost did not. Soon after, Virginia's younger sister, Mea, burst into the drawing room at twilight one evening, trembling badly, and proclaimed that "something" had chased her down the stairs. She said whoever or whatever it was — she apparently hadn't seen it — had been in high heel shoes that tapped loudly on the oak stairs as she descended from the upper chamber to the parlor. Still, Mr. Hawes insisted that no one talk of the occurrences.

Next, Alice Hawes, Virginia's 14-year-old sister, and a cousin visiting the house, encountered the phenomenon. Sent to bed at nine o'clock, they instead slipped into the parlor and sat before the fireplace talking for about an hour. When they went back into the hall to go to the bedroom they found it dark. The lamp had burned out.

Brilliant moonlight, however, streamed through the great window on the lower staircase, showering the stairway up to the upper landing. They stared, transfixed, as they saw a "white figure" moving down the steps. At first, they thought it was just one of the boys sneaking down for a glass of water or a snack. The figure appeared to have a trailing nightgown or nightshirt, and it seemed to the girls that there was something white cast over the head.

As the figure moved nearer, the front door suddenly opened and in walked all the boys of the house, back from a nighttime stroll. At the same instant the white thing descending the stairs disappeared before the girls' eyes. Alice said it didn't go backward or forward. It just vanished. Understandably, the girls screamed in unison, arousing everyone in the house.

The next morning, Mr. Hawes called the family together and told them: "It is useless to try to hide from ourselves any longer that there is something wrong with this house. I have known it for a year or more. In fact, we had not lived here three months before I was made aware that some mystery hung about it.

"One windy November night I had gone to bed as usual before your mother. I lay with closed eyes listening to wind and rain when somebody touched my feet." He stressed that it was somebody, not something, before continuing. "Hands were laid lightly upon them; were lifted and laid in the same way on my knees, and so on until they lay more heavily upon my chest and I felt someone was looking in my face. Up to that moment I had not a doubt but that it was your mother arranging the covers to keep out draughts. I opened my eyes to thank her. She was not there! I raised myself on my elbows and looked towards the fireplace. Your mother was deep in her book!

"I have never spoken of this event to your mother until this moment. But it has happened to me not 20, but 50 times or more. It is always the same thing. The hands, I have settled in my mind, are those of a small woman, or child. Sometimes the hands rest on my

chest a whole minute. Something looks into my face and is gone."
Looking at Virginia, Mr. Hawes said: "You can see, my daughter,
why I was not incredulous when you brought your ghost upon the
scene. I have been on the lookout for further manifestations. By all
means do not let the servants hear of this. You girls are old enough
to understand that the value of this property would be destroyed
were this story to creep abroad. Better burn the house down than
attempt to sell it at any time within the next 50 years with a ghost
story tagged to it."

Everyone dutifully pledged to remain silent, including, apparently, the ghost, at least for a while. But it resurfaced once more at
some period later, this time with almost comical overtones. That
was when a distant relative, described as a "sanctimonious uncle-
in-law," came for a visit. He usually stayed several days at the

least; a fact which caused the family some concern because they were expecting other guests and needed the spare bedroom. However, to their surprise, he abruptly announced on the morning after his arrival that he had to leave immediately for Olney.

Later, a relative who lived in Olney was at the Hawes House and asked if the house was haunted. Everyone, as if on cue, acted innocently, and inquired why she should ask such a silly question. "Well," she told them, the uncle "had an awful scare the night he was here. He declared he was standing at the window looking out into the moonlight in the garden when somebody came up behind him and took him by the elbow and turned him clear around! He felt plainly the two hands that grabbed hold of him. He looked under the bed and in the closet. There was nobody in the room but himself, and the door was locked. He said he would not sleep in that room again for one thousand dollars!"

Such is the saga of the "Gray Lady" of Hawes House. Neither Virginia Hawes nor any other member of her family was ever able to determine the identity of the apparition they had seen and felt. Often, such phenomena are closely associated with either the house involved or the family. But no historical tie-in could be found in this case.

A footnote to the story, though, offers some clues. After the death of Mr. Hawes, and the marriage of the sons and daughters, Mrs. Hawes sold the house to St. Paul's Episcopal Church, and it was subsequently converted into an orphanage. During the construction modifications, workmen dug an areaway in front of the premises. Four feet down they unearthed the skeletal remains of a small woman. She lay less than six feet away from the wall of the house and directly under the drawing room window.

And, oh yes, under the woman's skull, workmen found a richly carved tortoise shell comb!

There are some who speculate that the woman was either murdered or at least died under suspicious circumstances. Such a theory is supported by the fact that no sign of a coffin or coffin plate was found. Nor had the woman been buried in a cap or shroud as was common in that day. Also, there were no known interments in that residential district. In fact, the grave had been dug in the front garden so close to the house that it could not be reasonably conceived that the plot was ever part of a family burying ground.

All of this would explain — at least to those who study the common denominators of the supernatural — why the woman continued to haunt Hawes House. She was, in the parlance of ghost followers, in a state of perpetual unrest, either seeking retribution for whatever evil had befallen her, or not gaining that, determined to expose that evil.

CHAPTER 57

The Unhappy Bride
of Tuckahoe

(near Richmond)

"Today I wear these chains and am here! Tomorrow I shall be fetterless —
but where?"

— *The Imp of the Perverse*

Considered by architectural historians to be the finest existing early 18th century plantation in America, Tuckahoe stands today in its virtually undisturbed setting on a bluff overlooking the James River valley." Those words are the lead-in to a brochure on this truly splendid mansion located about 15 miles west of Richmond off River Road in Goochland County.

One author described the entrance into Tuckahoe in these elegant terms: "The oldest of these trees in their lusty age extend arms farther afield than in their youth, their naked trunks standing stiff and upright, so like the pipes of some cathedral organ that one would not start at the sound of deep, reverential tones coming along the lane. It is most impressive.

"Down the lofty nave of this forest cathedral gleams, at the end, under the open sky, the old, white gateway which bars the lane from the lawn. And straight ahead in the distance, upon a little rise of ground, the old house stands like some fading seventeenth-century picture shut away in its immediate world."

The name Tuckahoe, according to one 17th century historian,

comes from the Indian word "Tockawaugh," which was an edible root found in the area. It was "of the greatness and taste of a potatoe, which passeth a fiery purgation before they may eate it being poison while it is raw."

The oldest portion of the house, the north wing, says a Virginia Historic Landmarks Commission report, was built by Thomas Randolph, perhaps as early as 1712. This means it predates such other famous James River plantation homes as Westover, Carter's Grove and Shirley. Thomas was the son of William Randolph of Turkey Island (1651-1711), who had emigrated to Virginia about 1673.

The mansion, built in part of colonial brick and in part of wood, is of unusual design. There are two major wings, each 25 feet deep and 40 feet long, connected by a hall 24 feet wide and 40 feet long. Arched doorways open at either end into the wings — giving the house the shape of the letter H. It is thus in effect two houses in one, connected by the great hall. It is believed to have been modeled after the Virginia Capitol building in Williamsburg, which was erected on such an H-plan in 1699.

Probably unique in American architecture are the rare outbuildings along "plantation street." They include a kitchen, slaves' quarters, a smokehouse, storage structures, and a small, one-room, one-story school house.

Thomas Randolph died in 1729, willing Tuckahoe to his only son, William, who was a burgess for Goochland. He died in 1745, leaving a large estate. He bequeathed 1,200 pounds in sterling — a fortune in those days — to each of his two daughters, and requested that Peter Jefferson come to Tuckahoe as an overseer and guardian, and hired a tutor to teach his young son, Thomas Mann Randolph. Jefferson did, bringing with him his young son, Thomas, who spent seven of his first nine years at the plantation going to classes with the Randolph children in the tiny school house on the grounds.

Tuckahoe remained in the possession of the Randolph family until 1830, when it was sold and subsequently passed through a succession of owners. The current "squires" of the land are the A. B. Thompsons.

As with many of the great plantation homes in Virginia, especially along the James, and including Brandon, Berkeley, Carter's Grove, Westover and Shirley — Tuckahoe has its share of ghostly legends, some of which have been experienced by highly credible witnesses and are fairly well documented. Others are more sketchy.

There is, for example, the story of the itinerant peddler. In days gone by these horse and wagon forerunners to the modern traveling salesmen used to ply their trades to the great outlying, plantations, selling everything from primitive cosmetics and miracle healing substances to trimmings and dress goods. Allegedly a lace peddler arrived at Tuckahoe one day to vend his wares, but instead got into a fierce altercation with a member of the household and was murdered. He is said to reappear at times, seeking retribution, in the southeast chamber of the house.

There also is "a little gray lady" at the site. Such ladies seem to be fairly common in old Virginia circles. There is a rather well known one at Sherwood Forest in Charles City County, home of President John Tyler. A Tyler descendent believes the specters of gray ladies, or rather ladies in gray, stem from the fact that most servants in the great houses along the James wore gray uniforms.

Anyway, in a book titled "Historical Gardens of Virginia," published in 1923, there is reference to a "dainty little Gray Lady (Incidentally, all of spectral gray ladies appear to be small for some reason) who, when the midnight hour has come, steps gently out from a cupboard in the lovely old 'Burnt Room' to mingle with the mortals for awhile." A second published reference to this particu-

Tuckahoe Plantation

lar phenomenon relates to Mrs. Richard S. Allen, whose husband, Joseph, bought Tuckahoe in 1850. She and a friend reportedly were standing in the dining room one day when "both of them saw distinctly the figure of a small woman in gray enter through the hall door and pass out the little entry door leading to the outer kitchen."

Mrs. Allen may have been mediumistic, because other strange things happened to her during her tenure at Tuckahoe. A Richmond *Times-Dispatch* article written more than 50 years ago recalled the time Mrs. Allen was sitting in the upstairs hall unpacking a box. The only other person around was a maid who was washing windows. Mrs. Allen heard someone call her name, "Jennie." She looked up, saw no one and continued her work. Then the call was repeated "in loud and anxious tones." The mystery voice fairly bellowed, "Jennie! Jennie!" This aroused her to her feet, and she hurried into the room where the maid was to see if something was wrong, knowing that only that would cause the maid to call her by her first name. But she found the servant quietly washing a window. Just then a loud crash startled them both. They raced back into the room where Mrs. Allen had been and found that a large portion of the ceiling had fallen and completely demolished the very chair upon which she had been sitting!

There is one other episode involving the Allens which is worthy of retelling. One evening family members and some guests were amusing themselves with a Planchette. This was a 19th century predecessor to the Ouija board. It is a small board supported on casters at two points and a vertical pencil at a third, and is believed to produce automatic writing when lightly touched by the finger.

Anyway, someone asked "who is your master," and the pencil spelled out "the devil." Then the question was posed, is Tuckahoe haunted? The answer was not only emphatic, but descriptive: "Yes, the red room upstairs, and it has an odd panel in the wall." This triggered a dash up the stairs to this room where indeed an odd panel was discovered that had not been previously noticed.

Then it was remembered that years earlier a traveling man who had spent a night in that room said he had been awakened in the middle of the night by a rocking chair rocking violently back and forth. He got up, lit a lamp and saw the chair rocking, but there was no one in it. No window was open, so no draft could have set the chair in motion. He went back to sleep only to be reawakened by the same manifestation. This was enough for him.

He hastily dressed, packed and vacated the house, telling a per-plexed servant along the way out that nothing on earth would induce him to stay in that room again.

There is an earlier tale, too, about a dream of a "fragile wraith" which led to "one of Tuckahoe's most loved chatelaines" being brought to preside in the house. It was the dream of Thomas Mann Randolph III, great-grandson of the builder of the house. After the death of his first wife, he envisioned one evening that a young lady opened a closet door in his bedroom and brought him a glass of water. The next day he spoke of the apparition and said the face was so clear that if he ever saw it again he would instantly recog-nize it. Accordingly, years later he did meet the woman of his dreams in Paterson, New Jersey, proposed to her, married her, and brought her back to the mansion!

Since moving into Tuckahoe a few years ago, Tad and Sue Thompson, a young modern couple with three small children, have either heard of, or personally experienced a few strange things at the house. "I guess the most distinct one," says Sue, "was one time in the middle of the night I woke up and heard the vague hum of voices downstairs, and a tinkling sound, like glasses of a chandelier. As I became fully awake, it sounded more like a party was going on, a really happy one. I roused Tad and said 'do you hear that,' and he said he did. It definitely sounded like a party, but it was muted. It was like it was far off somewhere. Tad went down to look but he didn't find anything. I'm not a great believer in this sort of thing, but it was very real that night. We heard something!

"There have been a couple of other things," Sue Thompson continues. "Once I saw someone or something in white at the little school house building. The door was open and I thought it was Tad. But it wasn't, and I never knew who it was. Other times I feel like I hear a baby crying in another part of the house, when I know all my children are accounted for."

On another occasion some friends were leaving Tuckahoe early one morning when they stopped to check a tire on the car. As they did, they happened to look toward the house. "They said they saw a figure in white near the garden toward the tool shed," Sue explains. "They said it was sort of hovering above the garden."

And one day Tad was showing a reporter about the house. They had just left one upstairs bedroom and crossed over to the Red Room when they heard a crash in the first room. It sounded like something had slid across a table and fallen to the floor, but when they went back in to look nothing was amiss. Yet the sound of the crash could be clearly heard on the reporter's tape recorder when they played it back.

Sue has a possible theory. "My feeling is that if there is an unhappy ghost at Tuckahoe, it might be Judith Randolph. She's buried here. She had a tragic life." The story behind this, as chronicled in "Mistress Nancy," and other books on Tuckahoe and the Randolph family, is that Judith was married to Richard Randolph many generations ago. There was an alleged scandal. Judith's younger sister, Nancy, was said to have had an affair with Richard and became pregnant. This was kept secret even from close family members. When the child arrived, delivered at another plantation by servants, it was either born dead or was killed, and the whole affair was hushed up. Nevertheless, ugly rumors circulated, so to clear up the matter, Richard, who was accused of snuffing out the baby's life, stood trial for murder. He was acquitted, as was Nancy, by a brilliant defense devised by none other than Patrick Henry.

Judith Randolph, however, later had a son who was born deaf. Deeply religious, she believed that in keeping quiet about what actually had transpired, the Lord was using this deafness to punish her, and she lived for years with guilt. Richard later died unexpectedly, and some have offered that he may have been poisoned by Judith. All of this leads Sue to wonder that if one of the ghosts of Tuckahoe is a sad one, could it be the return of Judith who grew up there so many years ago?

But by far the best known of all spirits at Tuckahoe is the "distressed bride with flowing hair" who, dressed in wedding veil and satin gown, wrings her hands as she "rushes along the Ghost Walk." This walk is a charming vista down a turfed alley lined with old fashioned or suffruticosa box, named in behalf of this spectral presence seen by many for more than 200 years. The legend is that she is running away from a husband she was forced to marry, who was three times her age.

One account, in a faded newspaper clip published decades ago, tells of "a sad little ghost, whose tragedy is a matter of family record." She had been married very young, and much against her own wishes, to a bridegroom many years her senior. "Shortly after her marriage, she died, presumably of that ailment dear in the memories of our ancestors — a broken heart — and lies in the family burial ground on the estate. We can let our fancy weave a very pretty story of an attractive if impecunious lover, whom her family would not permit her to marry rather than sacrificing her youth and beauty to age and wealth, an old familiar story."

Actually, we can do more than fancy that, because the facts in this case were set down in an absorbing monograph on Tuckahoe Plantation by Jessie Ball Thompson Krusen in 1975. From this we learn that sometime in the early 1730s one of the Randolph daugh-

Ghost Walk at Tuckahoe

ters named Mary, breaking with her family's wishes, married her uncle's overseer. His name was Isham and he apparently was not well liked by the landed gentry of the day.

Mary was, in fact, sternly censured by none less than Colonel William Byrd II, master of Westover and a longtime close family friend of the Randolphs. Byrd commented on what he viewed as an ill-advised union in this manner, as quoted by Ms. Krusen: "Besides the meanness of this mortal's (the overseer's) aspect, the man has not one visible qualification, except imprudence, to recommend him to a female's inclinations. But there is sometimes such a charm in that Hibernian endowment, that frail women can't withstand it, though it stands alone with any other recommendation. Had she run away with a gentleman or a pretty fellow, there might have been some excuse for her, though he were of inferior fortune: but to stoop to a dirty plebeian without any kind of merit is the lowest prostitution. I found the family justly enraged at it and though I had more good nature than to join in her condemnation, yet I could devise no excuse for so senseless a prank as this young gentlewoman had played."

Ms. Krusen adds that the "unfortunate Mary" was later brought home and forced to marry the much older Mr. James Keith, thus she speculates that it is Mary's pitiable figure that is seen wringing her hands as she flees her elderly husband along Ghost Walk.

The Lost Treasure of Whichello

(near Richmond)

"We had passed through walls and piled bones, with casks and puncheons intermingling, into the inmost recesses of the catacombs."
— *The Cask of Amontillado*

r. and Mrs. J. Donald DeVilbiss, who quietly celebrated their 50th wedding anniversary in November 1984, are gracious hosts who take obvious pride in showing their historic house at 9602 River Road on the outskirts of Richmond. It is subtly furnished with period pieces harmonious with the time it was built.

In the parlor to the right as you enter the house on the main floor is a large fireplace — there is one in nearly every room, in fact. And just to the right is an area once distinguished with elaborate wainscotting no longer visible. It is in this room that the legends persist. One is that the skeletal remains of a former owner are buried seven feet beneath the fireplace. The other is that treasure is secreted either somewhere in the structure or on its grounds, hence the reason for the missing wainscotting. Fortune hunters ripped it out years ago in a desperate search for the lost loot.

For this house is the famous Whichello.

Although the DeVilbisses say no one has gone into the history of the property thoroughly, quite a bit is known about Whichello, or the "Tall House," as it also has been called. The land on which it sits is believed to have been owned by the Randolphs of Tuckahoe. One of the family members gave this tract to his French barber, a man named Druin, who in turn passed it on to his daughter, Catherine Woodward, who built the house in 1827 at a cost of $2,000.

It has a center plan frame structure with a symmetrical five-bay facade, and exterior end chimneys of random American bond. It stands a full two stories and includes a basement and a fully finished loft. Walls are nearly a foot thick, with the exterior clapboard hung on brick and plaster.

From its earliest days, apparently, Whichello was used as a tavern for those traveling between Richmond and Charlottesville or Lynchburg.

After a few years, Catherine Woodward's daughter, Eliza Anne Woodward Winston, sold the house. There are conflicting accounts as to when this was done. Most say it was in 1838, although there are references to its sale in 1845. In either event, the new owner was an Englishman of questionable reputation named Richard Whichello who had arrived in the area by "sailing up the James River."

As owner and operator of the tavern, Whichello is said to have accumulated wealth, according to one old report, which "was not come by in manners befitting a Christian gentleman." He was described as being miserly and cruel to his slaves. And, it was rumored, he ran games of chance, perhaps including cock fighting, that were not always honest and above board. There is one reference to him as being the type of man who had "a willingness to turn a penny by whatsoever means..."

Here, the story is picked up by A. H. Moncure, who claimed he was born in the house, probably sometime during the Civil War or early post war years. Moncure was quoted in a feature article written more than half a century ago when he then was "well advanced in years." This is what he had to say:

"...One night about dusk in the year 1850, a cattle drover from the valley region to the West arrived at the tavern with a herd which he bedded in the corrals near the inn, and there he stayed overnight. The next day he continued into the Southern capitol, and sold his cattle, returning later to again spend the night with tavern keeper Whichello.

"After dinner that night...Whichello invited his guest to accompany him to the 'country store' which was in reality a crossroads barroom just a few steps from the tavern. There the two men had some drinks and it was reported that Whichello and the drover became engrossed in a poker game. Anyway, the result was that Whichello went home richer by the amount Richmond dealers paid for a herd of prime cattle, and the drover from the valley went to bed 'broke.'

"In the morning attendants found the inn keeper on the floor of his bedroom, brutally murdered, with his head beaten in with an axe. The drover was gone, so was his old red and white horse and all of the money Whichello was supposed to have had with him the night before. No trace was ever found of the cattleman, and no other solution for the tavern owner's death has ever been set forth."

Other sources say that the man's sudden death caused for what few friends he had, a curious problem. Where should they bury him? They were afraid that if his body was interred in a cemetery, that the slaves he had so harshly mistreated might dig up the remains and "treat it to varied indignities in retaliation."

Mr. Moncure tells what happened: "...That was a problem and this is the way it was solved. The friends secretly dug a hole along side the east chimney of the old tavern. Then, from this hole they tunneled to beneath the great brick chimney, and then shoved the coffin into the tunnel until it rested under the stack. That is Whichello's tomb, and from that fact, which later gained circulation, arose many of the reports of the ghost of the old owner returning to guard the treasure which his killer could not find, and which to this day is believed buried around the building."

The stories of the hidden cache of treasure have persisted, and there have been a number of fruitless searches for it through the years. At some point, the fireplace containing Whichello's remains was dug into, and the wall adjacent to it was ripped apart.

One of the most intriguing incidents was recalled by Mrs. Joseph Crenshaw, who ran a tea shop in the house in the 1930s. "Many attempts have been made to find the reputed treasure of the man," she stated, "and some tall tales are told, such as the one an old Negro told me. 'Uncle John' came to me one day and said he had a device which could locate all kinds of metal, but which wasn't any good for papers, and (he) wanted to try it out on the old Whichello hoard. He dug in what is now the kitchen...But alas, no riches, unless one count the richness of the yarn old 'Uncle John' spun me, a treasure.

"The old colored man assured me that no less than three times had he struck the very box which enclosed the wealth, only to have the 'spirit trove' vanish as such troves are said to do because the digger could not restrain an ejaculation or refrain from speaking at his fortune.

Whichello

" 'You really saw it, Uncle John?' I asked. 'I sure did, deed I did,' " Mrs. Crenshaw says he told her. "Each time, he said it sank down further out of sight, and the holes filled with water. This last is true enough. The holes in the old kitchen were veritable wells, and have had to be cemented over, the water flowing into them as fast as shovels made an opening."

While Mrs. Crenshaw may have had some difficulty believing Uncle John's story, even if it was told to her in dead seriousness, she nevertheless began to feel the house was haunted. For one thing, visitors to the tea room began to complain of a "feeling." It became so strong to some of them that they left their ordered refreshments before enjoying them and rushed out of the house.

Then there was the mysterious clicking noise that wouldn't go away. Mrs. Crenshaw said it sounded like an invisible telegraph key, and it seemed to follow her throughout the house from room to room. Her maid heard it, too. Says Mrs. Crenshaw: "No matter what room I went into, immediately the strange click was there, too. I told the maid it was an electric wire, but I knew that if it had been, the house would have burned up long ago.

"I became interested in the traditions and legends of the

house," Mrs. Crenshaw said, "and began to wonder on my own account what did cause so many strange incidents. One day in a spirit of daring, I braved the ridicule of my husband and friends, and decided to put my problems up to Lady Wonder, that fortune telling horse on the Petersburg Pike.

"After a few trivial questions, I said: 'Lady, is there treasure in my house?' The horse answered by spelling out the affirmative. 'Where is it?' was my next query. The horse spelled out the word 'Chimney,' and then I dared to ask again (dared for these questions are only answered when properly accompanied by the nominal amount the horse's owner collects) 'Which chimney?'

"This time, without hesitancy, the animal spelled out 'East,' which is true according to all the legends. My next try was at a more definite location, and the horse's answer was to spell out 'ten feet.' Returning home, you may be sure I eyed that fireplace and chimney many times, but I never did have faith enough to go ahead and tear up the property."

Mrs. Crenshaw continued her narrative: "The news (about the ghost) soon spread and I received several requests from Richmonders and others interested in that sort of phenomenon to hold a meeting in the old house. All of these I granted, and admit that I became intensely interested myself. The first group came out and we were sitting around the table in the tea room, the lights were all on and the fire in the fireplace added to the cheeriness. One of my guests, a well known Richmond woman, began to speak of a 'little girl' visitor we had with us. She said the little girl was giving a flower to one of the other women. Then she was gone, and the woman indicated admitted the description fitted her little niece. This was all done with the lights on and not a bit of gruesomeness.

"Next, the medium, if that was what she is called, turned to me and said an old Negro mammy was beside me. She described her and told how her head kerchief was tied in a peculiar way. It was my mother's old mammy who had taken care of me as a child. The woman said how glad the spirit seemed to have me know that she was with me again. Yes, it was Sabra all right, and this only added to my puzzlement.

"At last I asked this woman if she had noticed a queer feeling upon entering my tea room, and she said: 'Why yes, as soon as I arrived. Didn't you see me stop at the door?' I replied that I had noticed her delay in entering, and then she added: 'That was because there was a man standing just behind you. He was dressed in hunting clothes and seemed to live here.' That was my first actual contact with Richard Whichello's ghost. Since then, several others have told me of seeing the apparition, and each time it has been clothed in his hunting togs."

At another seance held in the house, Mrs. Crenshaw said the following letter in spirit writing was "materialized" at the sitting: "My treasure is not in the house, but in the yard. You should look in the backyard about 100 feet away from the house and marked by a little (here the ghost grew descriptive and drew what appears to be a small board fence on the paper) and it is about five feet under the earth. You should look toward the east when leaving the back steps and count until told to stop — then go back three paces." The writing, scrawled in a wild scribble, was signed with the initials "W. R. W."

And thus is the chronicle of the ghost of Whichello. The words of Mrs. Crenshaw, uttered more than 50 years ago, may well be the most prophetic: "There's something supernatural about that place," she said, "any many are the people who have confirmed my opinion."

The Sad Return of Sarah Henry

(near Ashland)

entlemen may cry, peace, peace — but there is no peace. The war is actually begun! The next gale that sweeps from the north will bring to our ears the clash of resounding arms! Our brethren are already in the field! Why stand we here idle? What is it that gentlemen wish? What would they have? Is life so dear, or peace so sweet, as to be purchased at the price of chains and slavery? Forbid it, Almighty God! I know not what course others may take; but as for me...give me liberty or give me death!"

Those, of course, were the words of the great patriot and orator Patrick Henry. They rank high among the most famous words ever spoken. They helped launch a war that won America's freedom. When he finished speaking on March 23, 1775, at St. John's Church in Richmond, the audience sat in silence, stunned. Edmund Randolph later said Henry's words reverberated so loudly, if not in the ears, at least in the memory of this audience, that no other member was venturous enough to interfere with that voice which had so recently subdued and captivated.

Today, practically every school child in America can recite lines from that remarkable speech. Yet very few people — then or now — were aware that the feisty Henry was heartsick the day he spoke from a still-burning deep personal tragedy. Only recently had his wife and the mother of the first six of his 17 children, Sarah Shelton Henry, died following a long, terrible illness which emotionally drained the entire family, and which haunted them, both literally and figuratively, long afterwards.

This all occurred during the seven years Henry lived at Scotchtown, a great sprawling estate in upper Hanover County a few miles west of Ashland off route 54. Scotchtown was the creation of Charles Chiswell who came to Virginia from Scotland late in the 17th century. He held nearly 10,000 acres of land in the area in 1717, and, according to local historians, he originally wanted to build a Scottish castle on the site. But after several of his native

Portrait of Patrick Henry at Scotchtown

craftsmen became ill and died of fever, he settled, instead, for the more modern "barnlike" house which stands today. It is believed that Scotchtown was built in 1719. The Virginia Landmarks Register calls it "probably the largest one-story colonial house in Virginia, with eight rooms and a center passage on the same floor." It is over 80 feet long and nearly 40 feet deep. It is only one story high, but that is deceiving, because there are eight additional rooms in the full height basement, and there is an enormous attic in which parties and balls were held. One author said of the attic: "It could have housed a swarm of merry and none too finicky guests, congregated for a dance or house party."

If Scotchtown has an aura of tragedy about it, it likely began with Colonel John Chiswell, who inherited the house from his father in 1737. Following a series of unfortunate investments including a lead mining company known as "Chiswell's Mine," he was forced to sell the plantation in 1760. John Chiswell, who was described as "a testy and choleric man," became "involved in a drunken brawl" at Ben Mosby's Tavern at Cumberland Court House in 1766, during which he ran a sword through his friend, Robert Routledge, killing him. He subsequently was charged with murder.

Before his trial came up, however, he died, on October 17, 1766, and there seems to be some confusion as to how he died. His physician said he expired from "nervous fits" owing to constant uneasiness of mind. Others speculate he committed suicide. In either case, when his body was brought back to Scotchtown for burial, a bizarre incident occurred. Routledge's friends followed the coffin and demanded that it be opened to verify that the corpse was that of Chiswell. When it was determined that indeed it was, he was buried in a small cemetery located about a mile in back of the house.

Debts also plagued John Robinson, who had bought the house from Chiswell and it was sold at auction. John and Mary Payne became owners during this period and for a short while they lived at Scotchtown with their daughter who later married James Madison, the fourth President of the United States. She was the famous Dolley Madison. Patrick Henry then bought the house and property in 1771 for about $18,000.

One biographer noted: "Here, Henry might have enjoyed the amenities of life on a large plantation with a number of slaves while continuing his legal and political activities. But again fate intervened. Did the tragic death of Colonel Chiswell cast a shadow over Scotchtown?" The author was referring to the distressing and traumatic illness of Sarah Henry that was to darken the great orator's days at the mansion.

Much has been written about Sarah's illness, and still there is considerable mystery surrounding it. In fact, in family accounts there is a singular absence of information about her Scotchtown years. There are scores of references from biographers, authors, historians and others. One wrote: "Family illness of a most distressing sort and the outbreak of the Revolution soon blasted Henry's hopes for happiness on the plantation." There are reports that her sickness began about the time of the birth of her sixth child, Edward, in 1771. A biographer speculated: "Perhaps she had an innate tendency to break under strain; the wife of a statesman often has to pay an even more onerous price for greatness than does her husband."

In another account, it is stated that Sarah suffered from a "protracted mental illness. Certain details are lacking, but the convincing family tradition is that several years before her death Sarah developed 'a strange antipathy' to her husband and children." Another insight as to the extreme seriousness of her condition was offered in a publication, years later, by the son of Patrick Henry's personal physician who attended to Sarah. He wrote: "Here (at Scotchtown) his family resided whilst Henry had to encounter many mental and personal afflictions known only to his family physician. Whilst his towering and master-spirit was arousing a nation to arms, his soul was bowed down and bleeding under the heaviest sorrows and personal distresses. His beloved companion had lost her reason, and could only be restrained from self-destruction by the strait-dress (a forerunner to today's straight jacket)"

Sarah was confined — for how long is uncertain — to two dungeon-like rooms in a cold basement of the house and watched after by a servant. Most evidence points to the fact that Henry was heartbroken over his wife's deteriorating condition. Henry once spoke of himself, while only about 40 years old, as "a distraught old man." When he was home from his frequent travels, he would visit Sarah by descending a secret staircase off the backhall of the building. However, one of Sarah's cousins asserted that Henry was hard on his wife, saying he was interested in outside projects and not in Sarah.

In those ill-informed days, people with mental illness were often considered to be demon possessed. And as time wore on with Sarah strapped in confinement and rarely seen by anyone other than immediate family members, fear spread through the plantation. Many workers, especially servants, were afraid to go in or near the house. Even when the tormented woman died, she was buried in an unmarked grave, which, again, was the custom in the 18th century for the burial of "crazy" people. It is not known today exactly where her body is located.

Although he was "crushed with grief," Henry was somehow able to put the finishing touches on his famous speech at St. Johns Church which he delivered only a short time after Sarah's death. For the next two or three years he was away much of the time, and in 1777 he sold Scotchtown to move to the newly-renovated Governor's Mansion in Williamsburg.

The great house in Hanover County went through several owners over the next 180 years and eventually became abandoned, with "infrequent and neglectful tenants." It was for a time even occupied by squatters who "quartered goats in the basement and raised chickens in one of the first-floor rooms. The plaster was falling, the roof was leaking and many of the windows on the main floor were gone."

In June 1958 the Association for the Preservation of Virginia Antiquities bought Scotchtown, then "in a sad state of repair," and began to plan for the mansion's restoration. This has been accomplished with dignity and integrity, and today the house is open to the public. It is now much like it must have been in 1782 when Baron Ludwig von Closen wrote in his journal after a visit: "The house is spacious and handsome, extremely well furnished and delightfully well ordered. In a word, it is one of the most pleasing establishments in America."

It also is haunted!

There are, conceivably, multiple spirits here, but certainly the predominant one — as attested to by many who have claimed to have seen and heard her — is Sarah Henry. "If this house wasn't haunted, it definitely should be," declares Ron Steele, Scotchtown's director today. "It is a very spooky place, especially at night when the wind is blowing. It can get very scary inside. You hear all kinds of noises. When the wind is blowing real hard, you can hear it whistling through the old house. It sounds kind of like a moaning."

Steele and his wife, Alice, keep check on the house during the off season — it is open from April through October — and he says there have been occasions when both he and the local police were reluctant to go into the house at night. "We have motion alarm systems inside, and someone or something has to be at least four feet tall to set them off," Steele says. "In the past two or three years the alarms have been set off a number of times, and when the police come out, they ask me to go in the place first. We only have lights in the hall, so it's pretty dark, and it can get kind of oppressive in the house." He adds that one of the most frightening phenomena has to do with the portrait of Joseph Shelton which hangs in the dining room. "You go in that room at night and his eyes follow you all across the room, no matter where you go. It is very scary."

Alice Steele had a terrifying experience of her own. "We had a bad storm one night, and the lights in the main house went out," she remembers. "I went out with a flashlight to turn them on. You have to open the door to the secret stairway to the cellar. I turned the key but the door wouldn't open. It was almost as if someone were on the other side holding it. It took all of my strength to get it open, and, finally as I opened the door the flashlight went dead, even though I had put fresh batteries in it. Well, have you ever had a feeling that someone was standing right behind you? I got that

Scotchtown

344

feeling. I could feel the hair on the back of my neck standing up. I just knew Sarah was there. There definitely was a presence. Even when I got the lights back on, I wouldn't dare turn around." Ron adds that when Alice got back to their house, she was as white as a sheet.

The Steeles also report that pieces of furniture seem to get moved around inexplicably at times. Once during the winter when the house was closed, they discovered a tea caddie had been moved from the center of a table and placed on a chair seat and the top of a tea pot had been taken off. "It appeared like someone was having a little tea party," says Alice. Several times a cradle in a downstairs bedroom which belonged to the Henry family has been out of place "It's happened to both Alice and me," Ron says. "Sometimes we go into that room in the dark and we bang our shins on the cradle, because somehow it has been moved from its place beside the bed to the middle of the room. This has happened periodically, yet we are the only ones who have keys to the house. How does the cradle get moved? Maybe we have it in the wrong place and 'Sarah' puts it back where it was 200 years ago."

But the Steeles are not the only ones who have experienced psychic manifestations. "Patrick Henry's great, great, great grand-

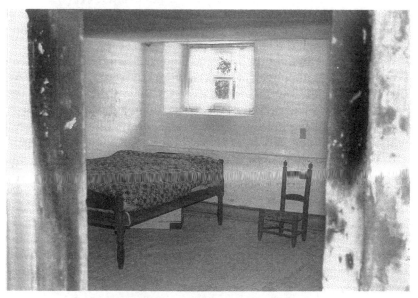

Sarah Henry's Room at Scotchtown

345

daughter was reluctant to talk about it, but she was convinced the house was haunted," Ron says. "She would never come here at night." Right after Halloween 1990, a police officer told Steele that a neighbor had told him she noticed what looked like a candle in one of the windows of the house. She had taken her kids out trick or treating when she saw the light. She pulled up into the yard and said the light suddenly disappeared, as if the candle had been blown out. She added that at that instant she saw a "fleeting image" which looked like someone holding a candle. Ron says the whole episode was strange because he and his wife were out of town at the time and there was no one in the house.

There are other questions which remain unanswered. Why can't the inner walls of the basement rooms in which Sarah Henry was confined be painted? The paint will not adhere. If there is a rational reason, the Steeles haven't found it yet. Why, on a breezy day in early April did a swarm of flies and wasps cluster against an attic window? What is the explanation for the sound of chains being dragged across the floor of the attic when no one is up there? Such sounds have been heard by more than one person.

"We know of at least one sound here that wasn't caused by ghosts," says Stuart Womeldorph, director of the Hanover County branch of the Association for the Preservation of Virginia Antiquities. "Once, the residents reported hearing the old piano being played downstairs when no one was downstairs. They went down to see what was causing it, and darned if a rat wasn't running up and down the keyboard!"

Alan Ward is another who has had supernatural feelings at Scotchtown. He now lives in Ruckersville, but several years ago he had what he calls "an incredible experience" during his first visit to the house. He had no prior knowledge of any ghostly legends.

"I was walking around in the basement area, by myself, and when I got into one particular room, I could feel something there. I didn't see anything," Ward recalls. "I just had this feeling that there was something there. There was a real sensation of presence there. Afterwards, I told Ron and Alice about my experience, and their eyes got wider and wider. When I described where I had been, they told me that was the room where Sarah Henry had been kept and where she had died. As they told me this, a really incredible feeling came over me. I'm not the kind of person who believes in ghosts or anything, but I really believe there was something there."

John Taylor of Ashland told a *New York Times* reporter 20 years ago, that when he and his brother were boys, they remembered seeing the "ghost of a lady at dusk passing from the basement of Scotchtown to the slave quarters." He said they tried to catch 'her' but she vanished before their eyes.

Several years ago, a tour guide was taking some tourists from Michigan through the house when they stopped to talk in the dining room, which is located directly above the room which Sarah occupied in the basement. When the guide started to tell the story of Sarah, suddenly the group heard shrill screams emanating from the basement. "They all ran from the house as fast as they could," Ron says.

Mary Adams, who lives in the small town of Montpelier nearby, (not to be confused with James Madison's home in Orange County) lived at Scotchtown from 1933 to 1940, before its deterioration, and says she experienced all sorts of psychic phenomena. "We were scared at first," she recalls, "but we got used to it. There were a lot of unnatural sounds. We would hear chains dragging across the floor and other real weird noises. But I really enjoyed living there. There was a lot of room to play, and you could whoop and holler and do whatever you wanted."

Mary says that once she was in the house playing with a group of kids. "I guess there were about eight or 10 of us, and the grownups were in the back part of the house, away from us. All of a sudden, we saw this figure. It looked like a person, like a woman with a long flowing gown. She was all in white. We all just stared at it. We were transfixed. Somehow, we knew it wasn't a real live person. The only thing that we could imagine was that it was a ghost. It was right scary. I can tell you that. We must have watched it for a half minute or more, and then it just disappeared. We bolted out of there and ran to our folks, but, of course, by the time they investigated, the room was empty. But even after I moved from there, I would always get the feeling whenever I went back to visit, that the ghost lady was there. I still think she is today.

"Was it Sarah Henry? I really don't know. It could have been."

C H A P T E R   6 0

The Ghost Brigade
of Centre Hill

(Petersburg)

*"...A great hero, in the heat of combat, not perceiving that he had
been fairly killed, continued to fight valiantly, dead as he was."*
— *How to Write a Blackwood Article*

lthough encroached upon by the trappings
of the modern world, Centre Hill stands
today, as it has for well over a century and a half, as the dominating architectural showpiece of Petersburg. It vividly recalls the antebellum splendor and prosperity of the old city. One early visitor to the mansion described it as a "superb" building offering a "grand and imposing view," and the wife of John Tyler, 10th President of the United States, said "the place is on a large and in some respects a really grand scale."

The grounds themselves are historic, for before the house was built, they served as a muster ground for the militia. It was, in fact, from this site that the famous company of Petersburg volunteers departed to distinguish themselves in battle in the War of 1812, and thus earn for Petersburg the title, "The Cockade City of the Union."

Perhaps this requires a little explanation, which is provided by Dr. James Bailey, city historian. "This is in reference to the fact that in the War of 1812, the volunteers marched to Ohio and fought with great valor at Fort Meigs," Dr. Bailey says. "During this period they wore cockades in their hats."

Centre Hill was built in 1823 for Robert Bolling, great grandson of the immigrant Robert Bolling, founder of a well-known Virginia family. Situated in a beautifully planted and enclosed park of over eight acres, it was constructed in "generous proportions" of over-size brick in Flemish bond, and is architecturally referred to as a "transitional Greek Revival style house."

Magnificent wolfhounds of Carrara marble guard the entrance to the columned portico, and the interior is adorned with hand-carved woodwork and lavish cornices. Remnants of a tunnel connecting the house with the Appomattox River can still be seen from the lower level of the house. It was built for the convenience of guests, mostly James River plantation owners who arrived there by barge.

Like other mansions of its size and prominence, Centre Hill has played host to its share of dignitaries over the years, including Abraham Lincoln. After the Confederate evacuation of the city, which ended the ten-months siege of Petersburg, the house became the headquarters of Major General G. L. Hartsuff, district commander for the Union. Lincoln met with him here on April 7, 1865. When the subject of rent was discussed, Lincoln said "our batteries have made rent enough here already."

It was officially opened as a Civil War era museum in 1950, and included exhibits and displays depicting the decisive and dramatic events in the history of Petersburg — Civil War portraits, uniforms, swords, pistols, shells, projectiles, rare maps, and the Confederate flag which flew above Hustings Courthouse until the day of the surrender. Centre Hill later was turned over to the City of Petersburg and today is a major tourist attraction.

With such an illustrious history, it is not surprising that the mansion is associated with some colorful ghostly legends. "Oh, yes, there are some interesting stories," says Dr. Bailey. One of the most common concerned "a beautifully dressed lady" who frequently sat at the second story window over the front door. She was seen by many people, but no one ever knew who she was. This occurred in the latter years of the 19th century. Once, during this time, a child living in the house told his mother of a "pretty lady" who had visited him during the night, sat on the side of his bed, held his hand, and talked to him. He indicated that he could see through her, meaning she gave a transparent appearance. The description he gave perfectly matched that of the woman others had seen in the window.

Mrs. Campbell Pryor, a direct descendent of the builder of

Centre Hill

Centre Hill, lived in the house in the 1880s and 1890s, and told of the spectral playing of a little melodeon that stood in a corner of the library. "Many, many times," she said, "familiar airs have been heard played by invisible hands, as no mortal was in the room."

Her husband also experienced the strange phenomena. He once tried to use as a bed chamber a small room on the first floor near an office, but apparently the ghost, or whatever it was, felt this room belonged to it. Every time Mr. Campbell retired and the lights were turned out, "invisible hands jerked the coverings off the bed and threw them onto the middle of the floor!"

But the oddest manifestation of all was the return of the troop of soldiers, presumably Civil War veterans, who for a number of years in succession tramped through the house precisely at 7:30 p.m. each January 24th. So regular was their procession, that the house owners at the time invited friends and neighbors in to witness the eerie spectacle.

This was best expressed by Margaret DuPont Lee in her 1930 book, "Virginia Ghosts." "On that day of the year," Mrs. Lee wrote, "the clock pointing to the half hour, the door leading into the office was heard to open. Then a noise such as a regiment of soldiers marching! The clank as of sabres suggested the occupation of those tramping along the passage; up the stairs and into a room over the office. After about twenty minutes the sound was again heard descending the steps, crossing the hall, then finally the slamming of a door and all was quiet."

C H A P T E R 6 1

Interludes of
Divine Intervention

(Southhampton County)

prinkled intermittently through Virginia's
history — and, in fact, involving some of the
most famous and infamous names in that history — are some curious vignette-footnotes that have to do with communicating with
spirit matter of the highest order. In a few instances, it has been
claimed that certain messages, in the form of signs, direct callings,
or otherwise, have come to mere mortals straight from the Holy
Ghost, or a close disciple. These messages have in turn been interpreted, by those who claim they have received them, or by others
who were witnesses, as expressions of Divine Providence. They
have been defined as inexorable destiny; unalterable fate.

Whether or not they involved some higher form of psychic
activity obviously would be arguable, but to those to whom these
occurrences happened, and often to others around them, there is no
way to convince them that they were not genuine. Take, for example, the charismatic aura which surrounded the legendary
Confederate general, Thomas "Stonewall" Jackson. As we know
from his many biographers, he was a deeply religious man — to the
point of fanaticism — who prayed incessantly. He was unanimous-
ly acknowledged to be a military genius, but many of his followers
felt the reasons for his at-times incredible successes went beyond
merely human capabilities. During the Shenandoah Valley cam-
paigns, for instance, it is said that his men came in time to believe
that Jackson was "in direct communication with the Almighty."

And what of the fate of John Wilkes Booth? For roughly two weeks after he fatally shot President Abraham Lincoln, Booth eluded trackers on a winding route which took him through part of the southern Maryland and into Virginia. Eventually, he wound up hiding in a barn on the Garrett farm in Caroline County. Tipped off to the assassin's whereabouts, a troop of 26 Union soldiers encircled the barn and demanded Booth to surrender. He refused. In an effort to smoke him out, the soldiers set fire to the barn.

They were under orders not to shoot; to take Booth alive. But as the flames began consuming the barn, an inexplicable thing happened. A single shot rang out, striking Booth in the back of the skull, oddly at virtually the same spot Booth's bullet had entered Lincoln's head. At first, soldiers who dragged Booth out, thought he had shot himself, but then a sergeant named Boston Corbett, a former hat cleaner known as the "Mad Hatter," admitted that he had pulled the trigger of his pistol, felling Booth. When he was asked why, Corbett said, "God Almighty directed me."

But probably the most bizarre "calling" of all — leading to one of the most notorious episodes in Virginia, or American history — occurred in 1831 in Southhampton County in the southeastern corner of the state. It was here, near the present town of Courtland, that the greatest slave uprising in the history of the United States took place. It was led by an intense, Bible-reading 31-year-old slave named Nat Turner. Turner seemed to have a hypnotic mesmerizing-type power over his fellow workers, and convinced them they should free themselves and "go to Jerusalem."

The rebellion began at a Sunday camp meeting in August 1831. "Exhorted to frenzy," by Turner, who they believed was guided by the spirits, this ill-fated group of slaves armed themselves with corn knives, axes, and scythes, and followed their leader in what was termed an orgy of butchery. They struck first at the Travis Plantation, where Turner worked, wiping out the entire family. Then they marched on into the country, plundering and gathering recruits as they went. Eventually, their force swelled to more than 50 as they proceeded from house to house, murdering all the whites they could find, men, women and children.

Once word of the insurrection got out, many houses were quickly evacuated, leading Turner to comment, "we found no more victims to gratify our thirst for blood." In all, 55 whites, including 12 pupils of a girls' school, were killed before troops summoned from Richmond and Norfolk arrived. Many (the exact number is not known) of the rioting slaves were slain by the soldiers, and 19 others later were hanged.

Turner escaped, for a time, as hundreds of men searched for him. Here is how he described his hiding: "...after having supplied myself with provisions from Mr. Travis,' I scratched a hole under a pile of fence-rails in a field, where I concealed myself for six weeks, never leaving my hiding place but for a few minutes in the dead of the night to get water, which was very near; thinking by this time I could venture out, I began to go about in the night, and eavesdrop the houses in the neighborhood; pursuing this course for about a fortnight, and gathering little or no intelligence, afraid of speaking to any human being, and returning every morning to my cave before the dawn of day."

Turner was eventually betrayed by a dog which had discovered food in his hidden sanctuary. Within days he was captured and later tried, sentenced and hanged.

Historians were to record their belief that Nat Turner appeared to have been a victim of superstition and fanaticism. He was able to arouse his fellow slaves to his cause, it was written, because he told them he was acting under "inspired direction."

In a confession he made while awaiting execution, Turner said that in his childhood a circumstance occurred which made an indelible impression on his mind and laid the groundwork of the enthusiasm which terminated so fatally to many. "Being at play with other children, when three or four years old, I told them something which my mother, overhearing, said happened before I was born. I stuck to my story, however, and related some things which went, in her opinion, to confirm it; others being called on were greatly astonished, knowing these things had happened, and caused them to say in my hearing, I surely would be a prophet, as the Lord had showed me things which happened before my birth."

His parents strengthened him in this belief, and said in his presence, that he was intended for "some great purpose," which they had always thought from "certain marks on his head and breast."

After a "variety of revelations from the spiritual world," Turner stated, in his confession, that, "On the 12th of May 1828, I heard a loud noise in the heavens, and the Spirit instantly appeared to me, and said the serpent was loosed...and that I should take it on and fight against the serpent, for the time was fast approaching when the first should be last and the last should be first — and by signs in the heavens that it would make known to me I should commence the great work."

The sign that appeared to Turner, in 1831, was the eclipse of the sun. He was to say it was this event "which determined me not to wait longer."

Curiously, Nat Turner ended up in Jerusalem, as he had prophesied. He was hanged there. The name of the town of Jerusalem, Virginia, was later changed to Courtland!

The Caretaker Bard
of Berry Hill

(Halifax County)

owhere else, perhaps, is the ante-bellum plantation to be found in equal architectural magnificence." This is how historian Fiske Kimball described Berry Hill, a monumental Greek Revival Mansion, erected in the 1840s, in Halifax County at the southern extreme of the state near South Boston. "Fronted by a heroic octa-style Doric portico reminiscent of the Parthenon," says the Virginia Landmarks Register, "the house is flanked by small porticoed dependencies, creating an exceptionally dramatic as well as romantic composition. No less impressive is the spacious interior with its grand divided stair that curves to meet a single flight."

James Coles Bruce, who built Berry Hill, was the oldest son of James Bruce, of Woodburn, Halifax County. By building a chain of small general stores and then expanding them, the older Bruce amassed one of the largest fortunes of his day. It was estimated at $4 million, and his empire included 3,000 slaves. Among the other valuable contents of the house was an extraordinary quantity of silver of the finest designs, including pitchers and basins. It is said the Bruces lived at Berry Hill like "lords of an English manor." The younger James Bruce ruled like "a sort of feudal chief on his great landed estate and in his county — where he was equally feared and admired. As he lay on his death bed in 1865, he said he "felt a grim satisfaction in leaving the world at that time, as he knew that nothing but ruin was in store for his class."

Berry Hill

Nevertheless, the mansion remained in the Bruce family for more than 100 years, and it frequently was the scene of lavish parties and elegant entertainment. Malcolm Bruce, last in the line to live at Berry HIll, died in the late 1940s, and the property was sold to Fred Watkins of Richmond. He, in turn, appointed Richard Cecil Rogers to be his caretaker, and Rogers lived alone in the 17-room house for about 17 years. Or rather it should be said that he was alone so far as mortal company was concerned. Apparently, according to Rogers, ghosts stalked about Berry Hill at will. He would tell stories of the haunting sights and sounds to just about anyone who would listen. In fact, he did better than that. Rogers wrote poetry about the spirits he experienced.

Following is his most famous work: "The Ghost of Berry Hill."

Did you ever see a Spook or a Ghost?
Did you ever have a Haunt, or something almost
Whisper, with warm breath close to your ear,
Till it froze up your blood with horror and fear?
Now, the story I tell, oh! it frightens me still!
While I worked on a plantation, called "Old Berry HIll."

In a big old house, with its sprawling lawn,
That was built 'way back, before Hector was born.

With its sky-high ceilings and transomed doors,
Long shuttered windows, and broad board floors,
That creaked and cried, if you walked or if you ran!
Lord, it wasn't no place, for an old Colored man!
Cause people had died on every floor —
From the cellar to the attic, now this I know;
For a record was kept in black and white,
But that record doesn't tell what happens at night!

No, that record will not tell, that the doors will slam!
That the windows will clatter, tho tightly jammed.
And that something tip-toes up the double stairs,
Like a Persian cat in her high-toned airs.
The record will not tell you, that while I slept,
That a woman came in, and raved and wept;
Hissing, and whispering, "Where can he be,"
Staring, glaring wild-eye, at me!

Oh! the cold chills ran the length of my spine,
My heart 'most stopped beating, I lost my weak mind,
And stared back at the woman, who stared at me,
And repeated her question, "Where can he be."
I thought of that woman, I'd promised to wed.
But why think of her, is my poor darling dead?
Has she come back to earth, in quest of me,
To kiss and whisper, "Where can he be?"

Oh, I shook, and I shivered, and covered my face.
And begged the Intruder, to please leave the place
But she stood and stared, thru her big eyes of brown,
Then pulled up a chair, and sat herself down.
She told me a tale, that I remember too well;
I promised her story, I never would tell.
Then there came a crash, like the breaking of morn!
I rolled out of bed, lo, the woman was gone!

Now, the story I tell, I have proof that backs
That this old Mansion still stands, in old Halifax.
With its sky-high ceilings and transomed doors.

And the Ghosts are still walking the creaky floors.
Big bats fly in from the grave yard hard by
And night Owls ask, "who, who, are youoooo?"
Then a voice cries, "Ise de Ghost, uf ol 'Mammy Louoooo!"

For eight long years, ah lived hearh a slave.
Toiled in de sun, an' lolled in de shade.
Heart sore an' foot sore, wid a strawbunk to lie in;
Fur a pone uv corn bread, an' a rock cabin to die in.
But ah sung an' ah prayed, ah laffed an' ah cried.
Yes, ah lived while ah lived, den ah died, den ah died!
Den mar good White-folks in splender, laid me 'way,
To res 'mar tired ol' bones, till de Judgement-day!

When de winder frames clatter, an' de lights all goes out,
An' de black cat purs de loudest, Ise some whar' bout!
Now, dar aint no use uv hidin! kaze every thing ah see!
While ah lived, not a soul, nor a critter feared me!
Little Chillun, dey loved me, both de Whites an' de Blacks';
Tho ah yanked dem fum mischief, an' spanked dey young backs!
Den rocked dem to sleep, an' tucked dem in bed.
Oh, it's de livin' dat hurts you an' never de Dead!
Fear de Livin', fear de Livin', and never de Dead!

Baffling Revelations
at Bacon's Castle

(Surry County)

I
t was, to the Virginia colonists, an ominous sign of impending disaster. It occurred sometime during "the latter months" of the year 1675. A great comet appeared in the sky sweeping across the heavens trailing a bright orange tail of fire. Soon after this eerie phenomenon came the flight of tens of thousands of passenger pigeons. For days they blanketed the sky, blotting out the sun. Then, in the spring of 1676 a plague of locusts ravaged the colony, devouring every plant in sight and stripping the trees of their budding leaves.

But to the colonists, the comet was the worst sign. Many remembered that another comet had streaked across the horizon just before the terrible Indian massacre of 1644. Thus, it was no real surprise to them — because they believed in such spectral omens — when, the following year, one of the bloodiest and most notorious chapters of Virginia History was written.

It began on a quiet summer Sunday when some colonists passing by the Stafford County plantation of Thomas Mathew on their way to church discovered the overseer, Robert Hen, lying in a pool of blood. Nearby lay an Indian servant, dead. Hen also was mortally wounded, but before he expired he managed to gasp, "Doegs! Doegs!" The words struck fear in the ears of the passersby, for Hen had mentioned the name of a tribe of Indians known for their fierce attacks on white men and women.

And so the seeds had been sown for what was to lead to the

largest and most violent insurrection of the colonial era up to that time — Bacon's Rebellion.

Dashing Nathanial Bacon — 18 years old — had arrived in the colony only three years earlier. Well educated and well endowed, he has been described by biographers as "a slender, attractive, dark-haired young man with an impetuous, sometimes fiery temperament and a persuasive tongue." But perhaps above all else, Bacon was a natural leader of men.

While Governor Berkeley remained inactive and inattentive in Jamestown, planters sought out Bacon to lead retaliatory strikes against the marauding Indians. When his own plantation was attacked and his overseer killed, Bacon agreed. He proved to be a skilled and capable military commander. On one march his forces drove the Pamunkey tribe deep into Dragon's Swamp. Later, Bacon overpowered the Susquehannocks, killing "at least 100 Indians," and capturing others.

Berkeley, furious at the unauthorized attacks launched by this rebellious group, dispatched his own troops to capture Bacon and his men. For the next several weeks the two men waged a cat-and-mouse game that involved daring, intrigue and bloodshed.

At one point Bacon surrendered, was brought before Berkeley and was forgiven when he repented. But then he escaped, returned with a force of 600 men and captured Jamestown, demanding a commission to fight the Indians, as well as the repeal of some harsh colonial laws. With no other choice under the show of arms, Berkeley granted the wishes, but when Bacon set out again chasing Indians, the Governor repudiated all agreements and sent his troops after the rebels.

After several skirmishes, Bacon recaptured Jamestown and had it sacked and burned to the ground. Berkeley, who had retreated to the Eastern Shore of Virginia, meanwhile, was regrouping his forces for a final and decisive confrontation. It never came to pass.

Bacon, who had suffered an attack of malaria at Jamestown, fell critically ill in Gloucester and died of dysentery there on October 16, 1676, at the age of 29. With the leader lost, the rebellion fell apart and Berkeley's forces captured many of Bacon's men. A large number of them were hanged, continuing for several more months the tragedy forewarned by the appearance of the comet.

For three months in 1676 about 70 of Bacon's followers occupied a large brick mansion in Surry County, just across the James River from Jamestown. Then called "Allen's Brick House." It has been known ever since as "Bacon's castle."

Now operated by the Association for the Preservation of Virginia Antiquities, this imposing brick structure was built some time after 1655. It stands amidst a large grove of oaks. There are two expansive, paneled first floor rooms, two more rooms on the second floor, and what has been described as a "dungeon-like" attic on the third.

There are several interesting love stories associated with Bacon's Castle — ranging from romantic to bitter sweet to tragic. Consider, for example, the relationship of Emmet (or Emmitt) Robinson and his wife Indigo (Indy). There is a window at the castle inscribed with a poem Dr. Robinson etched to his wife: "In storm or sunshine — joy and strife, thou art my own, my much loved wife, treasure blessings of my life."

There is the Civil War romance of Virginia Hankins, whose father owned the house at the time, and the dashing young Confederate soldier, Sidney Lanier, who later was to become one of the South's most famous and most eloquent poets. Stationed nearby, Lanier was a frequent visitor in 1863 and 1864, and became entranced with the lovely and well educated "Ginna." He wrote to friends that they had become "soul-friends," and that, as he read the works of great poets to her, "she is in a perfect blaze of enthusiasm."

Often during this idyllic interlude from the horrible war being waged around them, Ginna and Sidney would ride off into the green woods of Surry County, picnic, talk and plan. Lanier affectionately called her his "Little Brown Bird." And when, in August 1864, he was called away with his unit he pledged to return as soon as possible so they could be married.

They wrote to each other frequently but when Mrs. Hankins died, Ginna felt her first responsibility was to care for her grief-stricken father and his seven young sons. Sadly, she rejected Lanier's proposal. Still, although he eventually married, and created the works which are revered to this day, they corresponded faithfully for the rest of their lives in the form of poetry.

The third love story, though unsubstantiated, nevertheless has been passed down for generations. During the 1800s, a young girl was forced to meet her sweetheart, a boy from a nearby farm, in secret on the other side of a cornfield, because her father did not approve of him. Despite the predicament, Bacon's Castle hostesses will tell you, they shared the joy of young love and some measure of happiness.

That is, until one ill-fated evening when the girl was returning

Bacon's Castle

to the castle later than usual and had to light a candle to ascend the stairs leading to her room. She tripped on the stairs, and her long hair caught fire from the candle's flame. She didn't scream for help for fear of incurring the wrath of her father. Instead, she fled from the house in a state of shock, and ran through the cornfield desperately trying to reach her sweetheart. But by the time she got there she had been burned critically, and she died in his arms.

Is it any wonder, then, that in a setting of so much tragedy, anguish and lost love, there are so many occurrences of psychic phenomena?

Accounts of hauntings at the castle have been passed along, generation to generation, for more than 300 years. Many of those who have experienced strange sightings, noises, and "presences," believe they are manifestations of the devil. Others have felt it may be the spectral returning of Bacon's men, still seeking redress of the grievances they held against Governor Berkeley and the Colony so many years ago. Whatever, it is undisputed fact that the happenings which have occurred at the castle through the centuries have taken many forms.

Consider the revelations of Mrs. Charles Walker Warren, whose family once owned the castle. When she was a young woman, early in the 20th century, a visiting Baptist preacher who was spending the night, stayed up late reading his Bible. Sometime in the wee hours of the morning he heard footsteps descending the stairs from the second floor. Someone or something, he said later, opened the parlor door and walked past him. He saw no one, but felt the strong sensation that he was not alone. Then, mysteriously, a red velvet-covered rocking chair began moving back and forward as if someone were sitting in it, though the preacher could see no one. He put down his Bible and shouted "get thee behind me Satan," and the rocking stopped immediately.

Mrs. Warren and a number of guests reported hearing footsteps on the stairs late at night many times. One guest distinctly heard "horrible moaning" in the attic directly above her bedroom, though she was assured the next morning that no one could have been in the attic.

On another occasion, Mrs. Warren came into the downstairs parlor one morning and found the glass globe from a favorite nickel-plated reading lamp had been shattered into tiny fragments, yet, strangely, not a drop of kerosene from it had spilled onto the carpet. Also, a leather-bound dictionary had been "flung" across the room onto a sofa, and the iron stand upon which it normally rested had been hurled to a distant corner. No rational explanation could be offered to clear this up.

Richard Rennolds, curator of the castle from 1973 to 1981, used to tell of the time one morning at 3:30 when he was awakened by the sound of his two-and-a-half year old son laughing in his crib in an upstairs bedroom. "Daddy, where's the lady?" the child asked Rennolds when he reached him. "What lady?" Rennolds said. "The lady with the white hands. She was tickling me."

On another occasion, a few years later, a tour guide was standing in the great hall one morning before the castle was opened to the public when "something" ran by her from the outside passageway and went through the hall and into another chamber on the other side. She heard feet running on the hardwood floor but did not see anyone. As the sound of the steps were passing by, something brushed her arm and gave her a chill.

The same hostess also said there had been strange noises a number of times, most commonly loud popping and crackling sounds, which sometimes were heard by people in the video reception room. They were too much for one young couple who heard the noise and became so frightened they left the castle even before the tour started.

These and several other incidents, however, serve merely as preambles to the most shocking supernatural appearance at Bacon's Castle; one that reappears regularly at varying intervals over the years and has been seen and documented by a number of credible witnesses from several different generations.

It takes the form, say those who have seen it and been terrified by it, of a "pulsating, red ball of fire." It apparently rises near or from the graveyard of Old Lawne's Creek Church a few hundred yards south of the castle, soars about 30 to 40 feet in the air — always on dark nights — and then moves slowly northward. It seems to "float or hover" above the castle grounds before slowly moving back toward the ivy-covered walls of the ruins of Lawne's Creek Church, where it disappears.

One eyewitness, G. I. Price, a former caretaker at the castle, described the phenomenon to a local newspaper reporter in this manner: "I was standing, waiting in the evening for my wife to shut up the chickens, when a light about the size of a jack-me-lantern came out of the old loft door and went up a little...and traveled by, just floating along about 40 feet in the air toward the direction of the old graveyard."

Skeptics, of course, contend that the fireball is merely some form of physical manifestation that can be explained scientifically. But those who have seen it, including members of the Warren family and others, could never be convinced that it was not of a mystical, spiritual nature. Some even called it an appearance of the "Prince of Darkness."

One guest reportedly had "the wits frightened out of him" one night when the fiery red ball sailed into his bedroom at the castle, circled over his bed several times and then disappeared out the open window. A former owner of the castle told of seeing the fireball blaze overhead and enter his barn. Fearful of it igniting his stored hay, he ran toward the barn. Then the bright, glowing light turned and headed back toward the graveyard. In the 1930s, members of a local Baptist church, meeting at an evening revival session, collectively saw the strange sphere. It is said the praying that night was more intense than ever before in the congregation's memory.

What is the origin of this eerie fireball and why does it reappear every so often? One legend has it that a servant a century or so ago was late with his chores and as he was walking home in the darkness the red object overcame him, burst, and "covered him with a hellish mass of flames." burning him to death.

Another theory is that the light was somehow tied to hidden money in the castle. Some money was found years ago when two men were removing some bricks from the fireplace hearth in the second floor's west room. Apparently only a few people ever saw, or knew about the money, and since it was found, no one has seen the light. Still others say it may be associated with the spirit of Ginna Hankins going to the church where she and her sweetheart, Sidney Lanier, often lingered. Or could it be a recreation of the flaming hair of the young girl who ran to her lover across the cornfields so long ago?

Many oldtimers, however prefer to believe that the fireball is a periodic reminder of the brilliant comet that flashed across the same skies more than 300 years ago, forewarning that tragedy and bloodshed would soon follow. There are, in fact, those who are convinced that spirits frequent Bacon's Castle to this day; sad spirits from long ago, still seeking relief from their troubled and grief-stricken past.

C H A P T E R 6 4

A Tragic Toast
at Brandon

(Prince George County)

In a book on the homes and gardens of Virginia, it is written about Brandon Plantation that "it does not seem possible that so much loveliness can belong to one old house." Boxwood hedges, more than a century old, flank this superb manor home on a 4,500-acre farm located in Prince George County on the south side of the James River between Surry and Hopewell. Here, today, a dazzling array of flowers, every hue of the rainbow, gracefully coexist with giant elms, ancient yews, hollies, tulip poplars, dogwoods, redbuds, and varieties of magnolias, pecans, oaks, horse chestnuts, hickories, persimmons, hawthorns and locusts — to form magnificent gardens, open to the public, and leading to the banks of the James River.

The estate itself actually dates to 1616 when a vast grant of land was made to Captain John Martin who accompanied John Smith on the first voyage to Virginia. In 1720, the land was acquired by Nathaniel Harrison. The main part of the house was built about 1765 by Nathaniel Harrison II as a wedding present for his son, Benjamin, who was a friend of Thomas Jefferson. It is believed that Jefferson designed the center structure. The two extensive wings of Brandon predate Harrison ownership and were added to the main portion, creating a sweeping house frontage of 210 feet. The walls were riddled with gunfire during the Civil War, and, for a time, Brandon was occupied by Union troops. However,

Brandon

except for some living room paneling which was ripped out and used for firewood, little substantive damage was done.

During the latter part of the 18th century, and for most of the 19th, Brandon was a prime site for the gala social life enjoyed by plantation owners of the times. Lavish parties, dances and weddings were held here and the rich and well known gentlemen and ladies arrived in ornate coaches, and by boat from the north side of the river, from such great mansions as Shirley, Berkeley and Westover. It was from such an aura of refined gaiety that the main character in what evolved into a haunting tragedy emerges.

Her name was Jane Evelyn Harrison, the 18-year-old daughter of William Byrd Harrison of Williamsburg. She has been described as a charming heiress endowed with position and beauty, who, according to writer Hubert Davis who documented that era, "used her capricious blue eyes, winning smile, and every feminine wile she could summon to entrap and smash the hearts of young men." She was, in a very special sense, a real-life Scarlett O'Hara.

It was at a typically jubilant spring dance at Brandon that Jane met and immediately entranced a young Frenchman named Pierre Bondurant. He fell hopelessly in love with the fickle belle, and while details of their short but intense courtship are sketchy, he repeatedly proposed marriage to her. By applying an intriguing feminine mystique beyond her years, she left Pierre more or less dangling. She told him, as he was leaving for a lengthy trip to Paris, that such a union would only be possible with the expressed approval of her father, knowing very well that this would be all but impossible. Pierre was persistent, suggesting that they elope to France, but Jane demurred, saying that she planned to spend the summer at Brandon, partying with her friends.

Saddened, but ever hopeful, Pierre departed for Paris. He had hardly been there a month when he received a letter from a friend, the news of which devastatingly tore at his very fiber. William Byrd Harrison had announced the engagement of Jane. She was to wed Ralph Fitzhugh Cocke of Bacon's Castle in late November! The wedding was to be one of the grandest events of the year. It was to be held at Brandon so as to accommodate more than 100 guests, including Pierre Bondurant. And so, on the last day of November, a sumptuous feast was held, featuring the finest foods and the best wines and liquors in the Commonwealth.

Curiously, Pierre asked the prospective groom if he could propose the first toast at the wedding dinner and his request was granted. "Whatever fate may be," he said, "And this day alone will tell' May both of you be happy and free from sorrow, malice and ill." No one could imagine at the time what fate Pierre had in mind. The wedding took place at 4 p.m., and was followed by an extravagant reception.

At some point during the festivities, Pierre pulled Jane aside, handed her a glass of champagne, and asked her to exchange toasts with him. Delighted that he seemed to show no lingering bitterness from their past "fling," she agreed, and they each drank to the other's happiness. Just then Ralph walked up, unnoticed by the couple, and overheard Pierre offer a strange poem to Jane: 'Twas you I loved when we first met, I loved you then and I love you yet; 'Tis vain for me to try to forget, Lo! Both of us could die before sunset."

Obviously embarrassed when he realized Ralph had heard him, Pierre gulped down his champagne, made excuses, and nervously left the house. By the time all but the house guests had gone, Jane had become deathly ill and collapsed on the drawing room floor, gasping for breath. She was whisked to an upstairs bedroom and died that evening. Although it wasn't known then, she had been poisoned! As author Davis noted, "a veil of silence and sadness descended on everyone."

Oddly, as Jane's body was being prepared for burial it was noticed that her wedding ring was missing. No one could shed any light on this little mystery and she was laid to rest. A few days later, a messenger arrived from Williamsburg with the shocking news that Pierre Bondurant had been found dead in his carriage when it arrived in Williamsburg on the night of the wedding. Even more discomforting was the fact that Jane's wedding ring had been found — in Pierre's pocket!

The mistress of Brandon, Elizabeth Richardson Harrison, Jane's aunt, in an extraordinarily peculiar gesture, declared that the ring now bore a curse, and she had it embedded in the plaster on the ceiling above the spot where Jane had fallen.

Over the years following, there were periodic reports from residents, guests and servants, of seeing a wispy apparition of a young woman, in a flowing white gown, who seemed to appear only in late November, and Brandon slowly began gaining a reputation as being haunted. In fact, when Helen Lynne Thomas became mistress of the plantation, fully two generations after the tragedy, the real estate agent had casually referred to a "resident ghost."

That fall, Helen met the spectral being first-hand. It was on a stormy dark night as she was walking past the family cemetery. Amidst the weathered old tombstones she got a glimpse of a wraith-like figure seemingly drifting toward the main house. She trembled with fear, nearly fainted, then regained her composure and hurried into the great hall. There, she heard a thud which sounded like something heavy had fallen in the adjacent drawing room. She walked across the hall, opened the door, and saw that some plaster had fallen from the ceiling.

And then, as her eyes adjusted to the blackness, she saw something else — the same ethereal, white-robed phantom she had imagined she had seen outside. It appeared to hover about the room for a few seconds and then kind of settled over the pile of plaster as if it were searching for something. Helen could hardly breathe. Then either the door or a loose floorboard creaked and the figure straightened up, slid toward the door, and disappeared.

As it did, Helen screamed, and then fainted dead away. When she was aroused, more than an hour later, she told members of her family and the servants who had rushed to her what had happened. It was then that one of the servants, Hattie McCoy, told her about Jane Harrison and Pierre Bondurant. Hattie's grandmother had been at Brandon on the fateful wedding day.

After she recovered, Helen sorted through the fallen plaster and found a "blackened, tarnished" wedding ring. She had it suspended from the ceiling from a small wire several inches long. It can still be seen there today.

The estate was bought in 1926 by Robert W. Daniel, and his son, Robert Jr., lives there today. The Daniels have painstakingly helped restore Brandon to its former glory. He confirms the essence of the sad events which took place there so many years ago, and adds an updated spectral twist or two. "Oh, we've had a few things happen here which would be difficult to explain," he says. "There is one guest room door which seems to lock itself, and some visitors have said their things have been moved around in that room."

The most compelling and inexplicable phenomenon occurred in 1979. Daniel had been away from the house and there was no one inside when he returned one evening to find a light "in the guest room where the ghost seems to function." He went inside and in the room found water overflowing the bathtub. How could he be sure that no one had entered the house in his absence?

"It had been snowing for sometime," he answers, "and there were no tracks in the snow anywhere!"

The Psychic Wonders
of Haw Branch

(Amelia County)

"...a female voice from its recesses broke suddenly upon the night, in one wild, hysterical, and long-continued shriek."

— *The Assignation*

"A portrait taken after death."

— *Tamerlane*

he spirits seem to have settled down at last at Haw Branch Plantation, 35 miles southwest of Richmond. And that is something, because this historic home in Amelia County, Virginia, has probably had more manifestations of psychic phenomena than any other house in the greater Richmond area, if not the entire state.

These have included such familiar forms as: footsteps in the night; the sounds of heavy falling objects; the spectral form of a woman at night; and the recurrent fragrance of an attar of roses in an upstairs bedroom. But at Haw Branch, there also have been some rarer occurrences, too. There is, for example, the blood curdling scream of a woman, which happens only on specific dates, at six month intervals. There is the eerie swooping of a giant sized bird with at least a six foot wing span. And most strange of all is the story behind a portrait. It inexplicably turned from charcoal black and white to full color. And lastly, there is the haunting parallel between fiction and reality involving the portrait. It is in a short story written by Edgar Allan Poe.

But first, some historical background on the house is appropriate. Colonel Thomas Tabb and his wife, Rebecca Booker, were the first owners of Haw Branch. He settled the land in Amelia County before it was separated from Prince George County in 1735. Over the years Tabb increased his holdings from a single trading post to the point where he was recognized as one of the largest landowners in Virginia, and one of the most prosperous merchants.

According to a Virginia State Landmarks Commission report, the colonel purchased the nucleus of the land making up Haw Branch Plantation in 1743. A small house, believed to be incorporated in the western part of the present house, appears in the record in 1748. The plantation grew, reaching 2,700 acres by 1798. The house is thought to have been enlarged and given its present exterior appearance by John Tabb, son of the founder, sometime after the Revolutionary War.

The name Haw Branch is derived from a small stream on the property, the banks of which were lined with hawthorne trees. The large white mansion house is considered a splendid example of Georgian-Federal plantation architecture, and has been a familiar landmark in Amelia County for more than two centuries. It is set in acres of green lawn and is surrounded by large magnolia, elm and tulip trees. The house is built in a rectangular, brick-paved depression resembling a dry moat, which not only serves as a gutter, but also gives the rooms in the English basement as much light and air as the upper stories.

In 1965, William Cary McConnaughey and his wife, the former Mary Gibson Jefferson, bought the house and property, 120 acres, and began its restoration with loving care.

"I was nine years old when I first saw Haw Branch," Gibson McConnaughey says. "My grandmother brought me out to visit because the home had been in our family from the time the plantation was established in 1745 until Reconstruction days following the Civil War, and she lived here as a little girl, the daughter of Harriet and John Mason who owned it.

"The place was in dreadful condition. It was unoccupied, windows were out and cows were wandering through the English basement. An oil drum had been turned over in the drawing room, and when we started working on the house, that floor had to be sanded 11 times. The exterior hadn't been painted since 1929, and it absorbed fresh paint like a sponge."

Much of the renovation was completed, with the help of a construction crew of sometimes more than 25, over a three month period, and the McConnaugheys and their four children and two dogs moved in on August 13, 1965. Three months later a series of strange and singular events began. "I'm not a believer in ghosts myself, but I have to say I can't explain some of the things that have happened here," Gibson says.

In the early morning hours of November 23, 1965, the entire family was awakened by a woman's blood-curdling scream. It seemed to come from somewhere upstairs. Gibson and Cary raced up the stairs from their first floor bedroom and met their children, standing at the foot of the staircase leading from the second floor to the attic. The two dogs, Porkchop and Blackie, were reportedly "shaking with terror." The next day the attic was inspected and nothing was found awry.

Precisely six months later, on May 23, 1966, the McConnaugheys heard the woman's screams again. They resounded throughout the house just before dawn. No source was discovered. This strange phenomenon occurred once more on May 23, 1967. The following November 23, the family waited, this time armed with a tape recorder and flashlights, but there was no shrieking.

They tried again on May 23, 1968. This time, although no human scream was heard, the McConnaugheys and their children did hear "heavy footsteps" walking across the yard, and an eerie screeching wail outside the house. They went out on the porch, and Gibson recalls the definite sound of someone or something running. Then they heard the wail from somewhere behind the barn. The next morning the children said they had seen a giant bird in the moonlight which had a wingspan of about six feet. Although the bird was not seen again, its screeches were heard several other times, and always on or around May 23 or November 23.

"We never have learned anything about the significance of those dates," Gibson said during an interview in late 1984. "The screams of the woman stopped, but it seemed like something always happened on those days. One night I noticed a cardinal who kept flying at our fan light over the front door late at night. That's unusual because he should have long been in bed by then. But can you guess what the date was! It was November 23!"

But the puzzle of these dates is only one of Haw Branch's many mysteries. The family had been in the house only a few months when, while watching television one evening, they all heard a loud thud outside that shook the house. Recalls Gibson: "It sounded as though a very heavy solid object such as a safe had fallen from a great height and landed on the bricks of the moat. We rushed outside with flashlights expecting to find something lying there. But nothing unusual was found." This particular manifestation has occurred a number of times over the years, both at night and during the daytime.

The most recent occasion was early in 1985 when a draft copy of the manuscript for this chapter was sent to Gibson for her review. As she sat in the library in the evening to read the script she was startled by what she described as a "loud KA-WOMP" in the moat area just outside the room. "It was very loud and sounded heavy. I got up to look, but there was nothing there. It was the first time this particular phenomenon had happened in years."

There also have been some sightings of spectral forms. At one in the morning during the summer of 1967, for example, Gibson went into the dark kitchen to get a glass of milk before retiring. From the light shining out from the refrigerator, she caught a glimpse of something in the hall. "I could plainly see the silhouette of a slim girl in a floor-length dress with a full skirt," she says. "It was not the wide fullness of a hoop-skirt, but one from an earlier period. I could see no features, but she was not transparent, just a white silhouette. I saw her for perhaps 10 seconds. In the next instant she was gone. There was no gradual fading away; she simply disappeared from one instant to the next."

One of her daughters had a similar experience several days later. She ran to tell her mother about it, not knowing that her mother had seen a vision, too. The daughter described what she had seen in the drawing room as a "lady in white who was standing in front of the fireplace." She disappeared in front of her eyes.

Gibson later learned that earlier residents of Haw Branch had seen the same apparition. One relative told her that Gibson's great grandmother, Harriet B. Mason, had told of seeing the lady in white, and had once even been awakened from a deep sleep by a touch from the spirit. On other occasions, the McConnaugheys have heard footsteps descending from the second floor to the first.

The very mention of one of her great grandmother's girlhood friends apparently has been cause enough for other psychic happenings. Lights have gone on and off for no reason when her name came up in conversation. And once, when Gibson spoke of her at the dinner table, two bulbs in the electric chandelier over the dining room table glowed brilliantly and then went out.

There have been unexplained strange odors, also. Several times

375

Haw Branch

the strong scent of fresh oranges could be sensed in the library, though there were no fresh oranges in the house, and all frozen orange juice was unopened. Gibson also has smelled an attar of roses when there were no flowers in the house.

Aside from the screams, screeches, heavy thumpings, and footsteps, there have been other curious sounds heard at Haw Branch. One of the young McConnaughey sons and several friends, camping out one night in the surviving old slave cabin, heard the sound of a cowbell making a circuit around the building in narrowing circles all night. There are no bells on any of the cows on the plantation!

Other noises center in the attic. All family members at one time or another have reported hearing what sounded like furniture being dragged across the attic floor late at night. Yet when they went up to look, the dust covered furniture was unmoved, nor were there any traces of animals or birds in the attic. Sometimes a rocking chair is heard rocking in the attic, but the chair was broken and no one could sit in it.

On another occasion, a humming sound was heard in the basement. A musician friend of the family said it sounded like an old

English folk tune. In the basement, incidentally, there is a sealed room. It is a chamber about four by six feet in size and completely closed off by brick and masonry. The McConnaughey cats seem fascinated by it.

But of all the many and varied manifestations of psychic phenomena that have surfaced at Haw Branch, the most intriguing involves a portrait. It is a large pastel rendering of a young woman named Florence Wright. She was a distant relative by marriage, and little was known of her except that her parents had a summer home in Massachusetts, and that Florence died before the painting was completed, although she was only in her twenties.

After 20 years in storage, the painting was given to the McConnaugheys by a cousin, who told them it was a colored painting with beautiful pastels. This bewildered Gibson, because, in her words, "when the picture was uncrated and the massive gilt rococo frame and glass painstakingly dusted, the portrait appeared to be a charcoal rendering, rather than a pastel. No color was evident, everything was either a dirty white, gray or black." There was no signature of the artist to be found, and the back of the frame was tightly sealed. Gibson left it that way and hung the picture over the library fireplace.

A few days later, as Gibson remembers: "I heard women's voices in animated conversation on the first floor of the house. As Haw Branch (then) was open to the public, an occasional group of visitors will walk in without ringing the doorbell, not realizing the house is actually lived in. Calling, 'I'm coming right up,' (I) hurried upstairs from the English basement to find no one there. No car was in the parking lot nor the road leading away from the house. The unexplained sound of voices occurred five or six times in the library over a period of a year."

A few months later Cary McConnaughey was sitting in the library reading a newspaper when he looked up and noticed that the rose in the portrait seemed to have taken on a pink tinge. The girl's black hair also was beginning to lighten, and her grayish skin was turning flesh-colored. These changes continued gradually over the next year until the portrait miraculously transformed into pastel brilliance.

Says Gibson: "A partially opened rose in the portrait began to take on a definite pink cast, when previously it had been grayish-white. Other changes continued gradually for over a year. Several people connected with art departments of neighboring Virginia colleges saw the portrait from the time of its arrival and confirmed the change in coloring, but could offer no logical explanation."

A psychic expert from a neighboring county came over the investigate. He reported that Florence Wright's spirit was tied to the portrait because she died before it was completed, and that she had the power to remove the color from it when she was dissatisfied with where it was placed. She apparently liked Haw Branch, so with help from the spirits of two other young women (allegedly the ones Gibson heard talking in the library), she restored the original color to her portrait.

"Who can say his theory isn't correct," says Gibson. "When the color returned to the portrait and the changes ended, so did the sound of voices. Today, the girl's clear blue eyes look rather sadly out beneath her curly reddish-brown hair, and her pink and white complexion looks as if she were alive. The green and beige upholstery on the gnome-carved gilt chair she sits in is a deeper shade of the carved jade jar on a table near her. The rose that was first seen to change color slightly is now a clear, soft pink."

In 1971, Gibson wrote, "much about the portrait still remains a mystery. How did the young girl die? Did the partially opened pink rosebud in the crystal vase foretell her early death, or was it added symbolically after she died? Who was the artist, and why did the pastel portrait's coloring change without human assistance? There is a slight lead on the artist's name. When the portrait first arrived at Haw Branch, the owner had told (me) that it was painted by a famous American artist and signed by him, although she couldn't remember his name."

About a year later, some of the answers were learned — in a most curious fashion. One summer evening in 1972, one of Gibson's daughters and a friend of hers were sitting on the floor in the library beneath the portrait. They moved over to the sofa, and seconds later the supports of the picture's heavy frame pulled loose. The portrait slowly slid down the wall until the bottom of the frame reached the mantel shelf where it crushed a row of porcelain antiques, tipped forward slightly, slipped over the edge of the mantel and fell to the wide pine floorboards.

As the girls sat transfixed, glass shattered all across the floor. The portrait had fallen face down on the exact spot where the girls had been sitting only minutes before!

"Although the painting itself was undamaged, the big wooden frame was broken" says Gibson. "Lifting it up, we found underneath what had been the tightly sealed backing of the frame, a brass plate that gave the girl's full name, her birth date in Duxbury,

Massachusetts, and her date of death in the same place. Though we searched carefully for the artist's signature, both on the front and the back of the painting, it could not be found. The next day, the frame was repaired, the portrait placed back in it and the glass replaced. The man who did the work searched as carefully as we had searched to find the artist's signature, but with no success.

"It was late in the day when we arrived back at Haw Branch with the portrait. The sun was red and low in the sky. As my husband and I lifted the picture from the back of the station wagon, I happened to tilt my end of the frame slightly upward. Suddenly, as though a red neon sign had been lit, the name 'J. Wells Champney,' appeared. It had been signed in pencil on the apron of the dark mahogany table in the picture. Only under a certain angle of light could it be seen."

The McConnaugheys later learned that the girl in the portrait had been born into a wealthy family that owned several homes. Her parents commissioned Mr. Champney to paint the portrait. Before it could be finished, Florence Wright, who at age 24 was an accomplished musician who had studied piano abroad, slumped over a piano keyboard and died of a massive stroke. The artist completed the painting and added the partially opened rose to signify that his subject died an untimely death before the painting was completed. The McConnaugheys also found out that the artist was later killed when he fell down an elevator shaft in New York City.

Gibson adds that "many say that they can see the girl blush when they stare hard at her portrait. But now that Florence Wright's portrait has regained its original colors and hangs in a permanent home, it seems unlikely that she will ever again change her color, or need her 'spirit helpers.' "

There is yet a fascinating footnote to the saga; one with spine tingling parallels to the painting. Edgar Allan Poe wrote a short story called "The Oval Portrait." In the narrative, Poe tells of a man who spends a night in a strange chateau. He reads late into the night, and in repositioning the candelabrum he sees a portrait hanging on the wall of a beautiful young girl "just ripening into womanhood." He becomes absorbed by the painting which is in an oval frame, "richly gilded and filigreed in Moresque." He describes the portrait as having an "immortal beauty," with life-like characteristics. As Poe phrased it, the man had "found the spell of the picture in an absolute life-likeness of expression."

In a volume which discussed the paintings in the chateau and their histories, he reads of the background of the portrait. The girl was said to be a "maiden of rarest beauty, and not more lovely than full of glee...frolicsome as the young fawn." She fell in love with an artist and married him, but, Poe says, the artist was already married to his career.

He then decided to paint his bride's portrait. She was not pleased about it, but she obeyed, and so, for days and days he painted. He became so absorbed in his work that he did not notice her withering health and spirit. She grew "daily more dispirited and weak," but she continued to sit and smile for she loved her husband-artist so much.

As he neared completion of the portrait, he allowed no one into the turret, for he "had grown wild with the ardor of his work." Rarely turning from the canvas, he did not notice his bride's rapidly deteriorating health. At last he finished, and stood "entranced before the work which he had wrought."

As he admired the canvas, he cried in a loud voice, "This is indeed Life itself!" Then he turned suddenly to his beloved. "She was dead!"

Author L. B. Taylor, Jr., and illustrator Brenda Goens.
Photo courtesy of Michael Westfall

About the Author

L. B. Taylor, Jr. is a native Virginian. He was born in Lynchburg and has a BS degree in Journalism from Florida State University. He wrote about America's space programs for 16 years, for NASA and aerospace contractors, before moving to Williamsburg, Virginia, in 1974, as public affairs director for BASF Corporation. He retired in 1993. Taylor is the author of more than 300 national magazine articles and 40 non-fiction books. His research for the book, "Haunted Houses," published by Simon & Schuster in 1983, stimulated his interest in Virginia psychic phenomena, and led to the publication of 16 books on the subject.

The following books by L. B. Taylor, Jr., are available directly from the author:

The Ghosts of Virginia, Volumes II through XIII ...... $18.00 each

Civil War Ghosts of Virginia......................... $15.00

The Ghosts of Williamsburg, Volume I................... $8.00

The Ghosts of Williamsburg, Volume II $15.00

The Ghosts of Richmond $15.00

The Ghosts of Fredericksburg $15.00

The Ghosts of Charlottesville & Lynchburg $15.00

A Treasury of True Ghostly Humor.................... $15.00

Virginia Ghost Stories (CD) $10.00

Please add $3.00 postage for single book orders, $6.00 for multiple books.
Please specify to whom you wish the books signed.
Please, check or money order only.

L. B. Taylor, Jr.,
108 Elizabeth Merriwether
Williamsburg, VA 23185

Phone 757 - 253 - 2636
Fax 757 - 253 - 9415
E-mail - vaghosts@cox.net
www.vaghosts.com

....

L. B. Taylor, Jr. is available to speak on the subjects of Virginia ghosts and ghostly humor to civic, social, fraternal, business, school, library, and other groups. Call, email, or write for details.

If you have a ghostly or unusual psychic encounter you would like to share (for possible future publication), please contact the author.

OTHER BOOKS BY L. B. TAYLOR, JR.

PIECES OF EIGHT: Recovering the Riches of a Lost
Spanish Treasure Fleet

THAT OTHERS MAY LIVE (AIR FORCE RESCUE & RECOVERY SERVICE)

LIFTOFF: THE STORY OF AMERICA'S SPACEPORT

FOR ALL MANKIND

GIFTS FROM SPACE (SPINOFF BENEFITS FROM SPACE RESEARCH)

CHEMISTRY CAREERS

SPACE SHUTTLE

RESCUE (TRUE STORIES OF TEENAGE HEROISM)

THE DRAFT

SHOPLIFTING

SPACE: BATTLEGROUND OF THE FUTURE

THE NUCLEAR ARMS RACE

THE NEW RIGHT

SPOTLIGHT ON ... (FOUR TEENAGE IDOLS)

EMERGENCY SQUADS

SOUTHEAST AFRICA

DRIVING HIGH (EFFECTS OF ALCOHOL AND DRUGS ON DRIVING)

CHEMICAL AND BIOLOGICAL WARFARE

HAUNTED HOUSES

THE COMMERCIALIZATION OF SPACE

ELECTRONIC SURVEILLANCE

HOSTAGE